KNOW YOUR PLACE

essays on the working class
by the working class

KNOW YOUR PLACE

essays on the working class
by the working class

edited by
Nathan Connolly

dead ink

for my mum and every late night

Contributors

Abondance Matanda is an arts and culture writer and poet. Her home city, London, informs the subversive, colloquial voice she uses to dissect themes and identities like girlhood, class, blackness and language. Other influences range from Ms Dynamite to Toni Cade Bambara to old school Congolese music videos.

Alexandros Plasatis is an ethnographer who writes fiction in English, his second language. His work has appeared in UK and American anthologies and magazines. He is a volunteer at Leicester City of Sanctuary, where he helps find and develop new creative talent within the refugee and asylum seeker community.

Andrew McMillan was born in South Yorkshire in 1988. His debut collection was the multi-award winning *physical* (Jonathan Cape, 2015), a second collection is due in 2018. He is a senior lecturer at MMU.

Ben Gwalchmai is a maker, worker, writer who was Welsh National Opera's writer-in-residence, a Historical Novel Society 'Editor's Pick' for his novel *Purefinder*, and a shortlisted poet in the Melita Huma Poetry Prize 2016. From Powys, he still regularly works on farms and in pubs there. For more, see bengwalchmai.com

Cath Bore is a Liverpool-based writer. She writes about feminism, fandom and music for a number of publications. Her fiction is published in *Mslexia* magazine, many anthologies, and has placed in competitions at York's Festival of Writing, Writing on The Wall, Harrogate Crime

Writing Festival, plus Penguin/Random House's Write Now 2017.

Catherine O'Flynn is the author of three novels. Her debut, *What Was Lost*, won the 2008 Costa First Novel Award. She reviews books sometimes for the *Guardian* and turns up sporadically on Radio 4's *Saturday Review*. Her short stories and articles have appeared in *Granta*, *The New York Times*, the *Independent* and on BBC Radio.

Dominic Grace is a playwright and an award-winning short-fiction writer from South Leeds.

Durre Shahwar Mughal is a Welsh writer, an Associate Editor for *Wales Arts Review*, and a Word Factory Apprentice 2017. She studied for an MA in Creative Writing at Cardiff Metropolitan University. Her interests lie in a broad range of topics including race, identity, religion, gender and mental health. Durre's work has been featured in various publications and anthologies.

Gena-mour Barrett is a 24-year-old writer from South East London, currently working at BuzzFeed UK. Her work ranges from feature to humour writing, focusing largely on pop culture, race, and feminism. Gena also co-hosts the podcast *Well, Blactually*, and has appeared on national radio several times to discuss her work.

Kate Fox is a professional stand-up poet based in Thirsk, North Yorkshire. She has written and performed two comedy series for Radio 4 and is completing a PhD in class, gender and Northern English regional identity at the University of Leeds. www.katefox.co.uk

Kath McKay's publications include *End Notes* (co-editor); *Hard Wired* (Moth); *Collision Forces* (Wrecking Ball); *Telling the Bees* (Smiths Knoll); *Anyone Left Standing* (Smith Doorstop); *Waiting for the Morning* (The Women's Press) and short stories. She grew up in Kirkby and teaches creative writing at Hull University.

Kit de Waal is the author of debut novel *My Name is Leon*, a *Times* and international best seller, shortlisted for the Costa First Book Award.

Laura Waddell is a publisher, critic and writer based in Glasgow. Her writing has appeared in publications including the *Guardian*, *Times Literary Supplement*, *The List*, and books *Nasty Women* and *The Digital Critic*.

Lee Rourke is the author of the short story collection *Everyday*, the novel *The Canal* (winner of the *Guardian's* Not The Booker Prize 2010) and the poetry collection *Varroa Destructor*. His latest novel, *Vulgar Things* ('Poignant and unsettling' – Eimear McBride) is published by 4th Estate. Twitter: @leerourke

Peter Sutton is the author of *A Tiding of Magpies*, shortlisted for the British Fantasy Award 2017, and *Sick City Syndrome*, which is set in Bristol where he lives and helps organise Bristol Festival of Literature, Bristol HorrorCon & BristolCon.

Rebecca Winson grew up in Cumbria. She is a writer and activist who has organised around workers' rights, feminism and housing. Her work has appeared in the *Independent*, *New Statesman*, and the *Guardian*. She lives with her partner in Hampshire, where they are owned by a cat.

Rym Kechacha is a writer and teacher from London. She has an MA in Creative Writing from Goldsmiths and is working in her first novel. Twitter: @RymKechacha

Sam Mills is the author of *The Quiddity of Will Self* (Corsair) and several crossover novels published by Faber & Faber. She is the Managing Director of indie press Dodo Ink. She lives in South London.

Sian Norris is a novelist, poet and feminist activist. She is the founder of the Bristol Women's Literature Festival. She has written for the *Guardian*, *OD50:50*, the *New Statesman*, and more. Her first book came out in 2013 and she's now working on a novel set in 1920s Paris.

Sylvia Arthur (sylviaarthur.co.uk) is a writer from London whose essays and plays examine the intersection of race, gender, and class through the prism of popular culture. She's currently at work on her first book, *African, & Other Curse Words*, a collection of interconnected essays about identity, belonging, and language.

Wally Jiagoo is a writer for stage and screen. He's had his work performed at Soho Theatre, Theatre Royal Stratford East, Trafalgar Studios, and The Albany Theatre. In 2016 he won the BAFTA Rocliffe New Writing Prize for TV Drama.

Yvonne Singh is a journalist, writer and editor, who lives in Kent with her partner and two sons, not far from the seaside. Her work has appeared in the *Guardian*, the *Observer*, the *Mirror* and the *Evening Standard*, amongst others. She now works for the award-winning website *Middle East Eye*.

Introduction

As with so much of our political discourse in 2017, this book, fittingly, began life on Twitter. It was in response to a tweet that, in the aftermath of the EU referendum, requested someone produce a 'State of the Nation' book of working class voices. We agreed and took up the challenge.

Despite us not appreciating how much work this book would be when we began, it has been a joy to work on – and that is mainly because of the overwhelming amount of support that we have received right through the entire journey to publication. It isn't an exaggeration to say that this book wouldn't be here if it wasn't for the vocal support that we received when we announced it, the crowdfunders on *Kickstarter* who backed it and all of the generous help we've been offered to promote it. I hope that this book does all of those people proud. From the onset, it has felt like this book was part of a communal process, one that we at Dead Ink merely tried to channel.

At the time we began commissioning this book, it seemed as though a lot of commentators felt justified placing their own opinions in the mouths of the working class, and there was a lot of discussion of the Brexit vote being the voice of the working class too. What we rarely found was the working class allowed to speak for themselves. An awful lot could be justified in their name without actually giving them a chance to speak.

This concerned me on a number of levels, but it also felt personal, because my own background is working class. It felt depressingly familiar: politicians have always sought the blessing of the *common man*, but that hasn't always been synonymous with actually caring for their wellbeing or their wishes.

When putting *Know Your Place* together, our first concern was defining the working class, and it was something we were repeatedly questioned upon. From all levels of society, we were quizzed on who is and isn't working class. My own essay at the end of this book, *You're Not Working Class*, sums up my thoughts on this issue. What we eventually decided upon when requesting contributions was for the authors of the essays to self-identify as working class or from a working class background. Therefore, all of the contributors to this book felt that they fulfilled that criteria and, importantly, it allowed us to keep the submission process open to the public. We were always keen that this book should be made up of contributions that were open to everyone who felt they were eligible.

Our second concern was that class politics in the UK has been increasingly turbulent in recent years, and the very notion of what it means to be poor in this country has been a consistently recurring subject in our media. The topic was brought into even sharper relief following the horrific fire at Grenfell Tower and the subsequent response by the government and the local council. We originally set out to produce what would be described as a 'State of the Nation' book, but the state of the nation as it related to our subject was terrifyingly volatile and tense. Notions of class were becoming ever more intimately entwined with the daily political discourse.

It would have been an easy and perfectly viable route for us to have solely commissioned essays that engaged with the current political agenda. We tried to refrain from heading too far in that direction, though. Much of working class life, though directly impacted by it, is not about party politics. Most of working class life, like most of everybody's life, is about waking up, going about your day and then going to sleep again. And that too is political, it is important, and it is, unfortunately, so rarely allowed to voice itself. It is, in a way, the great irony of being working class; as a demographic they are so keenly placed on the receiving end of political decision making, and yet they are also so far removed from that process of power.

It might be expected that, given such a context, this book would be gloomy, pessimistic and angry. And some of it is – rightfully so, I would argue. But it isn't just that, it is also a celebration of working class life in all its guises. We tried to steer clear of flat caps and life down the pit as much as we could. Hopefully this is a record of the 21st century working class: one with smartphones, GCSEs, and 24-hour news. Though, if it is that, it is still one with a long memory and a sense of where it came from. The working class might have changed since *The Road to Wigan Pier*, *Love on the Dole* or *Kes*, but I think it is still recognisable and its challenges aren't all that different.

What we haven't done with this book is to try and achieve an authoritative or monolithic text representative of 'The Working Class Experience'. What we *have* tried to do is dispel any notions that such a book could ever exist. The working class is not singular and it is not possessed of any one set of ideals.

Know Your Place is a small space where we have tried to allow members of the working class to speak for themselves: an opportunity rarely afforded. If you are yourself working class, some essays may reflect parts of you – others may not. This is just a sample of the lives and the experiences out there, and we hope that, by creating this space, more room will be created for others to express themselves: when we deny people a voice, we provide room for someone else to speak for them.

Nathan
Editor

Contents

The First Galleries I Knew Were Black Homes

Abondance Matanda

Before I ever stepped foot in a 'proper' gallery or museum, I was already accustomed to how them spaces are set up and function, even though bare of these institutions never particularly had me or my experiences in mind upon their inception. Being a black working class woman, I exist on the peripheries, in the shadows of British society. It's scarily likely that you might not see me or my experiences portrayed at all, let alone wholesomely in our visual culture or art history. Me and my kind have been here making noise for a minute now though. I was born and raised in London, amongst an entire network of established art spaces – similar to how the Tate is a 'family' of four buildings dedicated to one central artistic vision. I'll focus on our capital city's working class landscapes though, as I tell you how black homes were the first galleries I knew.

Every Afro-Caribbean family probably has a pile of photo albums stacked somewhere nondescript, but these objects are special. As our official archives, these collections of amateur point-and-shoot pictures, taken for us and by us, represent our individual and collective histories in Britain more accurately, sensitively and tangibly than anything else. I remember going through all these rectangular film photos with my mother and aunties and cousins as a yute – I still do now – seeing where they lived when they first come over; what so and so looked like way back when; who their friends and neighbours was; how people used to dress day to day or on the way to functions like all-dayers and hall parties. Our makeshift archives were always accessible – never obscure or out of reach.

Beyond a biro scrawl of a year and location on the back of some photos, the only detailed information we got about how we came to be British kids by way of 'back home' came from our relatives-cum-archivists. They always entertained our curiosity, lest we forget who we are, indulging in pensive reminiscence upon our bombarding inquisitions like 'Who took this?' and 'How old were you then?' and 'What's this and that person's name?' We must've given them headaches, but oral history is ingrained in myriad African and diasporic cultures. We learnt to vocalise our thoughts about visual media long before we started stepping in white cube galleries, wondering why nobody laughs out loud or runs their mouths in there. I learnt about the intimacy and necessity of capturing and telling history as it is made, in black homes. I learnt how to curate a solid ontological narrative in order to stand up tall in my knowledge of self, in black homes.

My first galleries are evolving though, in accordance with developments in technology and social media. My upbringing was recorded on camcorders and VHS tapes, which the family watched gathered around lo-fi TVs. These days, flickers of my little cousins' first milestones get consumed in the vortexes of Facebook feeds and Snapchat stories. Front cameras rather than film photos shall affirm their visibility now and forever, since the future is literally in their hands, in the rectangular shapes of smartphones and tablets. The Internet is an Access All Areas pass into bare different worlds now, exposing and transforming how people see themselves and each other. This is an incredible power to take advantage of to challenge and affect social issues, especially when they intersect.

Tania Nwachukwu and Jojo Sonubi are two young Londoners who clocked this, so they founded a submission-based online archive called *Black In The Day* in July 2016. People upload scanned pictures from their family albums online, proving that Black Britons have existed all over this land, from Southwark to Scunthorpe for time, and our experiences are not monolithic. *Black In The Day*'s social, educational and political impacts unfold with every move they make, from projecting images from their ever-growing archive on Tate Britain's walls; to speaking about the project with the artist Ashley Holmes at Site Gallery in Sheffield; to hosting #ScanningSocials at East London's black-owned chocolate shop Dark Sugars and galleries including the Institute of Contemporary Arts (ICA), where people socialise and dance as the *Black In The Day* team scan your family photos. This is part of what the artist Jacob V Joyce identified in their 2017 Ted Talk as a cultural renaissance currently occurring in Britain. There is a movement of individuals and collectives building a solid bridge across the gaping gap between black communities and arts institutions, so that when we work in or visit these typically white, middle class spaces, we won't always have to jump across it only to stick out like a unslicked baby hair.

Alienation fully occurs when you touch a exhibition for whatever reason, only to feel eyes all on you like say you was mounted on them white walls yourself. How we look and how we are seen and received and othered as working class people can induce anxiety you know. When we feel cool and comfortable and creative, you call us 'ghetto' and 'chavvy'. Tracksuits and headscarves and big badgyal earrings don't always mean trouble you know, but they get read as intimidating if you also wear the double burden of being black and proletariat. Apparently, art was never meant to be a privilege reserved for our fiscal or temporal indulgence.

Capitalism would rather we remain preoccupied with our superficial image. But little does it know, as we stack and line our Adidas and Nike shoeboxes in our bedrooms, little working class kids with arguably low aspirations, ah so it go, are, essentially, unknowingly experimenting with sculptural forms. We might turn to illegal moneymaking methods and stash pink and purple paper in these cardboard boxes, attracting unprepared-for group visits by legions of feds, who are hungry to acquire such objects for their private collection. Without warning, they performatively run up and buss your front door to make unnecessarily noizy arrests. Off-site light installations of flashing, fluorescent, familiar red and blue soon ensue, communicating in code what working class life can be. Bodies become exhibits in prison cells like zoos, in exchange for their freedom to be visually, mentally stimulated, which they probably wasn't anyways if they hailed from industrial, bleak gutters like mine.

This is where that whole eye of the beholder thing comes through, though. The textures and sounds and colour palettes of the interiors and environs of many black homes in Britain are actually wicked stimuli you know. Samuel Ross is a multidisciplinary creative director, designer and filmmaker who's gone clear. His urban luxury label A-Cold-Wall has been referencing working class experiences and culture in Britain through fabric, ideas and semiotics since its inception. It gets more nuanced with every collection and their accompanying installations in the shops they are stocked in, from high end Harvey Nichols in London and Barneys in New York, to niche lickle shops in Tokyo and Rotterdam. Wherever he goes, Sam don't forget his upbringing as a poor black boy from ends and I love that. Growing up in-between London and Northampton, he was uniformly blacked out in Nike all day, listening to the grimiest music made by people not unlike him. He went from getting up to no good as well as being on the brutal end of a skinhead's boot, to graduating from university in the Midlands, like bare black kids are doing these days – some of whom credit him as a role model. Ain't it a madness how my man's gone from getting charged for grievous bodily harm to being dubbed by *Dazed and Confused* as 'British fashion's next working class hero'? Samuel Ross embodies the concept that black homes are galleries from whence one can go forth and tun the badness them experience or succumb to, in or around there, into something glorious.

When I look at A-Cold-Wall's clothes, I see the colours and textures of the blue plastic bags bossman gives me at the corner-shop. I take them home and stuff them in my kitchen cupboard and tie them round my head when it rains and I don't got an umbrella. The electric blue polystyrene ends up entangled and blown about in the branches of bony trees, eye-level outside my second-floor flat window. A-Cold-Wall references Aunty Anna's white lace curtains that billowed in the breeze when I'd go stay at hers in the summer holidays to give Mummy a break too. A-Cold-Wall is coloured by concrete, pebble dash walls and spray-paint graffiti, translating it all into grandeur somehow. The campaigns are always shot so striking, with their gully futurism. The posture and positioning of the models, who are beautiful in Samuel's way rather than the industry's, remind me of objects and images displayed in the National Gallery, the Victoria and Albert Museum, black homes. Samuel Ross has spoken about 'dusty glassware and crowded china – that shit you could never touch' that rarely comes outta them glass cabinets at the back of the front room. 'Do not touch the items on display' is always a tempting sign in galleries, but we are used to such rules from the days when we woulda got duppied by our mothers if they caught us even looking at that crockery too long.

My family is very much matriarchal. I am used to women's presence being acknowledged and exalted in the imagery around me. Colourful wall hangings and wooden carvings detail the long necks and saggy breasts and big bums of African women like the ones I come from, assigned the precious status they were crafted with when displayed and arranged with pride. Meanwhile, 'borrowed' artefacts from all over the continent live in limbo in the public and private collections of our European colonisers. In the homes we came to occupy here, we have had to visually and materially cultivate manifestations of our values, at times in line with and at others in resistance to the colonial ideas which essentially led to us ever becoming 'British'.

Gold frames adorn my nana's corridor, bedrooms and sitting room, but there is a distinction between the pictures in black and white and those in colour, simply down to where and when they was taken. The former ones got posed for in studios in Uganda, as was common practice all over 20th century Africa. A trilogy of them flew with the grace of Ugandan cranes to a wall in Nana's living room to communicate the beginnings of her life as a mother. First comes a photo of her wearing clogs and a pretty dress in 1977, heavily pregnant and standing alone except for a vase of tulips on a plinth. Not long after, the middle picture was captured of her and her younger sister, standing on either side of my seated great-grandmother who everyone called Ayaa, in whose arms are these two babies bathed in blankets who you can barely see. In the last frame, the twins are able to stand now. Their light skin looks so different next to Nana's northern Ugandan darkness, and my Pakistani granddad was never in the picture for anyone to see my mum and her brother's likeness to him.

I was raised in a network of art spaces. That's why the fourth picture in this sequence is on display in the corner of my mum's living room. She and her brother and her cousin are standing by their seated nanny, who they came to think was their mother, since Nana was busy working and raving and living in neighbouring countries in exile for most of their childhood. By the end of the next decade though, Nana and her twins came to England as political refugees, as a result of historical British interference in Ugandan affairs. They first shared a room with an Eritrean family in a similar predicament in a hostel, then viewed different flats around the South London borough of Lambeth, until settling for a fourth floor flat in Kennington. Current affairs will tell you how hostile and precarious immigrant experiences of Britain can be, so to secure a home is a mad milestone. Almost automatically you gotta adopt a working class life, whether you had one or not back home, in order to maintain what you have so graciously been granted – so it's only right that you then beautify your house until it is a home, with whatever means you have. Nana's flat was barely furnished when she first came here with her kids, but 30 years later it looks as lived in as it has been. Visual reminders of where the family comes from and how to carry ourselves stand firm on display in the galleries we have to make of our homes, lest we assimilate so much we disappear.

Part of my mum's permanent collection is a hand-hammered copper sculpture from Congo, gifted from the same don who gave her three kids but couldn't maintain a constant presence in their lives. Her curation has hung a lickle instrument she brought home from a trip to Uganda over one corner of it, and positioned the object next to the collection of CDs and DVDs of Congolese music my parents built together. It tells you about how they first met at a Congolese concert in London in the mid-'90s, as well as my own relationship with this man who toggled between physically absent and toxically present in my childhood. I remember him fucking off to Congo for a few years while I was in primary school yeah. When he come back now, he's brought this bronze-coloured copper ting of a topless man walking through his village with a knife and some sort of pouch on him like some any road yute, except he's got some fish hanging off some rod over his shoulder init. He's stood next to me now telling me it's him, and I just accept it as fact yeah, forgetting he lies, but all I could wonder was why my man looked so sad. My dad's from a place in Congo called Bandundu where the people apparently fish for tilapia.

One night, we was talking for time while my mother and brothers slept. Sky Sports mumbled in the background as he told me folk tales about the famous Queen Nzinga, and how people used to use this drum called a lokole to spread news through a specific sound system from town to town. It was so different to the regular rowdy and drunken discussions the uncles hilariously have at any given family link up, going round and round and nowhere about African politics and presidents and religion, until the sky goes blacker than us. I felt like I'd walked into a programmed talk at a Friday Late event at some next gallery about my heritage by accident. Just listening, I sat on the sofa of my black home which has been a haven for all kinds of conversations and performance pieces, mediating my identity as a Black British girl and a African one in a way I'd never had the headspace to before. My normal Clore Learning Studios are the bedrooms and kitchens and balconies where I laugh and gossip and see all kinds of madness and sweetness and nothingness with my aunties, my bredrins, my cousins. The first galleries I knew were black homes, big man ting.

Don't insult us with the label of culturally deprived because of the financial state of our communities here. We dun know already about art and heritage and all them things there, you get me? The art world is still set up way too elitist, bare moving like say race and class maladies ain't indelibly, historically ingrained in British culture and society. We haffi mash it up, then collectively build it back badder and better from the debris, whichever side of its white walls we're posted on – then we can gwan paint the ting rosy red, black art an' done.

> *'IT IS A STRIDE ALONG THE ROAD TO "SOMBODYNESS" FOR THE BLACK COMMUNITY.'*
> – Black Art An' Done Exhibition Handout, June 1981.

The Pleasure Button:
Low Income Food Inequality

Treats, when I was growing up, were true to the word. It's only now, as an adult with my own disposable income, I can overindulge in them, and render what was once rare and special, routine.

A hole in the wall pizza place in a neighbouring town was a particular joy metered out on uneven paydays. My mum would drive up to it and order. She'd have a pizza, loaded with mushrooms and ham, peculiar with pineapple, but I'd get a crisp baked potato to suit my plainer palate. The cardboard box and polystyrene container that emerged steaming from the counter, with a little round tub for the cheese and its matching little round opaque lid, contained riches of butter and salt. Memory mixes the taste of the food with the papery smell of the card and plastic packaging, and the feel of picking up food from inside it with salt-grained, grease-licked fingers. Taking it home, we might sit cross-legged on the floor to eat it: a small party.

Similarly, tea from a polystyrene cup meant being on holiday, buying one from the counter of a sizzling burger van, usually parked on a tarmac car park near a sodden beach, whilst en route to a caravan to listen to the same rain patter on the roof. Or, sometimes, not always, having the coins in my pocket to buy a hot drink from the canteen in the arcade market where, at 14 years old, I sold hair scrunchies, three garish ones for a pound (often picked as local football colours and worn stacked one atop the other, an earnest '90s/'00s scheme style now adopted by insouciant middle class art school kids. I, a council estate goth, stuck to solitary red velvet, which better matched a concrete backdrop not yet popularised by this decade's resurgence of think pieces on Brutalism). I'd bite circles into the foamy edges like overlapping flower petals with stupid sugary glee, and my grandfather would tell me not to eat the cup too whilst he fixed watch batteries nearby.

Fast food and junk food, when growing up in a small working class town, can be entertainment in itself. Perhaps you cannot afford to buy a ticket to a theme park, or a new video game; but you can afford some bars of chocolate or crisps. Maybe you can afford some cigarettes and cider. It's free to sit in the park or by the canal, or in your friend's bedroom. You can wander, winding around the newsagent's familiar aisles, before you wander around the streets. When the ice cream van bell chimes, run to it, slowing down as your heart is beating, to join the end of the queue of people from your street, if you have even ten pence for an ice pole or a mixture of sweets scrunched into a white paper bag. You can afford the small pocket pleasures decried in tabloid health scare features, or found in stock image libraries tagged 'ill health' and 'impoverished communities'. The streets I grew up in, where all of these scenes took place in food-colouring technicolour, rank within the top 5-10% most deprived areas of Scotland, according to the Scottish Index of

Multiple Deprivation[1] which analyses factors such as income, employment, health, education, skills, housing, geographic access and crime.

Treats, when there have been times when even the bus fare is a stretch too far, are always a compromise. The weighing up of pleasures and necessities means time divided into the immediate aching now and the austere later. The stomach veers between fixation and hesitation. A moment of deciding whether to step over the threshold of the window you've been looking in, taking fleeting hedonism after filing the gas bill in the back of your mind, out of sight. In a cartoon, a fox might consider whether snatching a cooling pie from a windowsill will result in the pane slamming down on his paw.

In these moments, treats are a taste of pure escapism. Carefully counted morsels or giddy impulse (occasionally with an aftertaste of regret). Now, years later, I press the same pleasure button, and can afford to do so more often. Celebration? Press the button. Feeling ill? Press the button. Tough day? Press the button. None of it tastes quite as special as when reaching up to press that button (or an adult pressing it for me) meant a temporary screening off of monetary confines, happiness blooming like sugar and salt through my bloodstream. I press the button now to order pizza, with the same eager expectation as the internet dial-up tone used to evoke, more specifically seeking the baked-in emotional thrill and comfort established at a young age and which has never left me. Press the button.

Andy Warhol's affinity for Coca Cola bottles, the everyday subject, like Campbell's soup cans, gracing hundreds of his screen prints, stemmed from the joy of knowing the experience

---

1. Measuring Deprivation Advisory Group. (2011, October 27). The Scottish Index of Multiple Deprivation. Retrieved from http://www.gov.scot/Topics/Statistics/SIMD

of drinking Coke was the same for everyone.

'You can be watching TV and see Coca-Cola, and you know that the President drinks Coke, Liz Taylor drinks Coke, and just think, you can drink Coke, too. A Coke is a Coke and no amount of money can get you a better Coke than the one the bum on the corner is drinking. All the Cokes are the same and all the Cokes are good. Liz Taylor knows it, the President knows it, the bum knows it, and you know it.'

Frequency of affordability aside, a democratising effect takes place when it appears a pleasure can be felt the same way by anyone from any social strata. More than the taste of the drink itself, what makes a Coke or the other everyday mass-manufactured foodstuffs fascinating enough to have been a motif for Warhol, and an emotional tripwire for me, is perhaps that brief intense moment where the socio-economic boundaries dissolve and bodily satisfaction is all there is.

Advertisements for fast food try to drill down into the same feelings, promising, alongside deliciousness, the happiness, friends, sunshine, glamour, and whatever else research data indicates consumers are really searching for when emotional impulse leads to spending money and brand loyalty, making kings of paupers when they bite into a stuffed crust.

One day as a child I was taken to the pizza chain I today have brand loyalty to, on a day out with adults who, notably, were not partaking themselves. Small or medium? I picked a medium, excitedly. When the cashier asked for £6, my cheeks burned with embarrassment and shame, the deep claret cringe of the consequences of my greed. I had made the wrong choice and asked for too much. An action taken in lightheartedness snapped back like a rubber band to sting me. The moment encapsulates a routine fear and doubt which circles leisure, days out, and fun on low incomes. It sounded like a lot of money, far too much for a solo lunch, and whilst it was willingly paid,

I ate each bite on my own feeling ashamed of myself. Possibly, it was entirely fine. It was left unspoken. To a young me, those six pounds I felt I'd caused to be spent felt like the epitome of wastefulness and selfishness.

Jarvis Cocker sings in searing class polemic 'Common People', on those who try on the lifestyle as a stylistic choice, wryly commenting their fast food grease will wash off. As an adult whose purse has wavered over the years, saving little and dipping at times into overdraft, I now often order pizza from that chain. I get deep pan margherita with barbecue sauce. I have a similar fondness for various brands of crisps. I buy chocolate, I buy cheese. I buy it all. I buy it when I feel up and down, I buy it when I feel sideways. I buy too much of it at the weekends, and I eat it all, and I feel, mostly, not physically or emotionally as satiated as expected but merely too full, glad of my metabolism and making a vague self promise to eat less calorific foods during weekdays.

A mental association has forged between this foodstuff of my youth, low in nutritional value and high in salt, sugar, fat and hollow carbs, with good times, or deservedness; with being kind to myself, happiness, birthdays, a life I ought to live, cheering myself up, distracting myself from depression, and many other balms. I associate bad food with free time; it has gotten into me that this is how to relax from weekday stresses. If I can buy it, even when using my overdraft, even by ignoring bills, I might just give in.

Until I lived in the city and could take in a wider variety of food, I looked for trussed up, plated versions of these simple foods on menus, taking comfort in the familiarity and trying to avoid showing ignorance on any occasion of eating out. Nor did I want to gamble money on the risk of something I might not like. Now, as an adult who recognises unfamiliarity is nothing to be ashamed of, I ask questions. Comedians sometimes laugh at the unsophistication of food in Glasgow or other working class areas. What they are really laughing at are the poor. These people, myself: we are no worse and no better by any moral or intellectual standard of judgement for where we have happened to fall at birth within a social order or geographical grid on a square that contains more takeaways than fresh bakeries.

While Andy Warhol's Coke bottles meant to him brief access to a glamorous uniformity, food more often marks out social differences. Routine meals on a low income can be a drudgery and stress, both the antithesis of and explanation for my joy in processed cheese prepared a different way by someone else.

School meals, provided free for children whose parents struggle financially, can cause the recipients to be set apart from others. Advances in technology have gone some way to soothing this, using cards invisibly topped up and on the surface, appearing all the same. In the United States, there are cases of 'lunch shaming', where children who cannot pay for lunch are made to clean, or given substandard fare. This is cruelty made official school policy.

The mere act of eating for these children can be a humiliation, when they are singled out by others, at an age where any differentiating behaviour or appearance is a target. In higher year groups when their peers may be venturing out of school to a chip shop nearby, the choice is be hungry and socialise, or stay behind and eat separately. Young social groupings predicated by wealth form in moments such as these. In cases of bullying for accepting free school meals, a necessity of life, to simply eat is the vehicle by which they suffer.

This can be seen in other basic necessities. Poorer children, like adults, can be picked on for their mode of shelter, in a council house or high rise flat, and their protection from the elements, in the clothing that they wear. The argument for a school uniform, that it should remove this jeopardy, did not work for the children at my high school whose parents could not afford the branded uniform either and who were sent to school in slightly off-kilter approximations or different clothes entirely.

It may be difficult to imagine what it is like to be a child who is hungry but who knows when they collect their lunch they may be picked upon for doing so. In this way, financial anxiety over food is written into everyday meal experiences from an early age, and children are set apart from each other. School trips take this to the next level. 'I need payment and parent forms back by Friday,' spoken by a teacher is a stressful line for those uncertain that asking parents for money will produce enough. If the poorest children can afford to go at all, pocket money limitations forbid the fun at the gift shop and snacks their classmates may be having, as they watch on silently and hope nobody will notice the difference. Poverty builds invisible assault courses into getting through the day for children who should, instead, be carelessly swinging from the bars of jungle gyms.

Children who grow up alongside peers who are even marginally more comfortable than themselves notice the differences: small and big; everyday and overarching. I was not one of the poorest children in my school, but I noticed that the own brand supermarket crisps I had in my lunchbox, 30p for a bag of six, did not match the Walkers my best friend ate. The sliced baguette habitually on her kitchen table was bought in a run-down Asda but seemed exotic to me. I did not learn how to eat with a knife and fork until later in life because I did not have a dinner table, or room for one, and found a fork alone easier to balance with a plate on my lap. Even though as a student I worked as a waitress in numerous workplaces, including serving food I could not myself afford to eat in a five-star hotel, residual self-doubt means I still feel daunted before setting cutlery.

Noticing the differences creates an interior narrative of fear and anticipation of awkward moments; of not just struggling to pay for a basic need or moment of leisure, but being set upon for it. Reflexive self-protection double-checks the pennies before getting to the counter to hand them over, and tries to act naturally in front of the shopkeeper. Poverty puts people from a very young age into isolated boxes, sometimes clearly stamped, but sometimes hidden, invisible, and fragile, like clear glass. Poverty can make people feel like they don't belong for the rest of their lives, even in moments when they can more easily count out the money.

For those without a car, poorly served by public transport or reluctant to spend bus fare, or for the time-poor or workers of antisocial shift patterns, the cost alone of fresh fruit and vegetables is only part of the problem. In recession-hit towns, where independent grocers and other businesses have gradually switched off their shop lights, hit by the double blow of squeezed margins and supermarket dominance, it can be easier to buy sachets of powdered soup and other cheap cupboard staples from a pound shop. Malnutrition is not a problem confined to the Victorians of history lessons, with millions of people in the UK, particularly those with low income or mobility problems, suffering from undernourishment in the present day.[2] Access to good food varies across the country. The term 'food desert' was coined in the '90s, applying to both urban and rural areas.

Finding fresh fruit and vegetables can mean a lengthy trip to a retail park supermarket on the outskirts of town as the only

2. Pells, R. (2017, April 17). Poor children returning to school 'malnourished' following increase in 'school holiday hunger'. Retrieved from http://www.independent.co.uk/news/education/education-news/poor-children-hunger-malnourished-rising-numbers-returning-free-school-meals-a7687091.html

alternative to the limp pickings of a newsagent or what can be found immersed in icy cabinets in bargain frozen food shops. Shops like Farmfoods with rows of cabinets and strip lighting psychologically evoke the harvesting of richly turned fields in name only and far-removed in actuality, similar to street names which reference old geographical landmarks that no longer exist on new housing estates; the ponds and glades long paved over. A bag of processed hockey-puck burgers or cartons of long-life concentrated juice can be found in buy-one-get-one-free promotions, but it is not so easy to stock the shelves with leafy greens high in protein, iron, and vitamins. Neither is it cheap to be poor, unable to benefit from the scale of economy a bigger purchasing budget can stretch to.

Forget the difficulty of finding pomegranate molasses for a celebrity cookbook recipe or deciding whether to spend 30 pence more for organic apples: it can be a challenge to find basics that satisfy daily nutritional requirements.

Public Health England, an executive agency of the UK Government's Department of Health, has found that diet is the primary cause of poor health in the UK.[3] Features with this statistic are common in newspapers, disseminating the information in a disdainful tone, making succumbing to the trappings of poverty a target of pious, head-shaking morality.

'Cutting down on junk food diets, couch potato lifestyles, cigarettes and booze could make Britain one of the healthiest places to live in the world,' said Oxford-educated Simon Stevens in 2015, chief executive of the NHS, who has spoken in

---

3. Donnelly, L. (2015, September 15). Britain's poor diet more deadly than its smoking habit as alcohol related deaths soar. Retrieved from http://www.telegraph.co.uk/news/health/news/11865074/Britains-poor-diet-more-deadly-than-its-smoking-habit-as-alcohol-related-deaths-soar.html

favour of increased privatisation.[4] Putting the onus of blame on the individual for their lifestyle choices when there are so few choices available is to ignore the more pressing political factors of austerity and inequality which directly cause food poverty and illiteracy.

As hunger in the UK grows, with food banks and charities more strained than ever, and people in low paid work struggling to cope with welfare cuts amidst inflation, initiatives to combat food inequality are up against the bigger political structures which perpetuate class inequality. Pop-up food markets and cookery lessons can only go so far. Yellowing posters about nutrition flap dog-eared from the walls of local surgery waiting rooms with five-a-day photographs of vegetables even less visually appealing than those on the front of frozen food store freezer packs. I don't want to eat those apples, clinically dissected into units of health, peeled of enjoyment.

The knock-on effect of food poverty spins out in all directions. Poor diets contribute to a plethora of health problems, with low income demographics more likely to suffer from diabetes, cancer, lower life expectancy and obesity. Cheap foods high in saturated fat, sugar, salt and empty carbs leave the eater unsatisfied. On a low nutrition diet, a cycle of fatigued slumps and cravings compound other factors working class people can face in their working day. The energy to work a manual job or ability to focus becomes strained. Children struggle to pay attention to their studies. Mental health, already under-resourced and under discussed, can take a toll as moods dip, eaten into by hunger and stress.

4. Donnelly, L. (2015, September 15). Britain's poor diet more deadly than its smoking habit as alcohol related deaths soar. Retrieved from http://www.telegraph.co.uk/news/health/news/11865074/Britains-poor-diet-more-deadly-than-its-smoking-habit-as-alcohol-related-deaths-soar.html

In food desert areas, food literacy levels are lower,[5] as a little varied routine of industrialised, processed foods creates a barrier to informed health choices or the ability to develop kitchen skills and confidence. For many years, I'd eat plain pasta with margarine and salt, suspicious of sauces whose herbed depths seemed mysterious and not for the likes of me. Benefiting from the affluent area of the city where I can just about afford to rent a flat now, I consult the cookbooks I bought from a local bookshop, I buy fresh herbs and vegetables from a well-stocked greengrocer, and trying new meals is an active process where, before I get to instruction one, I take an additional invisible step zero of reaffirming that the food inequality factors which have held me back were not merely failings of my own will.

Until it is at the forefront of discourse that ideological politics are behind the societal inequality which causes many communities to be fundamentally impoverished, with lesser access to food, education, employment, transport and all the other building blocks of informed choice, to blame the working class individual for the flaws in their lifestyle is a deception worse than the non-existent farm names printed on budget food packaging.

I take joy in a little round plastic tub of cheese, with its matching round plastic lid, because it was one of the purest pleasures I've ever known. I press the pleasure button to order pizza. I press the pleasure button to temporarily forget all of this. I press the pleasure button because the other buttons were disconnected, ringing out.

5. Press, V. (2004). *Nutrition and Food Poverty toolkit: Developing a local nutrition and food poverty strategy* (pp. 93-124, Rep.) (M. Mwastsama, Ed.). National Heart Forum.

More Than Just a Dream Land:
Why the British Seaside Means So Much to the Working Class

Yvonne Singh

There's a photo I treasure of my late mother and me at Southend. We are both ankle-deep in moss-coloured water, sea foam puddling at our legs. I am about three years old, my chubby fingers sealed around the flimsy handle of a shiny red bucket, a fake plastic policeman's hat, complete with golden braid, balanced lopsided on my head, while a frilled swimsuit droops around my shoulders. My mother's beige trousers are rolled up to her knees while splodges of water blot her pale T-shirt. Seaweed lies in front of us on the beach like matted hair, its pods blistering the muddy surface, while a hoard of smooth pebbles and broken mussel shells glisten in the sun like undiscovered treasure. In the background a grey-haired man in a worn woollen waistcoat and rolled shirtsleeves balances the edge of his flannelled bum cheeks precariously on the rail of The Dreadnought pleasure-seeker. Mum and I are both smiling. We are both so happy. And so my love affair with the British seaside begins…

When we were kids, growing up in 1970s Romford, we couldn't afford to go on holidays abroad. In fact, I don't think anyone could. I only heard of one person in my school going to Disneyland in Florida – Claire Watkins in the 5th year – and she was treated like a minor celebrity. I remember her coming back to school (these were the days before the term-time holiday ban), looking like Olivia Newton-John, honey-blonde hair striking against a rosewood tan, sporting a fluffy pink Minnie Mouse sweatshirt and baseball boots. We younger girls all crowded around her, eager to know what the land that brought us *Fame* and Ronald Reagan was like. 'Did you meet Mickey/Coco (from *Fame*)/Mr T?'; 'What was the food like?'; 'Was it scary going on a plane?' Claire answered our many questions in her newly acquired Texan drawl, superior in her newfound knowledge and keen to furnish us lacking airmiles with information. An older boy striding past the gaggle of girls surrounding her, and threatened by the attention she was getting, decided to put her in her place:

'Oi Claire! You look like a fuckin' Paki!'

Silence, except for his sniggers. Her face fell for a brief moment and then she carried on, ignoring the 'insult', the boy's laughter still ringing in her ears. I tried not to bristle, my sister and I being the only 'Pakis' in the school. The lesson: holidays abroad may seem glamorous but don't try to act better than you are, or someone will come along and knock you right back down to earth.

Which was a shame, really: we could have done with more Claires and tales of different, glowing Technicolour lands. Grey concrete was the bulwark of my childhood: concrete subways, concrete fountains, concrete flats. I could amp it up as pewter, but that would just be a lie. And with the concrete came the graffiti – 'KEEP BRITAIN WHITE'; 'PAKS [sic] out'; 'NF' – the types of slogans that made you *really* feel at home. Even the Dolphin swimming pool, the only leisure place for kids for miles, with its much-vaunted tidal wave machine (note: only switched on twice a day between 9.15-10.15am and 4-5pm), was a huge grey edifice stuck in the middle of a roundabout. It wasn't pretty.

So as a kid to get away from it all, to go on day-trips to the seaside and experience a magical landscape unlike anything I'd ever known: miles of pebbly beach meeting the vast mirror of the sea; a place where the light refracts in a certain way so that everything sparkles – even the concrete bollards – why that was just amazing.

The seaside had everything: sand (possibly), shingle (most definitely), and the sea (the ultimate waterpark where the tidal machine was never switched off). It instilled in me a hope, a hope that things could be better.

It must have been a mission for my parents, though, three kids, no car. My dad was a postman so he'd always take a couple of weeks off in August and we'd fit in a few day-trips then. We'd hop on the train at Romford to the end of the line. Southend was the nearest beach: shingly with a long pier. I'd come to appreciate it later as a seaside in miniature. As small kids, we would paddle and mess about on the beach, battering the plastic buckets and fragile fishing nets we'd picked up at the quirky shops that lined the seafront. And when we'd indulged our primal instinct for messing about in sand and water, so exhausted by wave jumping, sand tunnelling, and the rest, we would go to the tiny amusement park with its miniature railway that would snake around the edge of the pier. Back then, we were the only brown faces on the beach, but we didn't experience any racism. The seaside brought with it a universal camaraderie, and that made it even more special. I'd come home exhausted and happy, sea salt crusting my hair and eyebrows, sand molehills in my patent shoes, a visible reminder the next day to nag my parents to take me again.

Occasionally we would venture further afield to resorts like Clacton, which I remember as prettier, with sandier beaches than Southend and a lot more shells. But by far my favourite resort on the east coast was Margate, with its broad golden expanse of sand, bordered by elegant whitewashed villas and overlooked by its grand Victorian clock tower. Margate had swings and donkey rides on the beach, and there were even Punch and Judy shows on the promenade for the sand shy. This Kent beach did everything better than its muddier Essex cousin.

Of course, it follows that if the beach was better, the amusement park was, too. The aptly named Dreamland was a kids' paradise. There was stuff for us younger kids – the ghost train, the old-fashioned carousel – but it was the thrill-seeking, gravity-defying rides for the older kids that held my attention. I was too small back then to go on them, but I'd watch wide-eyed as teenagers stumbled off, legs buckling like young foals, after braving the Big Wheel, the Dipper, or the Scenic Railway Rollercoaster, a vast wooden skeletal structure that dominated that edge of the beach.

The first time we went, a tall, skinny youth clad in double denim stood a few feet away from me and my brother, and chucked his guts up as we struggled to devour a wodge of candyfloss.

'Just wotcha looking at?' he sneered, using the back of his hand to mop his mouth.

'Nothing,' I said, switching my gaze from him to the pool of chunky yellow vomit on the floor, worried that my dream was about to turn into a nightmare.

At this point, his equally lanky friend strode up and placed his arm around his queasy pal, which seemed to calm him down. 'Oh, don't worry about him, sweetheart. Some people just don't have the constitution,' he said, patting his stomach, his brown eyes twinkling.

'How did you manage to stay on – up there?' I asked, my eyes watching the next group of riders scream as the Rotor Ride spun like a washing machine drum, the floor slowly disappearing with each turn.

He touched the side of his nose. 'Gravity, sweetheart. It's like being on the moon. You're free. Nothing to hold you down. It's great.' And he stomped off in pretend Neil Armstrong boots, dragging his limp pal, his flares flapping around his ankles. Lessons learned that day: the seaside embodied freedom, it was a place where you could let go of all inhibitions; either that, or it was a place where the sicker you got, the more fun was to be had.

Over time I acquired my own battle scars: friction burns on the Helter Skelter, a sore head from the Dodgems. Away from the rides there were the fairground games: hook-a-duck, rifle ranges, where for a few coppers you could experience the thrill of winning something, even if it was just a cuddly toy.

Margate also had an arty side that embraced its tackier edge. I loved the little shops that sold jewellery, and ornaments delicately crafted of bone and shell. Every time we visited I would purchase a carefully chosen memento. Most of the trinkets didn't survive the years, but my eldest son now owns a tiny, shell-covered treasure chest I picked up at Margate when I was seven.

Sadly, all good things are destined to come to an end. The last time we visited Dreamland, it had been taken over and renamed Bembom Brothers Theme Park by its new Dutch owners. It didn't have quite the same ring. My parents refused to join the huge queues or pay the newly introduced entrance fee, so at ten my particular dream land was over, although the memories still linger.[1]

My friend Gillian is sucking her bottle-green school tie, her grey-blue eyes steeled with concentration. The bony fingers of her right hand are tensed, pressing all three large red buttons in unison, as if she is trying to elicit a tune out of the boxy Perspex machine in front of her. Her left hand nudges the joystick operating the claw grabber, desperate to get at one of the pound notes that are wedged between a mound of blue Smurfs. Its metal fingers descend and tantalisingly scrape the edge of the note. She clicks the button, the grabber refuses to grip. It glides past the note, brushing Papa Smurf's hat.

'For fuck's sake.' She looks at me and smiles. Her eyes have settled on a bank of penny pusher machines. She may only have pennies left but she still has a chance to win.

Fast-forward to the mid-1980s. Like the sand that clings to your feet following a visit to the beach, I hadn't quite shaken off the sense of freedom that being at the seaside brings. Times back then were hard. The grocer's daughter was in power and seemed dead set on entrenching the deep divisions within society, making the lot of the working classes even harder. Both the miners' strike and the Wapping dispute were supported by my dad's Communication Workers Union, so even at 14 I was well aware of the inequality and unjustness of it all. High unemployment plagued the nation and presented fewer opportunities for teenagers. Plus, in the words of dearly departed Prince, 'a big disease with a little name' was terrifying the hell out of the young, thanks to the government's Don't Die of

---

1. Note to Ed. After a few incarnations and several years of trying to save the site from redevelopment, the Dreamland Trust Restoration Project was established in 2010 by people with similar fond memories to mine. The site reopened in 2015, but was dogged by financial troubles and closed. Thanks to a new injection of funds, Dreamland reopened again in April 2017.

Ignorance campaign.

So when the doom and gloom got all too much, when I would think what was the point of school, if the inevitable destination was the dole queue or some dodgy YTS scheme, I'd bunk off school with my best mates, we'd jump on the train in our uniforms and head down to Southend – our very own version of 'taking the cure'.

Were we somehow trying to recapture the sense of freedom the seaside gave us when we were small kids, before the responsibilities of early adulthood loomed? Quite possibly. Or could it have been that the vastness and enduring nature of the sea gave us a sense of perspective? Any worries and anxieties could be nudged away like flotsam by the rolling tides.

All of the above – but in the days before people had game consoles in their bedrooms, it was the bright lights and buttons of the cavern-like arcades that drew us like moths.

We'd spend hours in the arcades, eating ghosts on Pac-Man or dodging fireballs in Donkey Kong, as synth Europop thudded out of the speakers. My friends Kim and Eleri were an unassailable double act on Space Invaders, racking up thousands of points for blasting aliens with lasers, even drawing admiring crowds of onlookers.

Gillian was an ace at the penny pusher machines. She would walk around the banks of piled copper, sussing out which one was close to spilling its contents and which toy was closest to the edge. She'd watch to see if the attendant was looking and then give the machine a sly nudge: the more coins we had, the more fish and chips or pints of prawns later.

I'd watch her slowly choke the machine's throat with copper. *Watch and wait.* It was an art, timing the coin's descent, watching each one as it trickled down through a maze of plastic. She would always win. The win would make up for everything: a shit week at school, a shit week at home.

And when we'd done with the machines and the imaginary worlds that were so much better than ours, we'd head to the beach for fish and chips, or wander around the rides. Most were cordoned off with chewed-up red tape, but some we could access, a playground that seemed strangely desolate out of season, but one where we could still scream at the top of our lungs as the Waltzer spun round and round.

'If you'd hit my dress, you would have to pay for it.'

The dress is a smoky emerald with glints of gold. In a former life it could have been a sofa cover.

The tidal pull has been too strong to resist. I am back at the seaside, working as a silver service waitress in my summer breaks from university. I was one of a handful from my school to go on into further education. I get a full grant but I need to supplement my income over the summer. The five-star hotels on the Cornish coast pay the best and provide accommodation, plus: they are by the sea, what could be better?

I blink and then I squint. A microdot of gravy has landed on her napkin. Haddock is one of the most requested dishes for dinner but fish is notoriously difficult to silver serve. The flesh always crumbles, so she could count herself lucky to get away with just a spot.

She is still looking at me crossly over her cat's-eye spectacles. Her grey hair is pulled severely into a french roll, tightening the flesh around her jaw – or she could just be clenching her teeth.

'Five hundred pounds it cost me.'

More than I would make in a whole season waitressing.

'I'm so sorry,' I mumble.

'And so you should be, so you should be,' she tuts.

At that moment I want to tip the platter of fishy gravy over her head.

The people I waited on at the hotel were lords and ladies,

judges, sometimes actors, the odd successful author (he'd tip very well), the very definition of high society. To them, a stay at the seaside was booking into luxury hotels and having a three-course dinner every night served by a chump like me. I wonder how many of them have played the arcades, or had fish and chips on the beach, or ridden a rollercoaster, and I can't help thinking that they're the ones that are missing out. (I could be wrong, of course. Lady Ermine could well have been a Dodgem fiend.)

You see, the seaside symbolised hope and freedom for many working people. So when broadsheet columnists denounce the 'cross-me-quick' beaches or the so-called tawdriness or decline of our beaches, I want them to look beyond that myopic vision to the hope it instils.

Yes, there is poverty – Margate, Hastings and Blackpool all have pockets of deprivation – but if we coveted our coastline, invested in it more, less of that would exist.

Last summer I cycled past Margate seafront on the first hot day of the year and spied a group of people down from London enjoying themselves on the beach. They were a mixed crowd of all ages and all races, gathered around a soundsystem, dancing freely while the midday sun lit the scene: a sapphire sea, a saffron sand – rich streaks of colour reminiscent of a Renaissance painting. The group's unadulterated joy was wonderful to behold and made me think that if the seaside is such a unifying force for working people, if its memories bring us such happiness and such comfort, we really need to take the initiative and look after it more.

The Death of a Pub

Dominic Grace

I am currently unattached. I have had six key drinking relationships in my life. Half of those establishments no longer exist or are so utterly changed that they are no longer the places I knew. The others are geographically out of reach and so I am currently without a pub that I can call my own. It is not a feeling I'm accustomed to and I don't like it. I'm not someone who takes well to the fancy-free existence of drinking wherever I happen to find myself. I've always needed a significant boozer.

Pubs have never been a trivial matter for me – just somewhere to slake my thirst or have the occasional knees-up. I have made serious commitments to pubs. Once I've entered into this sacred relationship these places have become both lodestone and lodestar for me, drawing me to them and guiding my path. Not only that but they have become a second domicile, the place other than my home where I can best relax and be myself.

While others might remember what pop songs were in the charts at a particular time, or who was PM, I can pinpoint significant events in my life depending on which pub or club I was drinking in. Just as I measure my life in terms of dogs (dogs I have had and the number I have left to have) so I demarcate and cross-reference eras in terms of drinking dens. Where I can name both boozer and mutt, I can probably narrow it down to months or weeks.

Just as these pubs have provided me with this home-away-from-home, so they have also been the key to my identity. In these days of identity politics, one of the key building blocks in creating my self-image has been the bars I've consumed alcohol in.

The pubs I've frequented are as much a part of my identity as the accent I have, the clothes I've worn, the haircuts I've had, the books I've read and the music I've listened to. And, just as some of those things have linked me to wider groups with a shared identity, the pubs I've used have always been a way of immediately plugging into the zeitgeist of working class community.

Each of my favourite pubs has in some part been an extension of home. The Welsh have a beautiful word – hiraeth – which is even more apposite when I consider the disappearance of some of these temporary homes; although there is allegedly no perfect translation into English of *hiraeth*, Wikipedia says that it is 'homesickness tinged with grief or sadness over the lost or departed... a mix of longing, yearning, nostalgia, wistfulness...' and so on. This is true. For me, every local will open doors on faces of those who are no longer with us. It's almost impossible to think of any of the pubs without at some point sighing and shaking my head. A proper working class pub brings up not just the memories of my past, but the folk memory of the decade before I was born and nearly all my family lived in the same terraced street – I am always wanting to return to a sense of community. And it's clearly not just me who has seen that the pub is a key and emotive element of who we are; the world of screen cottoned onto this a good while ago. One shorthand that the entertainment industry in Britain has used since the Second World War: if you want to portray a person or a group of people as working class then you film a scene in a traditional pub. From *Passport to Pimlico*, through *Get Carter* and *Kes* (actually a working man's club) up to the greatest of them all, Terence Davies' remarkable *Distant Voices, Still Lives*, the creators of drama have used, with varying degrees of accuracy and success, licensed premises as a milieu that immediately tells the audience what social group they are dealing with. These are the workers at play. The manual workers, the labourers, the unskilled, the poorly-paid and those who inherited nothing better than the gene for male-pattern-baldness are letting off steam.

Younger readers, especially those who do their drinking in town centres, might struggle to identify with the pubs they see on screen and perhaps wonder if these idealised boozers, where all age-groups mix and mingle, ever existed.

Of course, the working class are still visiting the pub on a nightly basis, but the trade is swallowed whole by just three premises – the Rovers Return, The Queen Victoria and The Woolpack. Meanwhile, in the real world, pubs close on a daily basis and this most British of institutions reels. And the reason you'd have been watching pubs instead of being in them is all part of the direction this country has moved in over the past 40 years.

It's another essay entirely to list the reasons that pubs are dying but economies of scale (spelling the death of 'small and local' in favour of 'large and out-of-town') and the drift of society towards being a nation of car-owning, cheap-beer supermarket-shopping, satellite or cable TV-watching, social-media-using hermits gives some clues. We can drink beer very cheaply at home while still chatting to people online. Plus we can smoke while we're doing it.

But what are we losing? As one who lived abroad for a while, I know the truth in the cliché that the Great British Pub is a thing to be missed like few others (decent tea and sitcoms were the other factors for me). We're not just losing bricks and mortar, an 'experience' to be ticked off tourist-style, or even a part of our 'heritage' (more on this shortly). We're losing living, breathing, vibrant cells in the body of our country. These are places where, for centuries, people have come together as one, to reaffirm their community bonds, to feel part of something bigger than themselves, and to sense that they are part of something intangible but even bigger – the country itself and all the other workers within it. The written history of the country may concern itself with the actions of kings and queens but the driving force and lifeblood has always been the groundlings – the peasants who have now traded the life bucolic for that of industry, the factory and the warehouse or the pick, the shovel and the open road. Who will speak for the amusement palaces of the ordinary man and woman? Themselves alone.

Government has done little to reverse this loss, perhaps seeing no merits in a working class that is in touch with itself and can feel not just its muscles but sense the power that resides within itself. Meanwhile, heritage and preservation industries in the UK are worth millions and employ thousands, but the heritage they wish to preserve has nothing to do with the cultural endowment resting in the reservoir of working class communities. Instead, it concerns itself mainly with the houses of the aristocracy and the arcane history of the moneyed and powerful – I've often thought that if legend claimed a king had once pissed on an oak the state would raise money to preserve it, but would do nothing to save the Royal Oaks around which communities in working class districts had been nourished and fostered.

The pub has always been 'our place'. Unlike the workplace we might have been in just half an hour ago, this is a place without hierarchy where we are truly judged on the content of our character above all else. In your local no one is going to look down on your accent, your income or where you live. The only time the pub strays into any kind of hierarchy is on Darts-and-Doms night when it becomes a meritocracy: your family's wealth won't buy you a place in the Fives-and-Threes squad – it must be earned! In 'our place' you can also swear and call each other names. If you can't handle that then maybe it isn't the place for you. These places are bawdy, brawling, unfettered houses of mirth. They are the exact opposite of a Safe Space and all the better for it.

I've known true joy in pubs and shebeens (the unlicensed drinking dens belonging to immigrant communities that are even more precise in their definition of membership) in a way that I never have at the theatre or in an art gallery or museum. Simple things like the combination of a Monday and the words 'rained-off' – the finest hyphenated words in English, rivalled only by 'lock-in' – and suddenly a quiet afternoon drink for one or two old men has turned into a wild, cartwheeling, careering, shambolic drinking session with a sideshow of gambling thrown in for good measure, when the pub has filled with blokes who should have been digging the road, except for one of them has ruptured a gas main. If you've gone to work on a Monday feeling rough and expecting a day-long battle of hard physical work and then you're given a reprieve, it would be rude not to use that gift, to spend that time, in a tantrum of jubilation, an explosion of exuberance. It was days like this that turned me into one of the 'twilight people' as my dad referred to anyone who drank between 3pm and 5.30pm – the hours that pubs used to be closed before a change to the Licensing Act.

For years, I incorrectly presumed that all pubs were working class. I thought the middle class joined golf clubs or perhaps went to country clubs. I believed that pubs were full of people like me. It was only when I started to venture outside of my comfort zone that I discovered otherwise.

The city of Leeds is divided north and south by the River Aire. The south side of the city is working class, the north side contains areas which are very well-to-do as well as housing near- ly all the city's university students. I am from the south side, from the entirely working class district of Middleton.

Everyone knows that South Leeds is the 'real' Leeds. Even people who live in other parts of Leeds know it, although they might not admit it. Deep down, they know.

Years ago I was having a drink in the Skyrack in Headingley with a friend of mine called Jason. He'd been sitting in silence for a few minutes, thinking, and I waited expectantly, knowing he was on the verge of saying something important. I knew this because, while he was by no means an unintelligent man (despite freely admitting to only ever having read one book – the autobiography of Wally Lewis, Australian Rugby League legend), quiet introspection was not the trait for which he was most notable. He'd been looking around the bar at the other customers and I waited for him to speak. Eventually he turned to me and said, 'They've even got different bone-structures to us.' I wasn't necessarily expecting, 'It's your round,' but it still sur- prised me until I looked for myself and almost immediately grasped what he was saying. Everyone else in the pub, bar none, was better-looking than us.

A lot of them may well have been students, and thus from various parts of the country, but as we continued our pub crawl around North Leeds we observed the same phenomenon in every establishment we went in. People's faces were generally more symmetrical than our own and, as if to rub our noses in it, they nearly all had better hair and clothes. We returned across the River Aire – that narrow band of water but that awesome gulf – two Cro-Magnon men, chastened by our very bones, our identities betrayed. We were Of South Leeds. We would return to the safety of Our Leeds, and the pubs we knew: 'So we beat on, boats against the current, borne ceaselessly into the past.' Because that's where the place we drank in those days, the Middleton Arms, now belongs. The past. Generations of the same families went in that pub. Groups of brothers, fathers and sons; for it was above all a Man's pub and they were men who worked in scrapyards and who dug foundations, men who were scaffolders, roofers, concrete-finishers, former miners and men who worked in tanneries and foundries. It was a pub where thirsts were quenched after a hard day's graft. I once took the members of my work's five-a-side football team, men from all parts of Leeds, in there for a pint after one match and while one of the team said, 'Let's just drink quick and go,' another said, 'Why are they all so big in here?'

I told them to relax. I knew the place. I loved it.

It was the place where for a very long time I saw it as my birthright to win the pop quiz, and with it a gallon of beer, to be shared with my team-mate Martyn. This weekly free beano came to an end when a man of diminutive stature but encyclopedic pop-trivia knowledge started drinking there, regularly prompting Martyn to toss a beer mat on the table and exclaim, 'Sod it! Pop dwarf's just walked in!'

What happens when a pub dies? What happens to all the stories, the laughs, the first flirtations that turned into love, and yes, the fights too – what happens to all that?

I could talk to you for hours about that pub. About some of the silly things that made me laugh – a 17-year-old girl coming in with her friends one Saturday night on possibly their first visit, all dressed in short skirts and low-cut tops, and a shout from the other side of the pub from her elder brother: 'Someone throw a coat on our lass!' Or the time they decided that Sunday lunchtime would be enlivened by strippers, and a customer answering the phone on the bar (a common practice because it was OUR pub), nodding, listening, and then turning to the pub and shouting in a hoarse, gruff voice, 'Exotic dancer's on t'phone – she wants directions from Wakefield.' Or the stripper who put her snake in a customer's pint, much to their displeasure and, as the story was told to me, 'T'bloke knocked t'bloody snake out!'

But I prefer to think of another time when Jason's dad had come with us for the Middleton Marauders' rugby side's end-of-season awards, and after a couple more pints than he was used to, found himself on the stage with the microphone in his hand and a break in his voice as he said, with genuine emotion, 'They might think we're nothing because we're from round here but we've got hearts like lions.' I knew that he had lost the run of himself but I didn't feel embarrassed – I agreed with every word.

A woman I worked with back then said she'd never go in there because of its reputation but for me its reputation rang other bells, those of friendship and brotherhood. Not long after the demolition process had begun, a friend called round one evening in his car and I asked him to run me up the hill from LS11 to LS10 so I could take some photos. I stood and looked at the half-chewed remains of the place as the light around us died and I could hear all those laughs, see the beginnings of those love stories, all flashbacks coming thick and fast as the sounds of the place were being silenced forever. And I thought of all those people in our community for whom the place had been such an important part of their story, their past, and how a line had been drawn under it so that we could have another supermarket. It took every ounce of strength not to weep for all that was gone in the years and to know that the past would soon be half-remembered things, fading away alongside those of us who had drunk there.

That woman who thought she knew the pub's reputation lived in North Leeds. She didn't understand us. That we're different. I went home and fell into a dark mood.

To paraphrase Fitzgerald, I sat there brooding on the old, unknown world and how our dreams had seemed so close that we could hardly fail to grasp them. But I knew they were already behind me, somewhere in that vast obscurity beyond the city.

Britain's Invisible Black Middle Class

Sylvia Arthur

I.

When I was 14, and counting down the days until I'd finish school and be free to conquer the world, my cousin Linda, who was two years my senior, got a job at her local council. I remember exactly where I was when I heard the news. I was loitering in our kitchen in Kingsbury, North West London, listening in on a conversation between my uncle and my mother when, over a coffee and a Rothman's cigarette, he relayed the story of his youngest daughter. Though he spoke in his characteristic mild-mannered tone, the broad smile that graced his face betrayed an inner pride that moved me. It was as if in ascending to the council, an institution of government, my cousin had satisfied something deep within him.

My uncle was a minicab driver. Like most of the adult males I knew at the time – relatives, pseudo-relatives, and friends of my parents from 'back home' in Ghana – they'd come to the UK in the 1960s in pursuit of higher education, but ended up trading short-term plans for long-term dreams as reality forced them to forget who they were and confront who they'd become. It was a memory they struggled to relinquish. They drove their cabs in suits, spoke the formal English of academia, and carried out their chauffeuring duties with a diligence their punters, mostly leathered young men on a night out, generally failed to appreciate. They weren't just out of place, they were out of context, which was, perhaps, worse.

My father, who worked as a British Telecom engineer, died before he suffered a similar fate. Before he succumbed to a stroke at the age of 43, he and my mother had, through hard work and determination, shepherded us from a two-bedroom council flat to a three-bedroom home in a North London sub-urb that was slowly transforming from working class to middle class with each influx of new residents. After my father's death, my mother invested her grief in the future, toiling 18-hour days on her industrial sewing machine to send me to a private board-ing school in the country. Her thinking was it would give me the best chance of making something of myself at a time when social mobility was practically public policy, but race was still a defining factor. Yet, for my parents, class wasn't a driving force; it was an insignificant by-product of progress.

I was still at boarding school when my cousin got her job. It was 1991, and I had high hopes for myself; I was restless to step into Oprah's shoes. Even as a teenager I knew I'd have to leave Britain to do this because Britain offered few opportunities for people like me to 'make it'. The snubbing of Soul II Soul at the 1990 Brit Awards proved that. Despite this, although Linda's council job was a basic administrative role, I was surprisingly energised by it, as if she'd been appointed chief executive.

To my African circle, a position in the council represented

more than just a job. It signified acceptance from the powers-that-be, even if they were just local, and an official stamp of approval that said you were good enough to be let into their do-main. It wasn't just a stepping-stone to the professions preferred by African parents everywhere – lawyer, doctor, accountant. A job at the council was venerable in itself – safe and secure, with a pension and sickness benefits, an organisation in which you could spend your life and that would take care of you for the duration.

I idolised Linda. I aspired to her savvy. Everything she did seemed so grown up to me. I wanted to dress like her, act like her, and be like her. In short, I now wanted to work at the council.

II.

My first job was somewhat less auspicious than filing papers in the respectability of an office. But having arrived back in Lon-don from five years in educational exile in the country, I was keen to do anything that would prove to my new classmates I was still one of them.

At sixth-form college, I was reunited with a number of kids from primary school who treated me like the intellectual equiv-alent of the Hottentot Venus. At break times, they'd gather around me and get me to speak so they could marvel at my ac-cent. They'd probe me about what music I liked and which stars I fancied, expecting me to say Nirvana and Kurt Cobain rather than Snoop Dog and R. Kelly. Whenever a question was asked in class about something nobody had the answer to, they'd look to me to provide a response. I couldn't decide whether they hat-ed me or were proud of me. When my classmate, Betty, said she could get me a job at the local McDonald's where she worked part-time, I felt like I'd finally been let back into the fold.

The restaurant was a franchise. Its owner was a rotund, balding, middle-aged businessman who barked orders at his staff as if commanding a dog. Working conditions, which were already questionable, were dependent on the colour of his mood, which changed shade by the hour.

I was scheduled to work all day Saturday and Sunday mornings. 'But you may be called to come in on other days if we're busy,' Franklin, the owner, advised. I was on £2.75 an hour. My bus pass, which I relied on to take me from home to college and work, cost £7.50 a week, not to mention books, food, clothes, and other necessities.

Franklin assigned me to the shop floor, a responsibility he insisted was 'immense'. In reality, this meant floor mopping, tray collecting, bin emptying, and tissue and straw dispenser refilling but, within weeks, I was promoted to the burger station before finally making it to the tills. I was on my way up.

About a month into my contract, things took a downturn. I'd turn up to the restaurant as scheduled only to be told by Franklin: 'We're not busy this morning. Go home.' There was no explanation, no apology, and no money, just an instruction I was forced to abide by. Almost every week, I'd show up as required and would be turned away without pay. The cash I'd spent on my transport never came into the equation.

I put up with this erratic situation for six months before I hung up my apron and quit. It had become uneconomic for me to continue. But there were others, like baby-faced Barry, who left school at 16; jack-the-lad, Wei, who supported his mother and younger sister; and single father, John, with a child back in the Bahamas, who depended on the wage for survival. No one ever complained. Though they could live without the shitty conditions and piss-poor pay, they couldn't live without the job, and staff were as disposable as paper napkins.

My initiation into the labour market had begun. If I'd been under the illusion that work, like education, was a route to progress, then my time at McDonald's showed me otherwise.

III.

It seemed fitting that I should be working at the elite of super-markets while studying at the elite of universities. Though my uncle urged me to apply to Oxbridge because, he insisted, 'It's the only way to get ahead in this country,' I resisted the pressure and opted to stay closer to home.

UCL offered a new level of immersion into Britain's class system. I endured three years at the university alone, finding nothing in common with my highbrow, upper middle class peers who showed little interest in their coloured classmate.

I'd spent the past two years downplaying everything about myself, from the way I spoke to what I read. At UCL, by contrast, everything was amplified – accents, achievements, aspirations, not to mention the familial connections whose roots had been harvested long before my associates arrived at Gower Street and from which they'd reap benefits long after they left.

The Waitrose gig arrived at the right time. The controversial Sunday Trading Act, which paved the way for seven day a week consumerism, had not long been introduced and the double pay offered for giving up what was, until 1994, capitalism's day of rest, proved too enticing to turn down. I'd gone from making an erratic £2.75 an hour to a solid £7.35, well above the £3 minimum wage for 18-21 year olds that would be introduced by the new Labour government a year later in 1998. Between my £700 a term grant cheque and my mother's incalculable provision, I was financially better off than I'd ever been.

But books were expensive. My mother was working long

hours on her sewing machine, stitching up clothes that would find their way onto the rails of major department stores. I needed a job to do my bit and Waitrose offered stability – a permanent three-day-a-week contract that provided for holiday and sick pay. More importantly, at Waitrose, we weren't mere employees; we were Partners. This meant we had a stake in ensuring the company's success as the size of our end-of-year profit share depended on it.

I was assigned to the patisserie section, where my duty was to serve customers the various breads and pastries we baked throughout the day. There were four of us on the department, three women and Gary, an amateur footballer and keen sportsman, but as far as Sally, my line manager, was concerned, only one of us was equipped to do the back-breaking labour needed to shift the boxes of bread from the fifth floor freezer to the shop floor oven.

One evening, when I'd been dispatched to the freezer one too many times and my back was at breaking point, I asked Sally: 'Why do you always send me up to the freezer?' Sally was a career retailer. She'd started at the company straight out of school and worked her way up from teenage shelf stacker to department manager in her fifties. My question appeared to take her by surprise. 'Because you're big and strong.' She was flustered. 'It's a lot easier for you than it is for us.' Just who this 'us' was I could only infer, but when I countered with, 'Oh, why's that?' my response was met with silence followed by sheepishness, as it dawned on her that she'd inadvertently told me everything I already knew about her assumptions of me and my body's abilities.

I was five-foot-two and nine stone, six inches shorter than Sharon and many pounds lighter than Gary, whose mammoth frame dwarfed me. Still, the idea of the Black body as a commodity for the execution of (free) manual labour runs deep, even today. We are the people who cart boxes, those who sweep floors, and those whose intellect is considered inferior to our superhuman physicality. Our Blackness is indivisible from the perception of us as proletarian, a centuries-old mythology that no amount of advancement has managed to dislodge. This archaic thinking would follow me throughout my working life, framing how those with power interacted with me and determining everything from pay to promotion.

I lasted about a year at Waitrose, but it remained a badge of honour. It represented a step up from the drudgery of McDonald's and the retail shop floor, and was symbolic of where I was, and where I was headed. Finally, my work or, rather, the company I worked for, matched my aspirations to get on in a Britain in which everything was stratified – race, class, gender – and all three were indivisibly linked.

IV.

In 2010, after New Labour's 13 years in power had come to an end, I moved to Brussels to take up a job with a communications agency. I decided it was now or never – either I left the UK for the sake of my career or I stayed stuck in my immovable place.

It took eight GCSEs, three A Levels, three degrees and many years later, but I'd finally followed in my cousin Linda's footsteps and become embroiled in the world of local government. Between 2002 and 2010, I'd worked a series of jobs in various councils all of which were characterised by cronyism and nepotism and, in all of which, I was overlooked for promotion on multiple occasions.

I managed to make a way out of the confines of the British imagination by going abroad and into the heart of European power. My secret weapons? Years of experience, a solid education, and the ability to communicate well in English, weapons deemed blunt in Britain.

There's a saying in Brussels that you either leave the city within two years of arrival or you end up staying 20, and in the first six months, the outlook was long-term. I had a beautiful, spacious, city centre apartment, the likes of which would've been unattainable in London, and a job in which I was professionally respected. Yet, within two years, I left, but not without having risen through the ranks and been entrusted with both human and financial resources.

When I return to Brussels today, I'm surprised how many Black British women are living and working in the city, many more than when I was there. Whenever I meet my sisters, curiosity gets the better of me, and I can't help but enquire what drew them there, and what keeps them away from home.

On my last trip, I was introduced to Sarah, a friend-of-a-friend who was coming up to her sixth anniversary in the city. A 30-something South Londoner of Nigerian heritage, she'd recently been promoted in her corporate job, and was buzzing from moving into her new flat the weekend before, excitedly picking out furnishings and decorations. It was a two-bedroom apartment in a good part of the city, she said, close to many amenities, and was a short tram ride away from her office, or a 20-minute walk. The cost? A mere €700 (£600) a month.

I remember reading an article in the *Independent* in 2011 titled, '*So where's our black middle class?*' In it, the columnist, Christina Patterson, argued that, unlike America, which boasts a significant class of 'black lawyers, and judges, and journalists, and academics,' Britain is lacking. My first reaction – to the headline as opposed to the content of the piece – was one of bemusement.

This is the thing about Britain's Black middle class: they/we exist, but many have had to go abroad to progress, whether it's our actors and musicians or our white-collar workers. Britain doesn't provide a route out of the class maze, especially for people of colour.

And that's the intersectional paradox of being Black and working class in Britain. You can possess all the education and experience you can acquire, but without the opportunity to apply it, you're stuck.

For many Black Brits, class isn't something we consciously consider, even as we aspire to its trappings. What we strive for are the accoutrements of class – the security of home ownership, the stability of a job, things that root us to a place in which our position is always tenuous – without necessarily being covetous of the title. The fact is, with their familial, educational and professional backgrounds, my parents would have been considered middle class had they not been immigrants. But class in Britain is about more than what socio-economic group you belong to, what education you have, and what profession you practice – it's about structure and governance, status and status quo. It's also about race because, fundamentally, it's about keeping the people in their physical, psychological, and racial place.

What keeps Black Britons in our place is that we have few networks we can tap into when we're looking for our first or next job. We have little generational wealth we can draw from or pass onto our children. We own few properties and few businesses; we tend to be employees rather than employers, renters rather than homeowners. What little money we make is used to take care of our needs in the here-and-now leaving little for savings and other investments that would help secure our future. A significant proportion of our take-home pay is literally taken *back home*, used to support families both here and abroad.

The African-American comedian, Chris Rock, has a joke that goes:

'Shit, there ain't a white man in this room that would change places with me [...] And I'm rich! [...] There's a white, one-legged busboy in here right now that won't change places with my black ass [...] That's right, 'cause when you white, the sky's the limit. When you black, the limit's the sky!'

The statistics speak for themselves. Black workers earn, on average, 23% less than similarly qualified white workers, at all levels of education.[1] Pay gaps are not due to the type of university attended, as they even extend to black workers with degrees from the most selective Russell Group of universities.[2] Black men consistently have the lowest employment rates in the UK.[3] In London, where black and mixed-race black men make up one in five of the population, 18% of black male graduates aged 16 to 24 are unemployed, compared to 10% of their white counterparts.

My hope is that young Black Brits will realise they're not stuck on this island. They may be up a creek, but they're not without a paddle. There's a whole world that awaits them. Leaving the UK for opportunities abroad isn't just for Hollywood stars. It is, in fact, what many of our parents did when they left their homelands in search of better outcomes. By seeking to improve ourselves, we're fulfilling their dreams of progress, whether we stay and fight, or choose to leave.

---

1. Richardson, H. (2016, February 01). Black workers 'earning less than white colleagues'. Retrieved from http://www.bbc.co.uk/news/education-35441833

2. Ibid.

3. Hunte, B. (2017, March 22). London's black male graduates less likely to get jobs. Retrieved from http://www.bbc.co.uk/news/uk-england-london-39302804?post_id=878971448856202_1335481953205147#_=_

This isn't about escaping being working class, but about getting out into the world and defining ourselves. It's about claiming our place rather than having it assigned, wherever that place may be.

An Open Invitation

Kit de Waal

I'm new to this writing game. I was 51 when I went to university to do an MA in Creative Writing. At 16 I got a job as a typist, then a filing clerk, an office manager, a paralegal in criminal and family law, a project manager in social services, a massage therapist, waitress and backing singer, became a Member of the Employment Tribunal, the Adoption Panel and then a Magistrate. I had a busy life. So, when I eventually started writing, I felt I had something to say.

Not only that, I'd paid my dues, eaten my way through the classics and a bit of contemporary literature, read too many books by old white men and loved them, avoided non-fiction and politics, dabbled in biography but only actors and nobodies, knew a bit of Shakespeare and swathes of Dickens, stumbled across the Channel and discovered Zola, Flaubert, Mauriac and Maupassant then headed in the other direction to Henry James, Mark Twain, Willa Cather and Edith Wharton, quite a journey for a child that grew up in a house without books.

At home, we had a narrow choice of reading matter; the *News of The World* that my Caribbean father bought every Sunday or a daily dose of The Bible from my Irish mother. The *News of the World* had racy bits of scandal but was overstuffed with sport and The Bible was pushed at us so often that by the time I was 15 I had read it cover to cover twice. And anyway, reading was what you did at school, why bring it home?

That is not to say that I didn't love the stories that we read in rote around the classroom but I never thought of reading as a voluntary pastime. In my careers essay I said I wanted to be a journalist, but working class with immigrant parents girls didn't go to university, they became secretaries and nurses, so I cheerfully left school at the first opportunity and read nothing until my mid-20s. Then through books I discovered the world.

The advice you're given when you start is 'write what you know'. What did I know? I knew about criminal lives, about women who lose their children, about foster care and angry kids, being broke, drugs, how to do a handbrake turn, burglaries, solicitors, barristers, social workers, bad flats, stale food, no food, cold, desperation, loving and laughing, survival and living. This wasn't suitable material for a book, at least not any of the books I'd read, so I looked again at the writers I loved because surely that's the place to go for inspiration. I found that it wasn't the prose style of writers like Somerset Maugham, Arnold Bennett and Patrick Hamilton that had me hooked all these years but it was the content of their stories, tales about the ordinary, about the woman at the edge of things, the man in the bedsit, the quiet domestic lives with huge micro-dramas, stories about ill-fitters or non-fitters, people like me, off-centre.

But when I looked closer still, I found that many of these writers were peering in on those lives from a place of relative privilege and ease. Arnold Bennett, a solicitor, Somerset

Maugham, a doctor, Patrick Hamilton, Graham Green, Gustave Flaubert all from the comfortable middle classes. Even George Orwell went to Eton, and I was the daughter of a bus driver and a childminder.

The truth is, and I heard this more than once, 'literature is a record of the middle classes for the middle classes.' Certainly the definitions of 'literature' and what constitutes 'good taste' are tightly bound up with class. What the working class or underclass produce is rarely included in the canon; street literature, songs, hymns, spoken word, dialect and oral storytelling is nowhere to be found, neither is it taught in schools or universities. After all, universal education has only been around for 100 years. How many working class writers would have been able to write a book even given the luxury of time, space and an audience?

The term *working class* has never had more problems. According to a BBC major survey using economic, social and cultural indicators there are now seven social classes, ranging from the elite at the top to a 'precariat' – the poor, precarious proletariat – at the bottom.[1] The closer you get to the bottom, the more likely you are to find marginalised communities and social exclusion and the less likely you are to find writing that speaks of those lives written by writers who live it every day. But why?

Well, for one thing, we need to be invited to the party. That invitation comes from the experience of seeing ourselves included, knowing that writing by us and about us and for us has a place at the table. I remember watching the BBC weather as a teenager and after the presenter had covered the cold in Lancashire and the rain in Kent he smiled and pointed at Switzerland.

---

1. Huge survey reveals seven social classes in UK. (2013, April 03). Retrieved from http://www.bbc.co.uk/news/uk-22007058

'At least we'll have some snow on the slopes for half-term', he said and went on to give the skiing forecast. No one I knew had ever been skiing. Skiing was for posh people. 'I'm not included,' I thought. He wasn't talking to me any more than Evelyn Waugh was talking to me when he wrote of grand country houses and Oxford's 'cloistral hush'. Even Jane Eyre, a 'poor' orphan, was well educated, spoke French and played the piano, ultimately and conveniently becoming a rich heiress. Who would I have been had I lived at Thornfield Hall with Mr. Rochester? The house-keeper? More likely I would have been Leah, the maid of whom we are given few details and no sense of her life and passions, or whether Charlotte Brontë considered her, like Jane, a 'free human being with an independent will.'

The more we reinforce the stereotypes of who writes and who reads, the more the notion of exclusivity is reinforced. It takes balls to gatecrash a party but some do it. They eke a few hours after working full-time, no mean feat in itself, but then find that a writer's life costs money. Even if you can't stretch to a £7,000 Creative Writing Masters Degree, joining a writers' group, net-working events, competition entry fees, manuscript assessment, hearing your favourite author give a talk, these things can run into the thousands. Even free events require money to get there and maybe a drink with your friends afterwards.

Let's say you can afford all of the above and say you live in Stoke-on-Trent or Paisley and, scribbling night after night after work, you've finally written something good, a novel about a council tenant in Stoke-on-Trent fighting a corrupt landlord. The agents are all in London. The big publishing houses ditto. You trawl through the Writers & Agents Yearbook (£20 incidentally), locate an agent you like the look of, post your manuscript at con-siderable cost and you wait.

Who is reading your book about Stoke-on-Trent or Pais-ley? Do they know where those places are? In a study exposing race, class, gender and pay inequalities, published in the journal 'Cultural Trends', researchers found that some 43% of people working in publishing, 28% in music and 26% in design come from a privileged background, compared with 14% of the population as a whole.[2] You have to hope that whoever reads your book doesn't equate working class with white trash sink estates populated by *chavs* and single mothers in tower blocks, that they don't reach for the lazy label, 'gritty', 'dark', and 'northern' when you're only halfway up the country, that their life experience and interests go beyond university and the London literati. You have to hope that the gatekeepers in literary agencies and publishing houses are open to alternative narratives about how we live now in a Britain of multiple, overlapping ethnic and cultural identities. It can all too easily become a vicious circle of exclusion and disappointment and even when you do break through, the typical income for a professional author in 2013 was just £11,000, more than £5,000 below the income level considered to be a socially acceptable standard of living.[3]

Some writers do get lucky. I was one. My debut novel, *My Name is Leon*, went to auction and I got a great advance. I got the chance to have my story heard, the story of a boy separated from his baby brother because his brother is white and he is not. It's about foster care and mental ill-health, about social workers and not having enough to eat, of riots and police brutality, of being adrift in the world and finding love and the unexpected people who get you through difficult times. I got the opportunity

2. O'Brien, D., Laurison, D., Miles, A., & Friedman, S. (2016). Are the creative industries meritocratic? An analysis of the 2014 British Labour Force Survey. *Cultural Trends, 25*(2), 116-131. doi:10.1080/09548963.2016.1170 943

3. What Are Words Worth Now? Not Enough. (2014, July 22). Retrieved from: https://www.alcs.co.uk/ALCS-News/2014/July-2014/Authors-Earnings

to give real voice to the outsiders. Three days after finding out I had a publishing deal, I went about setting up a Scholarship for a writer from a disadvantaged background to do a Creative Writing MA at Birkbeck University, fees paid, travel paid and a bit of subsistence so the scholar can have a cup of coffee and a sandwich in the campus café at the end of the day.

It was exciting stuff and I told people about it, asked them to spread the word deep into the communities that would least be able to afford two years of tuition fees for something they felt passionate about. The response was overwhelming, not only in that over a hundred and thirty people applied for the Scholarship, but professionals from the literary establishment, finding a mechanism for addressing their concerns, contacted me to get involved and their generosity has materialised. The staff at Waterstones Birmingham are paying for the books from the reading list, a friend is paying for a laptop and stationery, Arvon are donating a week at a writers' retreat. And then Penguin Random House, Spread the Word, The Literacy Consultancy, The Word Factory and my agent, Jo Unwin are all donating time, meetings, events, advice and support to another five runners up. And there's more, Birkbeck are running a Masterclass for a further 15 applicants with many well-known writers lecturing for free.

Publishing – like the rest of the arts – needs new markets. There are writers and readers in the working and underclasses, ready to see their lives depicted in literature, stories that speak of their concerns and their lifestyles, written with authenticity and humour from beyond the metropolitan elite. The publishing industry can no longer ignore the clamour for more inclusion and must begin to value the diverse experiences of people from under-represented communities.

The response I had to the Scholarship makes me believe that things are slowly changing. This year, Penguin Random House are taking #WriteNow, a new outreach and mentoring program, to Birmingham and Manchester to connect to local writers from diverse backgrounds and have, for the first time, relaxed the requirement for all job applicants to have a university degree. And their interns are paid. Faber's CEO recently said that publishing's London-centric nature 'had to stop' and many other organisations are waking up to the need for publishing to invite and embrace and include and support and help and recognise and champion **all** good writers, no matter where they're from.

The first recipient of the Kit de Waal Scholarship is a young, mixed race boxer from Birmingham who hid poems in his gloves. The author of the Stoke novel *Sitting Ducks* is Lisa Blower who got her book published by a tiny outfit called Fair Acre Press, one of a number of small regional publishing houses doing great things with very little money or recognition. We're still waiting for the Paisley novel. It's out there.

It's time for the industry, for the literary agents, for the editors and commissioners, for the judges of prizes and awards, for the organisers of literary festivals and all the many established authors who know what it's like to struggle at the bottom, to gather together and share their enthusiasm for change, to be outward facing and open-armed and to come together (count me in) and ensure that their initiatives are fairly distributed around the country, east and west, north and south and into those areas of London economically and culturally far beyond the reaches of Bloomsbury, to include white and black working class writers, writers with disabilities, those from small rural communities where poverty and isolation is often over-looked, writers who have looked at publishing and said 'They're not talking to me.' Let's invite them all.

There are stories already written which deserve to be read and new stories that will remain lost or untold until something changes.

Navigating Space

Durre Shahwar Mughal

The concept of 'space' that a working class writer may navigate can be broken down into two kinds. There are the obvious, physical spaces: rooms, houses, postcodes, workplaces, and social gatherings. Yet within these spaces is the sociocultural space that is also to be traversed. Both of these come to shape each other and, in time, even outgrow one another. Yet space defines us and, in turn, we it, and the psychological effects of being within certain spaces are more significant than we often give them value.

As a writer, I frequently think back to Virginia Woolf's concept of a room of one's own as I look at my own: a box room with a single bed, a single railed cupboard and a bookshelf. It is a bedroom, yet also a writer's room, void of a work desk. To have a separate writing room feels like a luxury reserved for the future. Instead, all my writing is done on the bed, sometimes with earphones in to drown out the noise of my family, the neighbours, or the neighbours' dog – a need for silence that finds me staying awake late most nights, though sometimes I think a part of me has become accustomed to the noise. The immediate view from my window is that of a large tree and the block of council flats 100 yards down the road. Lining the horizon beyond that is a whole city of houses, belonging to another postcode and another world. These tiny white triangles are what I sometimes look out to when I need perspective to look beyond my immediate surroundings.. I am still often embarrassed by my postcode and the blackening walls of the houses down my street, but do not feel the need to hide or lie about what is my reality as I did when younger. Being working class often comes with a heavy burden of internalised shame, as well as blame. Shame at being unable to afford yearly holidays and more aesthetically pleasing and roomier houses to bring friends home to. As a child, I remember I used to lie about going away every summer – I guess lying was easier in the early to mid-2000s when every trip was not backed up with photo albums on Instagram and Facebook.

The makeup of my neighbourhood mostly consists of families with young children due to the local school being at a walking distance. In the summer, days begin with kids devising adventures for the day to occupy themselves with, kicking balls against house walls, riding bikes or constructing makeshift cricket pitches. Meanwhile, the evenings end with parents calling their kids in, much like my own childhood. It is a neighbourhood in which private life is not always kept within the domestic space and hushed behind closed doors: childcare arguments break out into the street, afterschool exchanges take place openly and warmly between neighbours, cats get lost and found. I used to think it was not a life worth writing about, but a life worth keeping quiet about, rolling my eyes over, and distancing myself from. But gradually I find myself revaluating what it means to be working class today, and feeling a sense of ownership and duty to the environment that has shaped me.

It is interesting to think of what Woolf thought were two essential things that female writers needed in the 1920s in order to to write: financial independence and a room of their own. Both were luxuries that only upper middle class women from wealthy families with no burden of domestic labour were able to afford. This, coupled with the social capital that Woolf had access to, placed her at a great advantage. Yet today, Woolf's words become my mantra of encouragement as I realise that I have both a room and some financial security, in whatever shape or capacity. As social media never fails to remind me, my room is more than what some have in other parts of the world. More than what I would have if my parents had not migrated here 17 years ago while, at the same time, reminding me of those who have much more, balancing the two comparisons on parallel tightropes. And so write I must.

I think, over time, I have become accustomed to working within small rooms and small spaces. I sometimes wonder if that transfers to small expectations and ideas in my writing: whether this wide-eyed amazement that comes from being a small city girl from Cardiff, living in a small neighbourhood, in a country that has a stark lack of literature by minority writers makes my writing lazy and limited not only in subject matter, but also style. Whether I straitjacket myself as a working class, BAME writer with the themes that much of my work explores. But this self-doubt and need for external validity is dispelled by writers such as Zadie Smith, Monica Ali and Hanif Kureishi – writers who not only write about the working class experience, but also represent, in their own ways, those of us from BAME backgrounds – who have become my source of affirmation. Their work and presence in the book industry becomes an encouragement to stay adamant and write about what I know best in the face of mainstream, 'high class' dominantly white narratives.

The notion of the working class, on a simplistic level, is understood as to be something to do with economics. Yet the sociocultural aspect of it and how that determines an individual sense of self is something we carry into our work as writers. I think much of class culture is about confidence. Confidence that might come easier to the middle and higher classes, while the working classes are constantly riddled with self-doubt and imposter syndrome.

When I think of all the rooms I have navigated in my life, and walls I bounced ideas off of, I think of the room that was even smaller than the one I have now. It had barely enough space to stretch my legs out on; where 17-year-old me sat painting a canvas much larger than her for a college assignment. The canvas got a B, making the cramps and shifting of positions all night worthwhile.

There was the room that I shared at the age of 13 with my younger brother, who happened to have been kicked out of it on a particular Saturday so I could have friends over. The room is well furnished. I have a bookshelf, a wardrobe, a few stuffed toys – gifts from parents and friends that I treasured and placed on the highest shelf. I even have my own all-in-one radio, CD and cassette player. To me, I have everything I need; yet one of my friends tells me, 'You don't have much stuff.' I watch her bored face and think back to her room, which contains a TV, her own computer, a double bed, with toys of all shapes and sizes everywhere, making it impossible to find the floor. But, at 13, I hadn't quite learnt to defend myself, despite being hyperaware of the reasons why my room was not so full as hers, so I mumbled in agreement. Now I look back and wonder if I would change anything about that room, the room that allowed me to focus on the important things: the books. Reading for most people is a form of cultivation and escapism, but I feel that there is more at stake when reading as working class. The propelling of the imagination into other worlds was – and still is – a lifeline.

Growing up, stuffy toys, holidays, musical classes and school trips to France cost money, but books were accessible. Books were inexpensive and my plastic pink Cardiff library card with the maximum limit of 10 was used weekly to its full potential at my local library. The same library that, like many all over the country, has been shut down since due to the Tory government's cuts, putting pressure on local councils. The frequent closures of libraries and local arts and leisure centres in deprived areas takes chances away from those who need it most. People such as migrants, refugees and minorities who are criticised for not knowing the language or having other skills, while being deprived of those resources that would enable them to break these vicious cycles. Libraries are safe spaces and information access points. There are few publicly accessible venues that are completely free, as libraries are. There is no limit to a time you can spend in a library – no one peering over your shoulder to clear your plates or fill your cup. If it wasn't for the public library computers with the hourly bookings that allowed me to develop my computer skills and complete assignments until we could get our own as a family, I would not be here, would not have developed such a love for stories and the desire to tell my own. You see, the financial aspect of being working class is not as simplistic as having less 'stuff' or money, but is the barrier to skills, culture, and arts that a lack of money creates. Even today, there are still certain cultural and entertainment spaces such as theatres and literary festivals that are determined by or are more affordable to the middle or upper classes. Spaces in which I still feel anxious and out of place.

As I started accumulating more books, while physically growing into a 5'4" female, I inevitable took up more room. At 21 this meant making the most of my university library's summer opening hours. I remember making the walk up the hill in the hot, prickling July sun to it, simply because I needed to get some writing and reading done. When I got there, I was the only one in the library. Through the window, students threw a ball around – laughter and callouts before a car started up and drove away. When the librarian came around to stack the shelves, I sat still and almost ducked behind the cubicle so that I wouldn't draw any attention to myself. I felt criminal, being in a university library without any assignments to do, and a part of me thought that this might arouse suspicion and questions from the librarian. I also felt guilty and slightly ashamed for being in a university library just for the sake of silence and a working desk. A writing desk. At home, that is what I felt the most lack of: space. The way the walls of my class narrowed around me as I grew older.

I was also not the first in the family to go to university. Going to university was a must, not a miracle. South Asian cultures have a long emphasis on education. I was less confident as a student, yet university was a space I felt entitled to. Knowledge was what I felt I could have. But the choice of where I could get knowledge from was limited not only by my grades, as is the case for most, but also by financial security. To be able to do my Masters I had to rely on grades, university scholarships (which limited where I could apply) and staying at home, while many of my peers self-funded with family support.

If we are to really know what it is to be a working class writer today, we must dismiss skewed and monolithic examples of the working class and start from scratch. Representations of the working class as devoid of motivation, easily distracted, giving in to instant gratification and uneducated, with bad parents are false and damaging. It is only by taking into account various intersect of culture, gender and background can we begin to build an accurate picture: while my parents couldn't afford to give me a bigger room or more mindless stuffed toys to play with as a child, they gave me something else. The strictness when it came to studying, curfews, and pressure put on good grades despite going to the poorest school and living in the poorest neighbourhoods led me to form a connection with books and pens more personal than any. As with many migrant children, education was the first step in ensuring that we would at least make a crack in the class barriers, if not break them.

Yet I am conscious of the way that meritocracy only goes so far, and how every working class kid is not able to forge their way through with this alone. The concept itself is misleading, and I am also conscious of the way that the idea of the good working class girl who works hard and 'achieves things' is a misleading one: one that can be abused by the more privileged to perpetuate the myth that working hard is the answer to poverty and deprivation, not other factors. A myth that has placed the blame on the working class and away from those in more privileged positions for far too long. I'm conscious of the way that this trope can be used to glorify working class writers as though they are the exception in intelligence to their counterparts, or only worthy to talk about *because* of it – a trope I've found myself avoiding writing about altogether until this essay due to the sensitivity of the topic.

My first hand experiences of the sense of lacking and feelings of being an outsider that can occur when in a predominantly middle class environment came from work. My feelings of being pleased about landing a job loosely related to my two degrees soon turned into feelings of disillusionment, as I became more conscious of the way that my tongue did not round up the vowels and pronounce all the Ts – due to growing up in a 'rough neighbourhood', as well as being bilingually fluent in English and Urdu both. It soon became distressing trying to smooth out my words, especially since I hardly came across others who spoke the way I did in the industry. I also became more aware of my lack of knowledge and familiarity with things like exhibitions, festivals, galleries, or even cultural references. Things that other people may think common knowledge are things I still find myself shaking my head at, not knowing and constantly asking questions about. Much of it is also to do with embodying two cultures and two languages as a Pakistani-born, Welsh Muslim, as well as being working class, which makes me feel like I lag behind on all fronts.

Many literary spaces and events can also often overlook minority ethnic women and Muslim women like myself. If the working class are at a disadvantage entering a middle class publishing world, then BAME working class women are doubly disadvantaged. The industry needs to do better, not only in the representation of BAME faces and voices, but also in the atmosphere and accessibility of physical spaces. Events held in bars and pubs with a focus on alcohol can, by their very nature, dissuade people from attending. Similar applies to spaces that are not disabled-access friendly. It is the navigations of different spaces such as workplaces and social gatherings that can also often trigger mental health problems and anxiety.

While Wales still has some way to go when it comes to better representation of BAME writers in the arts and literature, as a country, it has a long history of nurturing and supporting local working class writers. As a devolved nation, it can often feel as though it becomes a separate space. There is a fine balancing between being a homegrown Welsh writer and reaching the wider global market. Yet the makeup of independent publishing in Wales is one that is more accessible to working class writers.

Many of those who are published are talented local writers, with no Oxford or Cambridge diplomas attached to their names. These are writers writing outside the bubble, who are often ignored by the 'bigger', more established and mainstream publishing houses. The makeup of indie publishing in Wales, and how approachable and open many of the editors of these houses are, allows for working class writers to carve out a name for themselves. Gatekeeping still exists, but to a lesser extent.

As a minority working class writer I'm constantly defining and expanding myself, as though trying to write myself into a new form. It is a layer of identity that you carry with you. You can learn to navigate the middle class spheres and even financially outgrow what would keep you in the working class 'bracket', yet the experiences that shape your formative years always stick. People often cry out 'political correctness' whenever discussions of class, ethnicity, gender or race take place, yet don't realise that what may seem like political correctness are the everyday navigations of our lives. As a brown, working class Welsh Muslim woman, I spent most of my time trying to draw attention away from these things until I realised they are an essential part of my identity. I guess now I see my presence in certain spaces as a necessary disruption.

The Benefit Cuts

Sam Mills

This is my first memory: I am three years old and my mum is guiding me down the corridor of a strange building. Its walls are white and the radiators make a gurgling sound, as if suffering from a watery indigestion. People are wandering about as though they are in the middle of some imaginary maze, seeking a centre. One woman has the cackling laugh of a fairytale witch. And there is my dad. He is sitting in a chair in his green dressing-gown. I wonder what has happened to him, this man who used to be a playful parent, indulging me in my favourite game whereby he would grab me by the ankles, swing me like a pendulum and cry, 'Tick, tock, tick, tock!' as my hair brushed his shoes. This new version of my dad remains silent when my mum greets him. When he finally raises his eyes to look at us, I see sadness fossilised in his pupils.

My parents were both from working class backgrounds. My mum grew up on a council estate in Elephant and Castle; my dad with a large family in Morden. My mum had been denied a good education by her chauvinistic father who said that university was a waste of time for a woman; my father had a few 'O' levels. But this was the late '70s, a time when social mobility was more fluid. My dad had got a good job in a factory and my parents had moved to the suburbs of Sutton. The house they'd bought was in a terrible state. Even the estate agent had looked bewildered and asked suspiciously, *Are you sure you want to buy this place?* It was a house on a fine street, but inside it was a mess of loose wires, crumbling brickwork and walls painted in those lurid colours that were inexplicably fashionable in the '60s, vomit-green and bright orange. The last owner had been an old man whose eccentricity had intensified into madness. His prints were still on the walls, black smudges of wrinkled fingers that looked eerie in their muddling of the elderly and the juvenile. But it held the promise that it might one day become a middle class dwelling, that over months and years they might enjoy a more prosperous existence.

Sadly, the dream failed to materialise. We ended up being a family who lived – or survived – on benefits. My dad lost his job and suffered a nervous breakdown; then, whilst staying in a psychiatric ward, he developed schizophrenia. We became a poor family in an area that was a patchwork of classes, where the middle classes covered the most squares. At school I became aware that I was different. The other children were dropped off by parents who had swish cars; they lived in comfortable houses; their clothes were crisp and their shoes shiny. My shoes had holes in them and when I changed out of uniform into my day clothes, they had a whiff of oddity about them. Someone asked me why I wore clothes from jumble sales; I wasn't entirely sure why I had been dressed in a ragged ra-ra skirt of mauve and lemon layers, which clashed with an off-white Mickey Mouse T-shirt. My mum scraped in some extra income by doing the odd cleaning job or babysitting. The local tax inspector called her for an interview about her tax return, asking how we could live on so little; he asked, 'But don't you ever eat out in restaurants...?' and looked (laughably) shocked when she replied in the negative. Nevertheless, the benefits we received held us together. Our lives were fraying, but the safety net of disability benefits prevented us from entirely unravelling. The payments were reliable, never stopped, arrived every week. My mum scrimped and saved so hard that she managed to keep up the small mortgage payments. And she lectured me and my brothers over and over that we had to get a good education, study like mad, and fight our way into better lives. I was lucky enough to end up with a place at Oxford.

But I doubt that I would ever have made it there if we had suffered what present families face when applying for benefits...

It began with the elections of 2010, when the Tories and Lib Dems formed a coalition government. Granted, they had a difficult task ahead as they grappled with a huge national debt, and some cuts were inevitable. But the government diverted the public anger this fuelled by creating scapegoats: immigrants and the working class. Most of the press – who lean towards the Tories – played along. SCROUNGERS! cried the headlines. SKIVERS! Regular articles ran telling stories of cheats going to jail, but this was a skewed perspective. Unemployment benefit is only 1% of our welfare spend,[1] benefit fraud is less than 1% of the benefits bill,[2] and most of the overall benefits bill is actually spent on pensions, tax credits and housing benefit, given that rents are so

1. ONS. (2016, March 16). How is the welfare budget spent? Retrieved from https://visual.ons.gov.uk/welfare-spending

2. Ball, J. (2013, February 03). Welfare fraud is a drop in the ocean compared to tax avoidance. Retrieved from https://www.theguardian.com/commentisfree/2013/feb/01/welfare-fraud-tax-avoidance

high. Owen Jones has pointed out that Cameron also inflated the numbers,[3] declaring a crackdown on 'fraud and error' – by combining the cost of fraud committed by welfare claimants, £1 billion a year, with errors made by officials, £4.2 billion a year – enabling him to argue that the taxpayer was suffering a cost of £5.2 billion a year and implying it was all the fault of cheats.

And so the cuts began. Those claiming sickness benefit had new assessments conducted by private firm Atos. The bedroom tax – a housing benefit cut on homes with a spare room – was introduced. This hit the disabled the hardest, for they are often unable to share a bedroom or have specially adapted homes. Those on Jobseeker's Allowance faced sanctions if they failed to look for work. If the latter had been implemented fairly, this would have been acceptable. But soon stories began to leak that people were being sanctioned for the most random and spurious excuses. For choosing to go to a job interview instead of their interview at the Job Centre. For turning up 5 minutes late (though, by their watch, on time). One Labour MP, Debbie Abraham, reported that one man's Atos assessment had to be stopped because he was having a heart attack; a few weeks later, he received a letter accusing him of withdrawing from the assessment halfway through, which meant he would be sanctioned.[4] Another MP, Ian Murray, reported that one claimant was on a mandatory computer course that ran from noon to 1 p.m. and had to sign on on the other side of the city; when he

---

3. Jones, O. (2012). *Chavs: The Demonization of Working Class*. London: Verso.

4. Heart-attack victim in cash-axe shock. (2014, January 31). Retrieved from http://www.oldham-chronicle.co.uk/news-features/8/news-headlines/84423/heartattack-victim-in-cashaxe-shock

turned up 15 minutes late, he was sanctioned.[5] Clearly, some claimants were being set up to fail; bureaucratic tripwires were being laid. And let's not forget that many of these people had previously been in work and paid N.I. contributions so that if they fell sick or became unemployed, a safety net would be in place.

The result? An explosion in the use of food banks. You'd think that Iain Duncan Smith (who at the time was Secretary of State for Work and Pensions), might have twigged at this point that there was a problem. It's not a hard logic to follow. If you take away someone's main income stream for a month, how are they going to feed themselves? But the government became intent on denying there that was any relationship between sanctions and starvation. Instead, the millionaires of the Tory Party made a series of Marie-Antoinette-style comments. Baroness Jenkin, who owns property in Kennington (where the average house price is £1.1 million), said that food banks were in demand because 'people don't know how to cook,'[6] though she later retracted her comments in shame.[7] Lord Freud was simply puzzled. 'It's hard to know why people go to food

---

5. Mcleod, K. (2015, August 26). Vulnerable are easy targets for benefits sanctions. Retrieved from http://www.dailyrecord.co.uk/news/scottish-news/vulnerable-easy-targets-job-centre-6320363

6. Roberts, G. (2014, December 08). Tory Baroness: Poor people use food banks because they 'don't know how to cook'. Retrieved August, from http://www.mirror.co.uk/news/uk-news/tory-baroness-slammed-saying-poor-4767987

7. Wright, O. (2014, December 08). Tory attitudes to poverty under fire amid benefit sanctions and Baroness Jenkin comment that poor 'don't know how to cook'. Retrieved from http://www.independent.co.uk/news/uk/politics/tory-attitudes-to-poverty-under-fire-over-benefit-sanctions-and-baroness-jenkin-comment-that-poor-9911580.html

banks,' he stated, and suggested that people were using them because more of them existed.[8] (Freud, the Welfare Minister, also caused an outcry by suggesting that disabled people are not worth the minimum wage.[9]) But you can't just rock up at a food bank because you fancy a free bag of food. You go there with a referral from a professional, from your social worker, a schools liaison officer, your Job Centre, your GP. You go because you are desperate.

Time after time, the government kept on refusing to accept any connection between benefits sanctions and the explosion in food banks – even when statistics and studies began to prove otherwise. Research conducted by the Oxford University proved the link; moreover, they found that people carried on using food banks even once the sanctions had tapered off, because their household finances were still unstable, still suffering after-tremors of shock, for several months after the initial penalty.[10] In 2016, the Trussell Trust – the charity that co-ordinates a nationwide network of food banks across the UK – warned that usage of food banks were at a record high: between 2015-16 they handed out over a million 3-day-supply food parcels. The causes? They cited low wages, insecure work, high living costs

8. Williams, Z. (2013, July 04). To Lord Freud, a food bank is an excuse for a free lunch | Zoe Williams. Retrieved from https://www.theguardian.com/commentisfree/2013/jul/04/lord-freud-food-banks

9. Dearden, L. (2014, October 15). Lord Freud: Past gaffes on welfare, food banks and 'bedroom tax' revealed. Retrieved from http://www.independent.co.uk/news/uk/politics/lord-freud-past-gaffes-on-welfare-food-banks-and-bedroom-tax-revealed-9797082.html

10. Butler, P. (2016, October 26). Benefit sanctions forcing people to use food banks, study confirms. Retrieved from https://www.theguardian.com/society/2016/oct/27/benefit-sanctions-food-banks-oxford-university-study

and problems accessing working benefits. Their data showed that benefit delays and changes were the biggest cause, accounting for 42% of all referrals.[11]

In 2016, David Cameron declared his belief in 'a compassionate nation', one that would protect the vulnerable. And yet the tragedy of the welfare reforms is that, ironically, those who tend to cheat the system, those who are savvy and have the nous to do it, are more likely to keep their benefits. The vulnerable, on the other hand, become victims. Six out of ten people who had their ESA stopped were vulnerable people with a learning disability or mental health condition.[12] I knew a man in the north who has mental health issues and had been on sickness benefit; his new 'assessment' merely consisted of his Job Centre saying to him, 'You're not depressed anymore now, are you? So we'll put you on Jobseekers instead.' He had no idea that this might be the wrong way to assess him, or that he might be able to appeal. Numerous doctors and whistleblowers have pointed out that the ESA assessments for mental health are rushed and inadequate. After all, mental health is not an easy thing to classify, nor is it predictable. When I was ten years old, my dad managed to work for a few years as a clerk, before he suddenly resigned, seemingly on a whim; yet this was the prelude to another semi-breakdown that occurred a few months later. Full-time work was something he simply couldn't cope with.

11. Bulman, M. (2017, April 26). Food bank use across UK at record high, reveals report. Retrieved from http://www.independent.co.uk/news/uk/ home-news/food-bank-use-uk-rise-continue-poverty-family-children-income-benefits-cuts-report-a7703451.html

12. Ryan, F. (2014, September 09). David Clapson's awful death was the result of grotesque government policies | Frances Ryan. Retrieved from https:// www.theguardian.com/commentisfree/2014/sep/09/david-clapson-benefit-sanctions-death-government-policies

With the vulnerable under attack, deaths became an inevitability. The full list is shocking, and the examples I list are only a few: David Clapson died two weeks after his benefits stopped. Staff at his Job Centre were aware that he had diabetes; unable to eat or afford electricity, he was unable to keep his fridge going, the fridge he stored his insulin in.[13] Paul Reekie, a Leith-based poet with a heart condition, committed suicide at the age of 48. Two letters were found nearby to his body. One notified him that his housing benefit was being stopped; the other notified him that his incapacity benefit was being stopped.[14] Nicholas Barker, a former farm labourer, who was paralysed on his left side due to a brain haemorrhage, shot himself after his benefits were stopped.[15] Dawn Amos, an ill mother was battling a lung condition that left her struggling to breathe, unable to walk or dress herself, was told that she no longer qualified for benefits for her personal care – a letter that arrived on her doorstep on the day that she died.[16] Lawrence Bond , who suffered from a

13. Ryan, F. (2014, September 09). David Clapson's awful death was the result of grotesque government policies | Frances Ryan. Retrieved from https://www.theguardian.com/commentisfree/2014/sep/09/david-clapson-benefit-sanctions-death-government-policies

14. Author's suicide 'due to slash in benefits'. (2010, July 24). Retrieved from http://www.scotsman.com/news/author-s-suicide-due-to-slash-in-benefits-1-1367963

15. Benefits withdrawal led to man's suicide. (2013, April 17). Retrieved from http://www.gazetteherald.co.uk/news/10360733.Benefits_withdrawal_led_to_man___s_suicide/

16. Henderson, E. (2016, January 07). Mother Dawn Amos told she was too healthy for sickness benefits on the day she died. Retrieved from http://www.independent.co.uk/news/uk/home-news/mother-told-she-was-too-healthy-for-sick-benefits-on-the-day-she-died-a6800921.html

heart condition, collapsed and died on the street after visiting the Kentish Town Job Centre in a state of distress, for his ESA had been stopped after he failed an assessment by Maximus.[17] The quote from the Department of Work and Pensions in response to his death was as dry as they come: 'Anyone who disagrees with a decision can ask for it to be reconsidered, and if they still disagree they can appeal.'[18] So, are the failed claimants to apply for their appeals in the afterlife?

Nor can any of this be easy for the Job Centre staff who have to implement these policies. Or doctors under pressure to sign off those who are mentally unwell as fit for work. One Job Centre whistleblower explained that they were under huge pressure to hit targets and suffered severe stress if they didn't dish out enough sanctions.[19] Staff were also shocked when the government sent them guidelines on how to deal with suicide threats from claimants; one Job Centre employee, who had been working at his centre for over 20 years, confided to the *Guardian,* 'Absolutely nobody has seen this guidance before... We were a bit shocked. Are we preparing

---

17. Alexander, S. (2017, January 25). Sick man ruled 'fit to work' collapses and dies in street after Jobcentre visit. Retrieved August, from http://www.mirror.co.uk/news/uk-news/sick-man-ruled-fit-work-9680115

18. Mann, T. (2017, January 20). Man dies after leaving Job Centre despite being found 'fit to work'. Retrieved from http://metro.co.uk/2017/01/20/man-dies-after-leaving-job-centre-despite-being-found-fit-to-work-6394339/

19. O'Hara, M. (2015, February 04). As a jobcentre adviser, I got 'brownie points' for cruelty | Mary O'Hara. Retrieved from https://www.theguardian.com/society/2015/feb/04/jobcentre-adviser-play-benefit-sanctions-angela-neville

ourselves to be like the Samaritans?'[20]

One might wonder if the government considers whether all this is really the best way to get people into work. Can someone focus on creating a good CV or preparing properly for a job interview if they are suffering the trauma of a potential eviction? Surely it would be of greater value to help someone who has literacy issues, rather than sanctioning them if they can't fill in a form properly. Or, if they are mentally ill, to offer help rather than declaring they are too lazy to hold down a 9 to 5. Theresa May, after all, wants to introduce grammar schools in order to improve social mobility. I was the beneficiary of a grammar school and, without a doubt, it helped me; but that was on the foundation of a safety net of benefits that stabilised our lives until my mum was able to find part-time work. Imagine a kid whose 11+ falls the same week that their parents have been sanctioned, a kid who might be underfed and picking up on the stress of their parents' terror that they could be made homeless: how are they supposed to excel in an exam?

The unemployed working class are not the only ones under attack. The homeless charity Shelter has recently warned that many recent evictions were for those in full-time employment, mostly public section jobs.[21] This is a problem mostly in the south of England, where the government freeze in housing benefit has clashed with steeply rising rents. In the end, it doesn't necessarily save money; councils are hit with bills for emergency

---

20. Domokos, J. (2011, May 08). Jobcentre staff 'sent guidelines on how to deal with claimants' suicide threats'. Retrieved from https://www.theguardian.com/society/2011/may/08/jobcentre-staff-guidelines-suicide-threats

21. Helm, T. (2017, March 04). Benefit freeze leaves families facing steep rent rise or eviction, Shelter warns. Retrieved from https://www.theguardian.com/society/2017/mar/05/housing-benefit-cap-forcing-families-homelessness

housing for the homeless, who are often shunted into B&Bs. As Philip Glanville, the mayor of Hackney, says, 'People assume that it is the unemployed who end up in emergency accommodation, but it is so much broader than that. We are finding it is people who are in work, who are striving and key jobs, such as teachers, nurses and trainee police officers. I don't know how the government expects people to go out to work, take their children to school and then return to one room.'[22]

'We're all in it together,' said George Osborne at the start of the austerity regime, but this has clearly not been the case. The recession was caused by banks creating too much money too quickly; in just seven years (2000-2007) they doubled the amount of debt and money flowing through the economy.[23] When the recession hit, when several banks nearly collapsed and had to be bailed out by the government, bankers became an unpopular species – but only for a time. The blame was soon shifted to immigrants and the working class, both employed and unemployed, who came under savage attack and were made scapegoats. The poor did not create the recession, but they have suffered the brunt of it. In the last decade, the top 20% wealthiest families in the country have become 64% richer, whilst the poorest have become 57% poorer.[24]

---

22. Helm, T. (2017, March 04). Benefit freeze leaves families facing steep rent rise or eviction, Shelter warns. Retrieved from https://www.theguardian.com/society/2017/mar/05/housing-benefit-cap-forcing-families-homelessness

23. What Caused the Financial Crisis & Recession? (n.d.). Retrieved from http://positivemoney.org/issues/recessions-crisis/

24. Morris, N. (2015, March 09). Britain's divided decade: the rich are 64% richer than before the recession, while the poor are 57% poorer. Retrieved from http://www.independent.co.uk/news/uk/home-news/britains-divided-decade-the-rich-are-64-richer-than-before-the-recession-while-the-poor-are-57-10097038.html

The average CEO now earns 386 times the salary of a worker on sa national living wage.[25] Inequality is bad for everybody – it's bad for growth, resulting in less consumer spending and lower tax revenues, which means we pay off our debts more slowly despite the austerity cuts. The result has been a society under stress and strain that has never seemed more fragmented and divided; I have no doubt that the welfare cuts contributed to the tensions that resulted in Brexit. The Tories need to stop denying and start listening, to burst their Westminster bubble and develop a conscience, before the gap between the rich and the poor becomes a gulf.

25. Allen, K. (2017, March 22). FTSE CEOs 'earn 386 times more than workers on national living wage'. Retrieved from https://www.theguardian.com/business/2017/mar/22/uk-ceos-national-living-wage-equality-trust-pay-gap

One of Us:
Some Thoughts on Sexuality

Andrew McMillan

N.B. I write this not from a position of authority, but simply to give some ideas about my own individual childhood and adolescence.

1.

It seems to me that people still approach class in the same way they approach sexuality, wanting something definite; wanting rigid definitions that don't fit into a new plurality of identities and hybridity which have come to define the 21st century. In terms of sexuality, that has meant, in popular culture, that the person stepping across heteronormative boundaries is portrayed as having the stereotypical outer characteristics of the male or female they are replacing in a typical heterosexual relationship – hence homosexual females oftentimes appearing on television or films as 'butch' or outwardly masculine, as they've 'replaced the male' in that relationship, and homosexual males being portrayed as feminine, and weaker, because they've assumed the status of a traditional woman in being attracted to a man.

*

Of course, I'm simplifying wildly and, of course, it is complete nonsense. Tied up in all of this too is an ingrained and deep-held misogyny in a society which might, on the whole, claim not to hold such views. The notion that a homosexual man is lesser because he is more feminine is still insidious in society, as is the idea that a homosexual man has, by being penetrated (never mind what any individual gay man's sexual inclinations might actually be), chosen to occupy the position generally reserved for a woman and, so questions the misogynistic mind, why would anyone choose to weaken themselves in such a way?

*

Well, where on earth to start? A culture that equates sexuality directly with sex has always baffled me; there are many men across the spectrum of sexuality who choose not to be penetrated, who express desire in different ways and there are, indeed, many heterosexual men who are regularly penetrated by their partners as part of well-rounded sexual relationships.

2.

I was at a house party some time last year to celebrate a friend's birthday and, a little after midnight and several bottles of wine (including one I'd brought as a present that I ended up opening myself) a few of us ended up in the kitchen. We'd been talking about education and schools and somewhere along the line had stumbled into a conversation about private education. Me and my boyfriend were stood by the fridge. I'm originally from Barnsley, he's from Lisburn in Northern Ireland; one party-goer interjected into the conversation and said, 'I can tell by the way you two speak that you haven't had the easiest start in life.'

*

...

*

That awkward pause you're doing now is exactly what I did as well. My Barnsley accent, which is softened but still there, or my boyfriend's speedy almost-Belfast phrases, marked us out as working class, or from working class stock: the way one speaks being incorrectly linked to education, which in turn is one of these rigid supposed indicators of class which people still cling to. It wasn't an assertion made with any malice and it wasn't meant to be confrontational, it was just a statement of as-they-saw-it fact; we spoke this way, therefore we were this thing.

*

Humans always want to taxonomise and categorise.

3.

As I said above, I was born in Barnsley, in 1988. When my debut collection, *physical*, was published in 2015, I was approached a couple of times to write pieces about what it had been like growing up in a small northern town as a young gay man. I had to disappoint people's stereotypes because actually – and I realise I'm lucky in this respect – I had a great time. I was bullied more for my obese body than my sexuality. I was going to a regular gay-night every Tuesday at the now burnt-down Chicago Rock Cafe. I walked through the streets of my proudly working class town to college and never really encountered any abuse, beyond the odd person shouting something out. I was never beaten up or faced the kind of hostility those down on Fleet Street might imagine a young queer lad could encounter on the grim streets of the North. I was only punched once, when I was about 16. Some kid came up to me at a bus stop and punched me in the face, breaking the cheap sunglasses I had on. He was small and it didn't hurt much, but he was able to go back over to his friends having proved something.

*

Being any kind of man is difficult in a post-industrial economy. I don't blame the lad who hit me.

4.

It's worth noting how many essays from 'The Academy' on the working class approach the subject almost as a zoological species to be observed and studied; they are already othered by the academic who strides in and tells them what their lives 'mean' or how they might be 'interpreted'.

*

These essays I'm about to mention are the ones that, by and

large, resist that urge.

*

David Rayside reminds us that 'Late in 1990, the Conservative Government introduced a Criminal Justice Bill,' which, in various measures, he saw as 'only the most recent episodes in a 300-year-long history of political measures designed to preserve the respectability of the realm by suppressing homosexual behaviour by denying it visibility.'[1] That word 'respectability', that idea of 'visibility' – hold on to them, we'll come back to them shortly.

*

Nicola Ingram makes a very general, but quite possibly true statement that 'having a working class identity cannot be separated from belong to a working class locality. For many working class children, life is lived mostly within their neighbourhood and it therefore becomes a strong force in identity formation.'[2]

*

J.C Walker tells us, on masculinity and young men, that 'practises which violated the dominant definition... were labelled

---

1. Rayside, D. (1992). Homophobia, Class and Party in England. *Canadian Journal of Political Science / Revue Canadienne De Science Politique, 25*(1), 121-149. Retrieved from http://www.jstor.org/stable/3228952

2. Ingram, N. (2009). Working-Class Boys, Educational Success and the Misrecognition of Working-Class Culture. *British Journal of Sociology of Education, 30*(4), 421-434. Retrieved from http://www.jstor.org/stable/40375441

negatively, as "poofter."[3] That seems such a quaint word now, but keep in mind that idea of violating the dominant definition of what it is to be a man.

5.

I was in a taxi coming back home the other night; we were coming through Moston in Manchester, the edge of which they're trying to call New Moston in an attempt to begin the process of gentrification, one of the more oppressive forms of violence enacted on the working class. A few minutes from my house we passed a large advertising billboard for a travel company that proclaimed *Manchester to Casablanca* and listed some very reasonable prices charged for such a trip. The message to this working class community: adventure is elsewhere, life is elsewhere, culture and exploration are elsewhere.

*

I wondered about taking the same journey in a similar suburb in London, close to the centre of the city, next to the transport links; there'd likely be an advertisement for the latest West End show or exhibition at one of the national galleries. The message: culture is here, adventure is on your doorstep, enrichment is just a couple of streets away. It's my lived experience that too often working class communities tend to look outside of their own communities or lives for a sense of enrichment or culture, just as Ingram suggested they might have to.

3. Walker, J. (1988). The Way Men Act: Dominant and Subordinate Male Cultures in an Inner-City School. *British Journal of Sociology of Education, 9*(1), 3-18. Retrieved from http://www.jstor.org/stable/1392996

*

In terms of sexuality that also poses a problem; it gives us the narrative of the young working class child, somewhere on the LGBTQ+ spectrum, who feels they must leave in order to fully become themselves. I did that, in a small way, by moving in with a friend after I first came out at 16, and then in a larger way by moving first to university and then to live in Manchester. Why must we leave? Why must the elusive *thing* be elsewhere? What happens to the ones who choose to stay, or lack the economic or social freedoms to be able to choose to leave?

*

With the high costs of cinema tickets, the extortionate prices of theatre tickets and the embedded social fear which comes from entering a space like a museum or gallery where certain working class people, particularly young people, might not feel comfortable, television, streamed or viewed live, becomes the main way of accessing culture.

*

What this access to television does, no doubt, is give the average working class family, and the average working class lad (or lass) struggling with their sexuality, visible LGBTQ+ people in their living rooms (though mainly just the L and the G of that acronym); maybe the only such encounters, knowingly, that might be had on a day-to-day basis.

So growing up in my small village there was Jack stealing the show every week on *Will and Grace* and flamboyant chat show hosts competing on a Friday night; there were other, quieter representations, a lovely romance on the Channel 4 soap

Hollyoaks, for example, but the most popular ones were the flamboyant, hyperbolic hosts and characters of just-post-watershed TV.

*

I always found it interesting that the people who might express homophobic sentiments at, say, a football game, or who wouldn't think twice at sneering at two men holding hands as they walked down the street, would also sit comfortably laughing along with openly gay TV presenters on a Friday night.

*

These sorts of TV celebrities or sitcom characters would seem to do what Walker talked about, violating the 'dominant definition' of what it was to be a traditional man; but they did it so overtly, so gregariously and bravely, that they were able to get away with it. Think back to those two ideas of Rayside's I said to keep in mind: in order to maintain the respectability of the realm, you denied homosexuality visibility. That's only partly true; if you can't keep it underground and pretend that it's not there, then the other option is to make it hyper-visible, so as to 'other' it and therefore make a clear distinction between a community and those that are to be considered outside it.

6.

This isn't an essay attacking notions of camp, or trying to push for the idea of masculine or feminine traits as being more or less desirable than any other, but just pointing out that it seemed to me that there was, as a young gay man growing up, a certain type of sexual identity which was shown to me on television – a sexuality that seemed hyperbolised, to take it beyond something physical into being something cartoonish and thus non-threatening; a sexuality so outrageously overt that it was easily distinct from the dominant masculine identity and thus could be safely ring-fenced off and observed – not unlike the way some academics write about the working class.

7.

Consider Robbie Rogers, the former Leeds United footballer, who came out as gay but was no longer playing for Leeds at the time, who has spoken about dressing room 'banter' and of the 'pack mentality – they're trying to get a laugh, they're trying to be the top guy. But it's brutal. It's like high school again – on steroids.'[4]

*

Consider Gareth Thomas, the rugby player, who spoke of his fear of his coming out in relation to his postman father: 'I used to be a postman myself and so I know that working environment. It's a macho world and I was worried about him going into work and hearing bad things about me. But I think he's 10 times prouder of me now than six months ago.'[5]

4. McRae, D. (2013, March 29). Robbie Rogers: why coming out as gay meant I had to leave football. Retrieved from https://www.theguardian.com/football/2013/mar/29/robbie-rogers-coming-out-gay

5. McRae, D. (2010, May 03). Gareth Thomas on being gay in sport and switching to rugby league. Retrieved from https://www.theguardian.com/sport/2010/may/04/gareth-thomas-gay-interview-crusaders

*

I think there would be something more difficult about coming out in spaces which occupy the 'dominant definition' of masculinity; so in these traditionally masculine working class spaces, the emergence of homosexuality cannot be othered, it has infiltrated the core, and is thus perceived as something more sinister. That could relate to a workplace, a particular community, even a particular family environment.

8.

Why does any of this matter? I think as a young gay man growing up in Barnsley, coming out at the age of 16 but wondering about it all from the age of about 11 – probably much younger – I was drawn to constructing a sense of myself in a certain way, partly because of a lack of role models in popular culture. If you regularly go to football matches, or witness exchanges in the playground where homophobic 'banter' and language is used frequently and casually, whilst simultaneously regularly witnessing those same people laughing with and enjoying a hyper-sexualised performance of homosexuality from on television, then this is likely to contribute to behaviour being socialised in a certain way.

*

I was not behaving, when I first came out, in a way which I was entirely comfortable with, but in a way which I felt would keep me sufficiently 'othered' so as to be beyond reproach. Luckily my after-school world was one of amateur drama or writing and so I didn't have to come out in places like the school football team, where I would have disrupted the 'dominant definition' of what it was to be a man.

*

If class is about knowing one's place, or telling other people what their place is, then the outsiders' approach to sexuality is similar: to tell people what their place is, to fence themselves off and to keep themselves (by which I mean their community) safe. The hyper-real sexuality of popular culture is sufficiently other, the footballer or the rugby player or the man in the WMC who turns out to be gay strikes much closer to home. It means that the traditional boundaries can no longer hold; like a working class academic, or a newsreader who speaks with a regional accent, it leads to a fluidity which, by its very nature, agitates and distorts the social order and thus has implications for the community.

9.

If any or all communities would benefit from a more rounded view of sexuality (and wouldn't everyone!) then it's the fault, mainly, of sex education in schools, which is still woefully inadequate to the task of discussing sexuality in an internet age, and popular culture which still, on the whole, portrays sexualised stereotypes rather than rounded characters.

10.

There is, also, a double-othering being enacted. Take down any gay magazine from the newsagents shelves, load up any porn website, and you'll see stereotypes of the working class played out for fetishistic pleasure; or, as Paul Johnson puts it much more academically, 'representations of chavs utilise various types of capital to invoke particular sexual subjects in a particular social space.'[6]

*

The gay community as a whole needs to reckon with the fact that they are enacting another type of othering, sexualising an economic and class stereotype in order to make it erotic rather than threatening.

11.

Of course, the ideal is plurality; a breadth of different queer identities spread throughout the different social classes, each being given equal status and representation in culture and art.

*

No more do we want the narrative of the young gay man who must move away from his small town in order to be himself without fear; its tied too intrinsically to that notion of working class as a transient identity, the idea that we should all be striving towards middle class living. Such a narrative means that working class becomes something you're meant to not want to be, you're not meant to stay working class, and if you do, then you become part of a narrative of being trapped or having

6. Johnson, P. (2008). 'Rude Boys: The Homosexual Eroticization of Class. *Sociology, 42*(1), 65-82. doi:10.1177/0038038507084825

failed, and the rich cultural and social history of the working class is hollowed out into a vacuum.

So too the narrative of the young gay man who grows and exaggerates his sexuality to sufficiently other himself into feeling safe grows it so large he finds his small town too small and moves away to a bigger city, leaving a vacuum too, a lack of post-teenage visible queer people. We need a plurality; young gay men on the football team as well as the ones like me, in the youth theatre groups, being equally accepted and celebrated. Both in terms of class and sexuality we need to accept that our old certainties and assumptions aren't enough anymore.

Glass Windows and Glass Ceilings

Wally Jiagoo

'Don't leave me hangin nuh, dread.'

Dean's fist has been pressed against the window now for nearly all of five seconds. His reaching out to me, calling me 'dread', accepting me as one of his own when it's him, and not me, that's rocking the salt and pepper locs, warms my jaded heart. So why am I hesitant to return the gesture?

There's a sheet of protective glass between us. We can't touch fists through the glass... can we? My eyes refocus. Dean's longing stare is full of expectation. That film scene flashes across my inappropriate mind. The one from *Midnight Express*, where two characters share an intimate moment through plexiglass in a Turkish prison. I snap out of it. Maintaining my decorum, I place my fist on the glass window, reaching out to Dean. We both smile.

As Dean leaves, I realise my appointment with him has overrun. Waiting outside my cubicle is a stressed mother with a crying baby. I gander at her notes...

Complex Overpayment.
Facing eviction.
Potentially Violent Person.
(That's a full house in Housing Benefit Bingo.)

Anticipating a stressful hour ahead, I remind myself of the upside of this job. *All the different people you meet, the stories you hear. They're a gift to you as a writer.*

You see, I lead a double life. One where I'm rooted, existing in the world of everyday working people, and one where I'm trying to spread my wings and fly away. I'm a Housing Benefit Officer for a local authority in South London. I'm also an emerging screenwriter. My job is to help those on the breadline, those demonised in society. My other job is to hobnob with upper echelon types, ingratiating myself in the hope of one day making it in the world of TV. The bridge that divides these two worlds is where I wait, patiently trying to convince the gatekeepers to let me cross. Rather innocently, I'd always believed that through talent and hard work I'd earn my place on that other side. Yet as others pass me by, I watch and wonder... *what is it that they have that I don't?*

'Don't take this the wrong way, but you're not very good "in the room" are you? Sometimes even I forget you're in the room!'

Despite asking for it, this honest critique from a writer friend stung deeply. I'd always taken pride in my ability to get on with all walks of life, so why was I so terrible at schmoozing with TV people? The reason is: cliques. As genuinely friendly as everybody is at networking events, unless you've worked or studied together, or have friends or family in common, you'll find yourself quickly and politely phased out of conversation with, '*You'll never guess what happened to so-and-so.*' It sucks but it's just human nature. Having spent the last 20 years working in entry-level jobs – far from this in-crowd – I knew I had *lots* of catching up to do. I didn't want to believe it, but hard work and talent will only get you so far. You have to be *'in the room'*. But how was I going to do that when I'm stuck down the benefit office, working hard to stay afloat in Tory austerity Britain?

'You've quite the knack for writing orrrdinary people,' purred Adrien.

I'm at a general meeting at Le Pain Quotidien on London's South Bank with Adrien, a development executive from a television production company. As he sips his coffee, I wonder whether he's clocked me putting four sugars into my tea.

'Um...thanks,' I mumble back.

What does he mean? These are just the people in my everyday life... does that make me orrrdinary? I snap back to attention.

'And you work... at the council?'

'For my sins, yes. Four days a week. Until I can afford to branch out writing full time, that is.'

'Oh, I know, it must be really hard,' he offers with sincerity. 'Still, your job sounds fassscinating. All those people, their different lives and such... great fodder for stories, yes?'

'Oh yeah,' I nod. 'It's a real gift.'

Back at the benefit office, I swallow hard as Thomas, a claimant in a well-worn Hackett polo shirt, puts me through the wringer. His white face is beetroot red, either from rage or rosacea, as he yells expletives from the other side of the glass. My mind flashes back to the meeting I had with Adrien. *It's a real gift, this.*

'Farkin... benefit cap??' Thomas splurts, his eyes fixed on me. He wants his pound of flesh.

'The government... they're capping your total benefits.' I gulp. 'You work less than 16 hours a week.'

'I'm on a farkin' zero-hour, mate! It's not like I ain't trying... there ain't none! How am I s'posed to feed my kids?'

Following the rules yet still struggling to get by, this welfare system is taking the piss out of people like Thomas. Weighing up his lot, he responds unexpectedly by letting out a loud, feral scream into his clenched fists. I suddenly realise who he is. *Tommy! Tommy Lown. Tommy who got expelled from our school in Year 10. I remember that raging red face.* After a moment, Thomas calms down, sheepish about his outburst.

'Sorry, I know it's not your fault.'

I nod politely. *Does Tommy remember me? I've smoothed over the edges of my Sarf Landan accent since school but he must realise who I am? Should I say something?* Then I remember Rukhsana, a girl in our class who turned up in my cubicle a few years ago. In my excitement I reminded Rukhsana of us being classmates. I recall how self-conscious she became. She'd not seen me for years and here she was, unemployed, asking *me* for help. It was without doubt the worst school reunion ever.

I commiserate with Thomas, imploring him desperately to complain to his local MP. He just sighs, defeated, slumping lower in to his chair having heard this all before. Thomas's attention then takes to the glass window.

'Why do youse lot have this, anyway? You scared of us or summink?' My eyes focus on the glass, and then on Thomas, his once red face now soothed to a light pink. I shrug apologetically.

'For our protection. But I think it's stupid and unnecessary, personally.'

Thomas allows himself the tiniest of smiles. I smile back, relieved. It's a sweet moment, but any poignancy is savagely undercut when my eyes refocus on the sheer amount of Thomas's spit on the window from all his yelling. Despite what I'd just told him, I was secretly grateful for not being drowned in saliva.

I remember Thomas vividly the following morning when writing in my notebook for an exercise.

It's Tuesday and, while I write every day, Tuesday is my official day off from work to focus on my writing. Although, as I'm now attending more networking events and meetings, these eat into my sacred writing time, which is frustrating. A silver lining arrives, however, as the head of a charitable trust emails me directly. '*Your grant application is very strong. You should apply for a higher amount.*' I'm overly excited by this. *Surely they don't go out of their way to directly email everybody?* I fantasise about the email I'll send to my employers announcing I'm going part-time, funded kindly by the grant money.

Later that day, I have a meeting at a production office in Clerkenwell. My producer, Janice, welcomes me with warm kisses on both my cheeks, making me feel like I'm part of the gang. Like I belong here. *My future will be full of kisses on both cheeks.*

'Have a seat, I'll be over shortly.'

I'm then greeted by a studious figure in glasses with a lustrous mop of hair, who looks about 15 years old. He's sat so confidently in his chair, I feel like I'm entering a job interview and he's the boss. Scribbling into his notebook, I offer the young lad my biggest smile and outstretched hand.

'Hey! I'm Wally.'

'Mylo,' he says formally, his handshake precociously firm.

'You're..?'

'Work experience. Yah.'

'Cool! To be doing it... here, like.'

Mylo shrugs with all the nonchalance of a Frenchman. I was a teenager once so I don't take offence. Seconds later, Janice enters.

'Mylo's at school with my son,' her eyebrows raised as a sort of explanation.

Janice then asks me questions about my latest piece. While I deliver my garbled response, I spy Mylo writing into his notebook. Not just one or two words. Actual sentences. Long sentences. *Is he really writing all this down?* Mylo then rests his pen on his lip for a moment, before returning to the page to write some more. *Another paragraph? When I was 15 I was busy drawing pictures of Ninja Turtles having sex.*

As Janice responds to my explanation, I can't help but drift off to find myself aged 15 again, being asked what I wanted to do for my work experience. I told my teacher that I wanted to be a filmmaker. Or a journalist. 'Hmm. *What about something more realistic... like electrics?'* And behold, I ended up at Trings Electrical Store in my home town of Mitcham. And while I didn't necessarily get the experience I craved, those summer days delivering washing machines to council estates and shadowing an electrician at close quarters, the walls of his work space devoted entirely to Page 3 tits, certainly made for a memorable excursion.

'Do you agree with that then?'

I snap back to attention, realising I have absolutely no idea what Janice has just said.

Luckily, Janice emails me later with the meeting notes. However, she also sets a brand new deadline for two weeks! This is nowhere near enough time, but I agree to it nonetheless as I want to meet her expectations.

The next morning I wake up at 5am, as I will every morning from now on whenever I have a pressing deadline. Half-awake, I write for a couple of hours before I head off to work. At lunchtime, my mum treats me to lunch at McDonald's. We both eat Filet-O-Fishes[1] as they just about qualify as halal. Mum can't help but notice the bags under my eyes.

'How's it going wiz the wrrrr-iting, garcon?' she asks sweetly, rolling the French Rs of her Mauritian accent.

'Slowly,' I sigh.

'Well don't give up your job until you get something, okay?'

---

1. (Or is it Filets-O-Fish?)

Mauritians are blunt. I have a proper teenage fit, admonishing my mum for never believing in me, before feeling terrible and apologising.

Deep down I know she believes in me, but her motherly instinct is to protect me from the rejection and disappointment that lies ahead. I want to allay her fears, telling her that one day I'll be a successful writer and that all of her hard work will one day be worth it. But I can't. We finish our Filets in polite silence.

The next day I'm off work as I'm invited to attend a writing workshop by the BBC. I love meeting all the other writers, hearing their stories. Turning up to a blank page can often feel like climbing a mountain, so it's always nice to meet other mountaineers. Some of us are older, some are very young. Some have cut-glass accents, and some, like me, are well-spoken enough to mask their humble beginnings. Sipping on my tea, I can't help but eavesdrop on a conversation between two writers.

'I saw your dad treading the boards at The Nash, he was superb,' beams one.

'Oh, he knows,' deadpans the other.

I make friends with Hattie, a much younger fellow emerging writer, and we hit it off instantly. Sharing the same sense of humour, we bond over bad script notes we've received, and our demanding day jobs. Hattie works as an intern for a leading production company.

'The pay's shit, but hey. I love eating toast for dinner.'

We're also both yet to land our first properly paid writing jobs, lamenting the catch-22 that you can't get hired unless you have experience, but you won't get experience until you get hired. Hattie then enthusiastically invites me over to her house party that weekend. I'm touched. *She really likes me. We're like two peas in a pod, me and her.* It's only upon arriving at Hattie's four-bedroom semi in Maida Vale that I realise it's just me living in the pod.

'This place is fucking amazing,' I yell over the music, eyes wide with wonder.

'Yeahhh,' Hattie sighs. 'Still living with the folks at the mo. Proper lame.'

Writing in my notebook at 5am on Monday morning, my admiration for my new acquaintance is literally scribbled all over the page. *I think I'm finally mixing in the right circles...*

Back at work, my first appointment brings me crashing down to earth as Suzie paws desperately through numerous shopping bags to find her eviction letter. Having visited several times last week, my colleagues have labelled her a nuisance. I immediately have a soft-spot for Suzie. She's a single mum doing her best to look after her two kids on a low wage, just like my mum did for me and my sister growing up. Suzie speaks, and her voice dissolves away as I momentarily daydream of winning big in the writing game, paying off the remainder of Mum's mortgage.

'I need somewhere new to live but landlords won't take me 'coz I'm DSS,' sniffles Suzie into her soggy tissue. 'People like me don't get leg-ups, do they?'

Holding my gaze with hope, I hate having to tell Suzie that we can't house her. We only deal with benefits here. Without saying goodbye, she gathers her bags and leaves.

'What's her sob story today, then?' asks my colleague Mo, twinkle firmly in his eye. Mo refused to see Suzie today. I tease him about being such a kind-hearted man.

'Nah, don't get me wrong, I feel sorry for her and that, but she don't half have a chip on her shoulder.'

Mo's comments stick with me. I realise that Suzie's completely valid complaints about her situation made him and my other colleagues feel uncomfortable. People don't like chippy. It makes them squirm. Little did I know, I'd soon be experiencing chippy feelings of my own.

Following another general meeting with a different company at Le Pain Quotidien[2], Hattie, my new BFF, enters just as the development exec Laura and I are leaving.

'Laura!' she screeches excitedly.

Laura and Hattie hug it out, genuinely pleased to see one another.

'Do you guys know each other?'

'Laura and I were at Cambridge together.'

It's a happy moment, so I sidestep away, leaving them both to catch up. Months later I bump into Hattie again at a writer's event.

'Wally!' she greets me with the same excited screech.

Hattie will then tell me that she's finally quit her job and landed her first paid writing gig on a new TV series out next year. I'm genuinely happy for her as I know how thrilled she must be to finally break through. But it's only later on that it twigs... *Laura works at the production company that makes that show...* I feel myself become suspicious and full of envy and I hate myself for it.

When I get home that night I scour through the dictionary to remind myself of who I don't want to be.

chippy
informal
noun BRITISH
a fish-and-chip shop.
a carpenter.
adjective
(of a person) touchy and defensive, especially on account of having a grievance or a sense of inferiority.

---

2. *(Why is it always Le Pain Quotidien?)*

I take comfort in the fact that I've only ever worked one shift frying chips, and that I don't know how to shape wood. The last point, mind, rings true.

I'm aware of the importance of fitting in, so I internalise these words: *don't be chippy*. Every time I hear of a writer contemporary landing another great job: *don't be chippy*. Every time I meet someone who doesn't work full-time, having more time to write than me: *don't be chippy*. Every time I meet a writer who's in all the right social circles: *don't be chippy*. Every time anything ever happens that doesn't go my way: *Don't. Be. Chippy.*

I make a concerted effort to use all my energy doing positive things, and not dwelling on my bad luck. I worm my way into the inner circle, attending a prestigious invite-only meet-up for writers and directors. And, slowly but surely, I start building up my own network, developing working relationships, and generating my own (unpaid) work. I feel great. I'm being pro-active, I'm not being chippy. And then I meet Leonard with the sweepy fringe.

Leonard edits a leading film magazine, and sits across the table from me at an artists club in Soho. Realising who he is, I talk to him about foreign cinema, impressing him with my non-obvious choices. We then talk about his job as a critic, and mine as a screenwriter. The hour is late, so I start to say my goodbyes. Leonard, now onto his third glass of red, tells me to stay for another. I politely decline; I need to leave.

'What you *need* to do is quit your job. Get out your comfort zone. Get hungry! Then you'll be working your little arse off so much, the gigs will come piling in.'

Leonard then flashes the most self-satisfied grin, like a class prefect who's answered correctly, his teeth and lips stained in Merlot.

'I can't afford the risk of an irregular income,' I begin, before being stunned into silence by Leonard, who's started playing an invisible violin. *An invisible violin! I've only just met the bumptious prick.* Leonard realises that perhaps he's being a tad rude, so offers to get me a drink to compensate. Not wanting to offend, I bite my tongue and stay for another.

The next morning I sleep through my alarm and miss my writing window. I'm furious at myself for being so weak-willed. I'm also late for work. Cycling frantically to the office, I can't help but wonder whether Leonard had a point. Did I need to get out of my comfort zone? Because the zone I'm in at present certainly doesn't feel comfortable. It doesn't feel comfortable to still be living out of my overdraft. It doesn't feel comfortable to not have a bank of Mum and Dad. It doesn't feel comfortable to neglect your significant other as you're always working or writing. I eventually calm down, remembering I'm a shoo-in for that grant I've applied for. Once that pays out I can go part-time and write more. *Things will change.*

Days later, I receive **the** email. '*Unfortunately you have not been successful on this occasion.*' I stare daggers at the screen. *But... they emailed me personally??*

This particular setback hits me hard and I beat myself up for falling short again. I don't bother to turn up to the page the next morning, nor for the next week or so. I don't wake up early to write before work. I don't even read or watch TV. The only consolation I muster is that someone in a similar situation to me got that grant money. I hope that it gives them the leg-up they need.

At the benefit office a few weeks later, I'm still consumed with existential brooding. *Why do I write? Have I ever written for pleasure? Or did I just view my talent as my ticket out of Mitcham? How many more times can I go through this?* The longer you wait at that bridge waiting to pass, the harder it is to not internalise that maybe you're just not good enough.

I'm very quickly shaken out of my funk by a familiar face: Suzie. Back with all of her plastic bags in tow, all of my colleagues groan. Suzie's well aware of how she's perceived around here, but yet she still turns up.

She still turns up.

'Look, I know youse only do benefits here, but I'm being evicted this week! No one wants to help.'

It's not within our remit to help her, so we've just accepted that we can't... but we can.

See, in the world I'm trying to enter, I'm waiting on someone to let me pass. But in this world... *I'm that someone.*

Staring at Suzie through the glass, I get out of my chair and leave the cubicle. Moments later I reappear on the other side of the window next to Suzie. She's completely flummoxed.

'What you doing?'

Pulling the telephone through the hatch, I take a seat next to her.

'We are calling all the landlords that I know accept benefit claimants. Let's get this ball rolling.'

For the first time since I've been dealing with her, Suzie smiles. As do I. All she needs is for someone to take a chance on her, just once. I hope one day someone will do the same for me.

All names have been changed, except for my own.

Heroes

Catherine O'Flynn

At my primary school there were two people into music.
John Mahoney and me. We both had a load of older brothers
and sisters and I guess that's what did it. Certainly our tastes
were shaped by our elders. I like to think I moved on from that,
and that John never really did, but I'm not sure how true that is.

Prior to acquiring my own independent tastes, I followed in
the family tradition of Bowie. He was a rarity in our household
by featuring in various of my siblings' record collections – this
to me was the original meaning of a crossover artist. Anyone
who could sit next to my brother's Pink Floyd and my sister's
Ohio State Players was bridging a significant chasm.

A few years later, in the early '80s, I would become tediously
obsessed with Bowie, haranguing idiot Duran Duran fan classmates at their failure to acknowledge his genius and influence.
Around the age of eight, though, my fondness for Bowie was
more low key and significantly cooler. He was the background

noise I'd grown up with. I didn't feel the need to evangelise him to the girls playing skipping games in the playground, or to incorporate him, as I would later do, into any story or poem I wrote for school. My allegiance was signalled only by a badge. This wasn't a button badge, which had yet to really dominate the pop badge market, but rather a slightly less comely, larger diameter model. The badge was a miniature of the 'Heroes' album cover. Bowie doffing that invisible hat, whilst holding his leather jacket collars close to protect him from the Berlin wind.

I wore the badge with pride, but without comment. At primary school it passed beneath everyone's scrutiny until a disastrous collision with David O'Brien during a typically bloodthirsty lunchtime game of British Bulldog. He grabbed at my jumper, I flailed and broke loose. Tearing madly to the safety of base, exultant at my freedom, I didn't notice David O'Brien weeping on the ground behind me, or his fingernail still attached to the back of the other David's head, snagged on the pin mechanism.

Heroes was released in 1977 just a year after Bowie's notorious Victoria Station incident. Whilst the Nazi salute was maybe nothing more than an unlucky freeze frame, some of Bowie's comments during his Thin White Duke phase were less easily explained away, though of course both he and I would try our best in the years to come.

My classmate John Mahoney, as far as I know, knew nothing of Bowie or his fascination with the occult and fascism, but he too would find himself drawn towards the lure of the Reich. John's older brother Jimmy had been to Borstal. I suppose it was this deferred cachet that gave John such influence in the playground. Certainly it's hard to fathom any other explanation. He wasn't good at football or fighting and he wasn't cheeky to the teachers. He was a skinny boy with ginger hair. And yet he drew other boys, and me, the pathetic tag-along tomboy, into his orbit like litter trapped in a cyclone.

John was knowing and snide, but snide in a way that impressed us. He wore a child-size black leather jacket, was the first boy at school to have his hair cut in a skinhead and declared himself a punk like his older brother. I'm not sure now that his brother was a punk. I think what Jimmy was, essentially, was a violent headcase. But John was our unquestionable authority on the matter. His main area of expertise was in distinguishing true punks from poseurs. Often this sorting of sheep from goats would be conducted from the window of Junior Two's classroom. John would point out a passerby with bleached hair, or a cap sleeved T-shirt and test our skills. We'd invariably get it wrong. Wearing Doctor Martens was punk, wearing monkey boots made you a poseur. Blondie were all poseurs, and Debbie Harry the biggest poseur of them all. As far as I could tell the key difference between punks and poseurs was something to do with hygiene. If someone looked as if they might have been a bit sick on themselves they were a punk.

All of Jimmy's behaviour was interpreted by his younger brother John as punk and so we absorbed Jimmy's Borstal ways along with his musical choices. We all wrote ACAB on our knuckles because we thought that was punk. When Sister Kathleen told us off for writing on our hands (without knowing what it was the letters signified), John taught us the prison code of simply putting a dot on each knuckle. We were thrilled. I remember serving PC Talbot in my Dad's shop on various occasions, terrified that he would notice the marks. Perhaps he did, but assumed the dots on a little girl's hand were more to do with a childish game than a conviction that he personally was a bastard. He was probably right.

The punk revolution upset the status quo, and so it was in the playground too. I, who had always been tolerated only for the free sweets and chocolate I could bring from the shop, now had a little kudos for the first time. My sister had The Clash's first album and I knew it pretty well. I could sing a few lines of 'I'm so bored with the USA' and John Mahoney would nod approvingly. He would sing back 'White Riot' and smile knowingly and I'd smile back, but I didn't yet know what it was I was smiling knowingly about.

It was around this time that the fights with the school across the road began. It's the natural order of things for neighbouring schools to scrap and throughout my time at St Vincent's I had known that pupils of Cromwell Road were the enemy. This enmity, though, was pretty latent and half-hearted until a dramatic incident changed everything. They made the first strike and it was both audacious and theatrical. Their leader Lloyd Blackford donned a cardboard dog collar, climbed up John Mahoney's garden fence, and there, leaning over, looking down onto the tiny council house patch of grass, waved his fist and shouted: 'I am Ian Paisley!' Thus started the great sectarian skirmishes of Nechells.

From that point on, our war with Cromwell Road was no longer just some tawdry territorial scuffle, but a holy war. Their school could hardly have been more aptly named. The Cromwell Road pupils were transformed from just the kids you never saw at church into Oliver's Army – hardcore protestant defenders of the faith – and we went from recalcitrant shuffling church attenders to an oppressed minority united by the communion wafers stuck to the roofs of our mouths.

I didn't see much action in the war. Being a girl and living outside the tiny epicentre of the fighting (the manmade hillock in front of the blocks of flats), I got only second-hand accounts of the skirmishes. But the images were vivid enough, fit for any gable wall: Lloyd Blackford, a latter day King Billy in a Fonz T-shirt, standing on top of the hill surrounded by his henchmen, swinging his belt around his head before descending on our brave boys.

I did manage to tag along to one battle but found it a pretty disappointing affair. There didn't seem to be any actual fighting, just a few limp fake kung-fu kicks followed by lots of running away. I began to secretly question the official propaganda.

I was distracted from the frontline, though, by the appearance on *Top of the Pops* one Thursday night of a new group. The sampled Prince Buster screech at the start of the song was a dog whistle. I stared at the screen and saw Terry Hall's bored, sulky face; Jerry Dammers' crazy leer and Neville Staples shouting about I really didn't know what. The Specials were calling directly to me.

From that point on, Saturdays had a new purpose. The ever-puzzling inconsistency and unpredictability of my mom 's anxieties about my safety meant that, whilst my bedroom window was tied shut with twine to keep me from falling out, I had been allowed to catch the bus into Birmingham city centre and wander around on my own from the age of eight. I'd previously spent my Saturday mornings wandering around the toy departments of the big stores, looking at the I-Spy books in Midland Educational, ordering the children's special lunch in Denny's and eating it on my own. Now, Saturday mornings were spent exploring every possible way of exchanging my pocket money for 2-Tone and 2-Tone-related products.

As an adult I find many other former 2-Tone fans were just children at the time of the label's heyday. I'm not sure what it was about the scene that attracted kids. Maybe the sharp Tonik suits. Maybe the cartoon figure of Walt Jabsco. Maybe the infectious Blue Beat sound. It's hard for me to have a view as I was entirely unaware of this junior groundswell at the time. My classmates at St Vincent's were immune to the charms of The Specials or even Madness, who I could see even then were the crowd pleasers of the scene. A new, more urgent craze was sweeping them away. Jimmy Mahoney's latest gift to his little brother was National Socialism.

Back in the infants' we often used to play Army or War or Soldiers. The country you fought for correlated with your power and influence in the classroom. John Mahoney and his right hand man, Mark Higgins, were the Americans. The boys on the next rung down played the British. The next the French. The Z-listers of the team were made to play the Germans and I, the girl, below even them, was made to single-handedly represent Italy. I didn't really know what Italy had got up to in the war – they didn't feature in many films – so I just used to stand near the school wall shaking a big imaginary saucepan and shouting: 'Don't shoot! I am a-making ze spaghetti.' The boys seemed happy to have me thus occupied.

Now, though, it was the A-listers who wanted to be the Germans. We didn't play Army anymore, we were too old for that, but copies of grown-up looking books by someone called Sven Hassel started changing hands amongst the boys. John Mahoney came to school one day wearing a swastika arm band, an action met with fury and an incredibly long lecture to all of us from Mr Winter the headmaster. I wasn't sure if this was all still to do with punk. I'd seen pictures of Sid Vicious wearing swastikas, but I'd thought that was just him being mad, not actually a Nazi. I didn't like the idea of being a Nazi – they were so obviously the baddies. But when John Mahoney started the Blitzkrieg Gang I forgot my reservations.

The Blitzkrieg Gang was the elite commando force to be unleashed upon the Cromwell Road rabble. It seemed odd to me – Nazis vs. Protestants – a weird mash up of history. Maybe I'd have found it less strange if I'd known then about the murky role of the Vatican during WW2, or maybe then I'd just have been truly confused. Already the figures of Rommel (John Mahoney's personal hero), Ian Paisley and Bobby Sands were all getting mixed up into one big, lumpy soup. To join the Blitzkrieg Gang you had to pass an initiation test. You weren't allowed to know what was involved in the initiation test in advance, and you couldn't back out once you'd been told. I didn't like the sound of that at all. I was essentially a good girl. I was also an enormous coward. My greatest fear was that it might involve playing on the railway tracks or in the storm drains of the canal, both things that many boys in the class used to do for fun and which filled me with absolute terror. Life outside the Blitzkrieg Gang, though, looked like a lonely existence and so in the end I said I'd do it. The leadership greeted the news with a shrug. They knew I'd tag along one way or another.

The initiation test turned out to be not so bad. In fact, I think some of the boys were a little embarrassed by it. It involved breaking into a building site and following a prescribed course, climbing over the half-finished factory unit. At one point you had to climb along some scaffolding, shout out: 'I am a commando' and then jump off. It seemed a bit silly. Even though it was a palpably soft test I still didn't get involved with the climbing and jumping. One of my many terrors along with being killed by a train, drowned in a storm drain and savaged by a guard dog was falling off half-finished buildings. I said I wasn't going to do it and the leadership decided that in my case just breaking into the building site was enough.

Once in the Blitzkrieg Gang, life was quite sweet for a while. We had a den underneath a tree on the wasteland at the side of one of the massive gasometers at Saltley power station. Out of school we'd hang out there quite a lot, throwing stones at the abandoned machinery that littered the ground. We were always engaged in target practice though none of us ever mentioned that we were unlikely to encounter the enemy, hidden away as we were in our little bunker.

At school the Nazi craze was slowly mutating into something more contemporary and British. I'd seen the graffiti 'NF' sprayed here and there in the area but Nottingham Forest were quite popular at the time and I thought it related to them. When John Mahoney started writing it on his hand, though, I knew that couldn't be right as he was a Villa supporter like the rest of us. I eventually discovered that NF stood for National Front. I knew all about the National Front. In fact, all I knew was what Jerry Dammers had taught me, but that was enough. I couldn't see it catching on at school; everyone in my class had immigrant parents, of one sort or another. Perhaps John Mahoney sensed this flaw too. Or perhaps his natural cowardice and barely concealed fear of confrontation made him choose the one ethnic group not represented at school, but for whatever reason a new acronym sprung up on his hand: APL.

This was not, as might have been at least consistent, an Anti Protestant League, but instead another of Jimmy's Borstal hand-me-downs – the Anti Paki League.

I thought Paki was a bad word. It wasn't one I'd ever heard at home. It seemed a toxic, hate-filled word even back then. There weren't many Asian families in the neighbourhood, which was predominantly a mixture of Brummie, Irish and Afro-Ca-ribbean. The only Asian children I ever saw were the children of the shopkeeper up the road. Sometimes they'd be out playing at the kerbside, two little girls with long plaits, and a smaller boy in what looked like a dress. Despite the weird clothes I felt the universal kinship of the offspring of retailers. I'd see them sometimes at the warehouse telling their dad which crisps to buy. I wondered if their dad paid any more attention to their advice than mine did.

Soon all the boys in the gang had white laces in their Docs, which meant you were APL. 'Paki-bashing' was apparently how they spent their free time. They spoke about it in coy terms, lots of nudges and winks, as perhaps they would speak in a few years about equally fictitious sexual escapades. They talked about 'christening' their Docs with the blood of their victims. I wondered where they were finding these victims. Did they mean the two little girls and their four-year-old brother?

The Blitzkrieg Gang still met in its den. It wasn't really much fun though. We didn't speak about punks anymore, they seemed to have disappeared from the face of the earth. None of the other members were allowed into town on their own, none of them had anything to say about music, not even rubbish music. The fights with Cromwell Road, in as much as they had ever really been fights, had died out. No peace agreement had been brokered, just a mutual recognition of the futility of that particular war. We spent long hot afternoons under the tree, throwing stones half-heartedly at bits of metal and each other until one day the long awaited, never truly expected invasion came.

The invaders were three big girls. I'd never seen them before. They looked as if they were at secondary school – some terrifying pubescent Amazonian tribe. They strolled right up to the den, while we sat and gawped. They sized us up and asked the inevitable starter question – the question to which there was never a good answer:

'What you looking at?'

I can't recall now how the conversation went. I remember that John was quiet and sheepish, the girls loud and aggressive. For some reason I was spared their attention. I'm not sure if this was an act of universal sistership, or because their only interest was in humiliating small boys. They made the others climb into the cradle of a JCB digger, which they then proceeded to pelt with stones and bricks. It didn't appear to be a particularly terrifying ordeal. Both attackers and victims seemed equally bored and embarrassed by the theatricality of it all. Eventually the girls lost interest and drifted off, shouting threats and warnings after them. The boys took their hands from their ears and climbed out of the cradle. Mark Higgins said the girls were lucky to have left when they did, before the boys had launched their counter-attack.

It would be tempting to say that that was the end of the Blitzkrieg Gang and the end of John Mahoney's spell of influence, but I don't suppose it was. It's impossible to recall the chronology now, but I'm sceptical of any neatness to the story. I did eventually start tagging along less with John and the others. I found standing in records shops on my own, endlessly looking at records I already possessed or very much wanted to possess, preferable to anything else really.

'Ghost Town' was released in June 1981, two years after 'Gangsters' and a few weeks before I left primary school. By the time I started secondary school in September, The Specials were history. The break from my primary school was absolute. I had no cause to walk up to the flats and maisonettes where most of my primary school classmates lived, I caught the bus early for my new school and came home late. My new classmates lived in quiet suburban Hall Green, or bohemian middle class Moseley in landscapes apparently free from storm drains and building sites. The Specials had deserted me and so I turned back to Bowie, clinging to him tightly for the next few years, obsessing over his classic '70s albums, covering my school jumper with new smaller badges to ward off the evils of New Romantics and Wham! fan hedonists.

I never saw John Mahoney again. I've no idea if he ever outgrew his racism, or his infatuation with his brother. Years later when I was 17 I bumped into his old lieutenant Mark Higgins in a pub in town. He told me John had got a girl pregnant whilst still at school and had ended up marrying her. 'Too much too young,' he said – six years too late – as he sipped his lager and black. He was dismissive of his former hero, laughing at his folly. I knew all about fallen idols. David was in his Glass Spider phase. We drank and chatted and reminisced about the rats in my dad's cellar. My dad was dead by then, the shop and the cellar sold, and I was living in a different part of the city. I found myself thinking back to one of the last conversations I'd had with John. In those last few weeks of primary school with Ghost Town at number one, The Specials had finally done enough to dent the consciousness of my classmates. John asked me:

'So are you a Mod?'

This was a common misconception. The Specials, Selecter, Madness, The Beat were all seen as Mods. Anyone in a suit basically. I wasn't a Mod. I knew very well that Mods liked Motown and Northern Soul, but followers of Ska were rude boys (or girls). I knew also that such a distinction would be far too finely graded and nuanced for anyone at school to get, even John Mahoney, the one-time great sifter of punks and poseurs, so I said simply:

'Yes.'

'I like the coats they wear. The parkas. They look good with the targets and stuff on the back. I might get one,' he said.

'Ok.'

'But if you're a Mod, do you have to like wogs?'

He knew the answer already, but I gave him what he wanted. 'Yeah, you do.'

'Do you have to dance next to them?'

'Yeah, you do.'

'Do you have to hold hands with them?' He was laughing now at his deliberate childishness.

I laughed too. 'Yeah, you do.'

John pretended he was choking on poison, holding his throat and sticking his tongue out, parodying his own disgust.

I laughed at the charade. He stopped choking but carried on smiling at me.

I'm not sure if we choose our idols or if they choose us. I think if it hadn't been for Borstal Jimmy, John might have been a different boy.

Disguised Malicious Murder:
The Working Class and Mental Health

Rebecca Winson

It was 2009, the awkward, fitful few months before gradu-ation. The economic depression was on the airwaves, on the bills for oversubscribed job fairs, on the lips of all my friends. For them, it meant a few months back in their childhood bedrooms, their parents footing the bill for their commute to unpaid internships. For me, it meant something else entirely. My parents couldn't afford to support me, at home or not, and I couldn't support myself either. I couldn't see any way of starting my adult life which wasn't going to be staggeringly crap. There wasn't one.

So a depression, of another kind entirely, was on every page of my journal, on every frantic phone call home to my mum, on the tip of my tongue whenever people congratulated me for getting a degree, watermarked into every CV I sent out, in every shaky breath I took to stave off the daily panic attacks.

And a depression was in my little brother's head. On Tuesday 9th June, 300 miles away, in the back bedroom of the little council terrace I was so desperate to avoid returning to, depression was in his 18-year-old hands, shaped like a rifle, it was in the long, bassist's fingers he wrapped round the trigger, it must have been buzzing in his ear, under his dark curly hair, as he put the gun inside it.

*

At the time – especially to an artsy English graduate only vaguely aware of what a mortgage was, let alone a subprime one – it wasn't clear what had caused the 'economic downturn'. The government at the time were quick to point to bankers and America, the opposition blamed it on people like me. I was from a family of scroungers, and I was a scrounger myself. Thirty quids' worth of Educational Maintenance Allowance, weekly, had paid for my bus and books during sixth form. Loans and grants paid for my degree. I'd grown up on a council estate; my parents had paid for our low rent with a mix of public sector wages, cash in hand jobs and, worst of all, benefits. I was about to sign on. We'd scrounged all the money, now there was none left.

I knew that was bollocks. I took a vicarious pleasure in refusing to be guilty, in staring coldly for a solid, silent minute, at the parent of a friend who asked me why I thought people like them should support 'people like you who haven't got jobs'; in arguing, gloriously incandescent, with the Job Centre worker who told me to say 'please' before she would authorise my benefits. I'd been brought up a socialist and, idiotically, I loved those first opportunities I had to really defend my class, our existence.

But after a while, I stopped finding it so easy. Because although I knew full well the working class weren't responsible for the economy's depression, I knew what, in a huge way, was responsible for mine. For my brother's. For me being dosed up on citalopram and Alex sitting alone in his room with his finger on the trigger of a gun. It was what I was defending. It was being poor. It was being working class.

Getting sick: 'Are you sure you're not bringing this on yourself?'

In 1844, a young Friedrich Engels wrote *The Condition of the English Working Class in England*. In it, he documented how the conditions the poor were kept in affected their cleanliness, nutrition, the air they breathed, the lengths of their lives, and he called out what that all amounted to:

> 'When one individual inflicts... injury upon another such that death results, we call the deed manslaughter; when the assailant knew in advance that the injury would be fatal, we call his deed murder. When society places hundreds of proletarians in such a position that they inevitably meet a too early and an unnatural death... its deed is murder just as surely as the deed of the single individual; disguised, malicious murder.'

He backed his accusation up with evidence: statistics on sickness and mortality in the towns he studied. Indisputable, black and white columns of numbers, totting up the slaughter of men, women and children, showing how the structure of society killed the poor.

Engels' findings weren't published in English until 40 years later. Today, if you want to find mortality rates, just Google it. The information is more accessible than ever: society does indeed know in advance what injuries it afflicts are fatal. But whilst miner's lung and mutilations in cotton mills are things of the past, the overall picture isn't so different from what Engels raged against. On mental illness alone, the inequality between rich and poor is startling.

Academics estimate that the austerity resulting from the 2008 recession caused an 'extra' 1000 men to commit suicide. The same figures say there were up to 40,000 more suicide attempts. Data from the Health Survey for England shows the poorest fifth of the population are almost 20% more likely to develop a mental illness than those in the richest.[1]

There's a bewildering number of reasons for those illnesses: not enough endorphins; too much dopamine, booze, fags, weed, or coffee; head or brain injury; genetics; streptococcus bacteria; mercury poisoning; physical abuse; underactive thyroid; divorce; anaemia; redundancy; lack of sunlight; financial stress; poor nutrition; childhood trauma; air pollution.

Less bewildering about mental illness is why working class people are more likely to have it than the rich. You don't have to be a statistician to look at that list above and see that the vast majority of that stuff is stuff we're more likely to go through, live with, even consider part of who we are. Two pints of lager and a packet of crisps: most Friday nights for you; a big red flag for any GP you might go to complaining that you're always sad, something for him to wag his finger at before he goes home to a pint of craft ale and some dauphinoise with his steak.

Forgive me for being cynical. I've seen far too many fingers wagged to be anything else. Very few people dispute that health inequality exists, that the poor are more likely to be mentally ill, but not everyone is like Engels, not everyone is on our side. We're not sick because of poverty, or trauma, or ill-health, some

---

1. The Poverty Site. (n.d.). Mental health. Retrieved from http://www.poverty. org.uk/62/index.shtml

people say. We're sick because we bring poverty, trauma, or illness on ourselves.

This belief is so ingrained in society that it's almost invisible, but the invention of the 'deserving poor', the culture of blame around poverty, extends into how our health problems are treated, and here it sticks out like a sore thumb: the working class are so tied up with castigation, that symptoms and causes of ill-health are punished before they're treated.

That's what happened to Alex. At school, I could see my little brother wasn't able to 'deal with stuff' as he should. He was constantly teary or full of a temper. He was paranoid, waiting for anyone who showed friendship to turn on him. He always wanted to be alone. He would come home and cry for hours. He was stuck in a vicious circle: he was depressed because he was being bullied, then he was bullied for being depressed.

One lunchtime, the bullies – nice, smartly dressed lads whose parents were on the PTA – finally went far enough that it couldn't be ignored anymore. Snotty and tearful, he told a teacher. The teacher went to the the boys. 'He cries at anything, Miss.' 'He's just a pain, he's always following us round, clingy.'

Miss – qualified enough to be Head of Year, with at least a decade's experience under her belt, and with enough awareness of physical and mental health to be a PE teacher – let the boys go back to class, unpunished, then returned to Alex. 'Are you sure,' she said, to a 13-year-old who cried openly at school, 'that you're not bringing this on yourself?'

A few months later Alex finally flipped, turning on the boys after they made fun of our 'small, shit house'. He punched one of them in the face. He was punished. Our parents were told. He got put on a 'cause for concern' list.

The ringleader of the bullies walked away without so much as a detention. He'd been going through some problems at home. He had such a big, nice house.

Being working class didn't exactly cause Alex's trauma, but it meant that, when it happened, things were worse. His story is black and white. He didn't bring mental illness on himself. But there are different types of trauma. Some are short, horrible, easily identified. Others drag on for so long that you consider them part of everyday life.

It's in these types of trauma that the grey areas start to open up. So much goes unsaid about working class life that it's easy for prejudice to fill the silences, and there are few things talked about less often or less accurately than the experience of being poor, of growing up poor: acutely crap and at the same time, beautiful. Responsible for all the fierce and funny and proud and best bits of you, for all the bright memories of the people you love. You don't want to slag it off, because everyone else already does.

It's difficult, for example, for me to admit that since I was old enough to worry about money, I have. We never went without food, but at some point I became aware that this wasn't guaranteed. Bills, rent payments, weekly shops and new school uniforms were all paid for, but discussed in quiet panic. I had nightmares about my mum and dad losing their jobs – nightmares I never told them about, because I was aware they probably worried about that themselves.

This behaviour – especially amongst guys – is often pointed out as emotional reticence, or reluctance to show a softer side. But saying 'I'm worried' would have been about as pointless as explaining that I was breathing. When you're working class, worry is just there, a constant background hum everyone can hear. Pointing out that you hear it too seems laughable, or selfish. It didn't even occur to me to let anyone know I felt a bit sick with nerves whenever I needed new shoes. Other working class kids behaved the same way. My friend Tom made sure he had his panic attacks quietly in his room so his mum wouldn't have 'another thing to deal with.' Like Tom said, this wasn't traumatising, at the time. It was fine. You just got on with it, just humming along, like everyone else.

When you're used to a background noise, sometimes you don't notice it getting louder until you're deaf.

Treatment options: 'Are you selling these? To get some money?'

Like my brother, my class didn't cause my illness, but it made it worse. Looking back, I'd been depressed for a while before I went to university. I was sick with something, anyway. I remember once having such an outburst of nervous, sick-with-dread panic, that I ripped my bedroom apart. Other times I would just lie awake and cry.

Really, university was my first attempt at getting better. When you're working class and depressed, sometimes you think becoming middle class is a treatment option. I moved as far down south as I could. I used my summer job wages to buy a good laptop and 'proper' clothes, including a big, bright red trench coat I thought was very art school.

I had a room in a halls of residence which was a castle, I had sushi for the first time, I had the big, wooden desk I'd always wanted, I had a boyfriend with such a posh voice he once answered my phone and my childhood friend thought he was messing around pretending to be Hugh Grant, and I had a breakdown. Four months into university, I was suicidal.

When I got older, I found out lots of my friends with a similar background to me had had 'episodes' at uni. We all thought we were going to finally be ourselves, and we spent three years realising that who we were was nothing like our professors, the authors on our reading lists, and the high-collared, aquiline, private school kids we encountered for the first time, but that all of a sudden we were also nothing like our friends or family back home anymore. You can't pretend that you're not poor just by wearing a nice coat and carrying round a Penguin classic, and you can't pretend that you tried to pretend not to be poor.

When my brilliant plan of tackling depression by completely changing everything about myself hit the totally unforeseen obstacle of being utterly arrogant and impractical, I ended up on citalopram. Citalopram was great.. Once it built up in my brain, it numbed my feelings, kept me constantly sleepy and, if I didn't take it, I'd get a headache, so it was nothing like anything I might have chosen to self-medicate with, like alcohol. Brilliantly for someone studying full time, it made me horrendously forgetful. I forgot essays, lectures, how to footnote, who wrote *Robinson Crusoe*. I forgot how to write. At my lowest point, one of my essays was just bullet points. It was handed back, ungraded, with a solitary red question mark at the bottom.

I also forgot about the citalopram itself. Sometimes my anxiety would get so overwhelming that there'd be a few blank hours and then I'd find myself back home. Once, I didn't pack anything but my purse, and had to go to my old surgery to get an emergency prescription. 'I do need to check something with you,' said the GP.

I swallowed. I didn't like being asked how I was, but a small part of me still appreciated people caring enough to ask. 'Are you selling these?'

I blinked. 'What?'

'I just need to check that you really forgot your prescription. I know how difficult it can be for some students, financially, and selling on prescriptions can seem…'

I stood up. I didn't know who she knew who was prepared to pay money for a drug that took four weeks to make you fall asleep in the middle of the day, but I didn't have the energy to argue. 'I'm not selling my medication,' I said. She gave me one day's worth, and made me come back the next day.

It was better to be safe than sorry, she said. It was my first lesson in how an accent, cheap clothes, class, could determine how you were treated by health workers. It wasn't going to be my last. There was the counsellor who told me I should stop watching *Coronation Street* because it was too violent and depressing, so I had energy to concentrate on my assignment on *Lord of the Flies*; the cognitive behavioural therapist I had when I was unemployed, who suggested I spend money on books and days out to keep me busy, and who sighed I was 'unwilling to participate' when I pointed out the whole reason I was depressed was because I couldn't afford things like that.

Then there was the aftermath of Tuesday 9th June 2009, and the gun in the back bedroom, the gun with the trigger that was never pulled. I'm still sick with thanks that I can write these words: my beautiful, funny, clever little brother didn't kill himself.

Mum and Dad found him with the rifle – the type which, by the way, you can buy freely in the UK, a high-powered air rifle which people use for hunting. He was hysterical. They had to wrestle the gun off him. He hit Dad. Mum rang the mental health crisis team. They couldn't get anyone out for at least 90 minutes. There were no GPs reachable. The only thing anyone could do, the mental health team said, was to get Alex arrested for assault, and then sectioned. They made it sound like a bizarre but necessary admin procedure. Faced with a suicidal son who no one would help, Mum rang the police.

So Alex didn't kill himself. He had a taser pointed at him instead. He was pinned down on the floor and handcuffed, instead. He was charged with assault, instead. He was stripped to his boxers, and put in a police cell, instead. He had swabs of his DNA and his fingerprints taken, instead. He was taken to hospital, handcuffed, and then taken to a mental health unit, and then sectioned, instead. He was left in a locked psych ward, with no one-to-one care, and no facilities to take a shower, and a schizophrenic fellow patient trying to get in his room, instead.

Getting better: 'You have nothing to lose but your chains'

It took Alex nearly two weeks to persuade 'a bunch of people with posh Parker pens' to let him go home. It took me two years to get off citalopram. I don't know how long it will take either of us to be really better, or if we ever will be. But we're both nearly there. We really are.

One thing that helps: we were both brought up by parents who taught us about people like Friedrich Engels and his mate Karl, what people like them wrote about, thought about, acted upon. They taught us so that we know what happened to Alex, what happened to me, what happens to people from our background, every day, up and down the country, isn't our fault.

It happens because society is happy to place the mentally ill, the poor, and those who are both, in situations where they may well meet 'early and unnatural death'. Or, as Alex says, better than Engels, I think: 'Being working class and being mentally ill are both just constantly shitting yourself. And no one cares.'

Knowing that helps, not just because we know it's not our fault, but because we know what we have to do to fix it. Because Engels never really meant that all of society wanted to murder the poor, and because Alex doesn't really mean that no one cares. He means 'They' don't care, the government doesn't care. People in power don't care. But we care: me and him, our mates, our family, our unions, our class.

So being poor might be the reason we got ill, but it's also the reason we've got solidarity. Against all of that. It's the reason we're both spending time and effort trying to make sure other poor people don't get ill too. What helps the most is knowing it doesn't have to be like this…

Where There's Shit, There's Gold

Ben Gwalchmai

Let's do something together, reader: picture the first street or road you think of when you think of a working class childhood. Now imagine the clothes they're wearing; imagine their accents; imagine what their mum and dad do; imagine whether they have both. What do you see?

Searching your mind for a cultural reference to match, would it be the *Kidulthood* series by Noel Clarke? Or Ken Loach's BAFTA-winning *I, Daniel Blake*? They're fine examples, but they represent urban and suburban working class people: there are a whole load of us that are *never* called working class.

We're the Rural Poor.

For a cultural representation, you might think of *Kes* or 2013's *The Selfish Giant*, but neither come quite near enough. I've only found one film that comes close to my experience of growing up: *Sleep Furiously*. It's a documentary on small, rural communities in mid-Wales that looks at the community as a whole – an overview, with a slight understanding of class. Let me give you a little more.

Our work can define our class, our families define our class, and yet class can be performed. We working class folks know this best.

My taid, pronounced 'tide' and the north-Welsh word for grandfather, told us that anyone can do any job, and necessity will force us to do whatever jobs are around. My taid also told me, 'Where there's shit, there's gold.' When your job at 12 involves battery-chickens shitting on you from above, it's fair to say that phrase comes as cold comfort. After that job, I worked clearing cesspits and sewers: don't let anyone tell you country life is easy... or idyllic. But, since my first job – cleaning toilets – things have looked rosier each time, even if they haven't smelt it.

My first job was before primary school had finished and remains a strong, disinfectant-smelling, happy memory. We were over the border in Shrewsbury, at the Shrewsbury Flower Show. A huge event. Thousands of people came to show off their gardens and appreciate those of others. I was nine. I helped with whatever my mam told me to: scrub here, stand there, smile at the people, refill those rolls, mop that piss, collect 10p from anyone who wants to use the toilet. Though I'm unsure if I'd been paid to work before that, this is the first time I remember feeling fully exhausted at the end of the day and having a plastic money-bag full of my 'wages'. That image of a money-bag with a little calculation of my wages on the white paper inside resonated with me for years and has stayed with me since. Being paid £1 per hour for 7 hours' work rated pretty highly on my achievements of 1994.

Little jobs would follow – a quid here, a quid there – but it was after turning 11 that work really began. Rarely did it *not* include poo in one form or another. 'Clean the pig shed' meant sweep the pig shit, shovel the pig shit, and move the pig shit: there was no 'cleaning' that shed – nor other animal sheds. 'Clear the sewer' was actually a fun job: get in the tractor cab, sit behind the driver, then take the pipe from the muck-spreader and climb down the sewer shaft, put the end of the pipe in, call up to activate the suction, and try not to fall in. Reader, I fell in. Plenty. 'Clear the field', aka 'Poop the field', meant push a wheelbarrow around and shovel the shit into it. 'Grind the fertiliser' meant sifting through the dry– well, you get the picture.

We weren't a farming family, not properly. 'Always the farmhand, never the farmer.' Always the difficult to navigate, porous borders between what we were and what we weren't. We kept animals as and when we could get them cheaply, but only to provide a service, or as meat to be fattened for Christmas. Benefits still put the majority of the food on the table and paid our rent: my mam managed to find us a disused farmhouse with dilapidated sheds to rent for the same Housing Benefit that the council were already paying. 'Do your chores': clean the fireplace, sieve the ashes through your hands to get any small leftover coals (a process I renamed 'Grind the coals' in honour of the aforementioned grinding of the fertiliser); chop logs, carry logs, dry the logs; check if the goat was ok, move the goat's station and water bucket if she'd chewed the grass enough in that area; feed the pig (or pigs) and the poultry; 'clean the pig shed'; feed the belligerent turkey, clean around the turkey; ensure they all have enough water; then light the fire and ensure its survival. That was in the winter evenings, if there was food and fuel enough. Weekends meant proper work in the day, chores at night, and homework on Sunday evenings.

We moved into that house when I was 11 and starting secondary school. Though cold, it was the biggest house we'd ever lived in; it felt amazing. My own room! Even now, when I think of '*home*' I think of the stretch of land near that house. Perhaps it's Montgomeryshire or perhaps it felt like becoming. We've all moved now but some within walking distance. When I stay with my family, I walk back there and admire it.

My mam certainly took my taid's words to heart and worked whatever jobs she could. As a single mother in the countryside, she worked hard to make sure we were 'respectable' and polite but always knew the value and difficulty of money.

Whether it was as immigrants to a new village or as poor people surrounded by what we saw as riches, we developed a kind of instinctive performativity. This was built on three core fears: we couldn't be seen to be so poor *as to admit to being poor*; we couldn't rock the boat too much with our English landlords, so *we were neither English nor Welsh*; we could do anything other kids could do *and we'd do it 'respectably'*. This notion of respectability would eventually be the main driver of my teenage rebellion's burning, speeding, auction-bought, £12 car that went crashing into a hedgerow.

I actually did buy a car for £12; I put in 5 and my friend put in 7. It lasted us about two months. We were 13. Fortunately, he was a farmer's son and the most damage we could do was on their fields (and they needed turning up anyway). We didn't crash it, it just burnt out. There was a lot of freedom to do strange and unlikely things in the countryside.

After starting my A Levels, I stopped working on farms or in sewers. The pay was worse than designing websites and I'd been picking that up progressively. Unless they were desperate, folks I'd worked with before wouldn't call on me because they knew I'd 'grown into an angry, weed-smoking little shit', as my mam put it. According to her, I'd become the steaming shit I'd hated.

It's easily done. I've seen it in so many of the young adults I've worked with in writing workshops, in interviews for articles, or as a carer: there are pressures and expectations on working class kids that are felt more keenly if you're caring or observant or – god forbid – both. My own family wanted me to be a good student but later feared that I'd 'swallowed a dictionary'. They wanted me to work and pay a fair rent, but I had to do well at school *and* 'get out more' – yet I couldn't do anything while out that might reflect badly on the respectable reputation of the family. These expectations only intensified as time and different jobs went by. As you've probably figured out, I was a disappointing teenager to my mam – I stopped being respectable at 14. I got less and less so.

Remember I was told, 'Where there's shit, there's gold'? There's a frank, funny kindness to my taid's phrase that I see more as each day passes – as children growing in the shit, we are the rose-gold. Thorns and all. Only with travel and the struggle to get that travel did I see how good I had it, how good and kind my family are in the face of an everyday struggle that continues even now.

On returning to Wales from a year away, I truly understood how tough it is to stay kind and caring in rural poverty. I was 19. I was damned sure then that I was going to help a lot more and be a lot kinder than I had been. And I'm damned sure now. It only took me a year to realise that to break that glass, class ceiling, we must out-think our situation. Work smarter *and* harder. Be respect*ful* not respect*able*. Thereafter, I channelled that anger into helping: helping my family and other families like ours.

Whenever a friend uses scatological humour, I smile. I rarely laugh a full laugh but I smile. Shit's a serious business some-times. Different strokes for different folks, different shits for different bits. Dog shit for leather, horse shit for fertiliser, cow pats for heating and insulating and throwing (it's funny when you're 12) – I could go on. You get it.

I am made of different shit to most. Most tell me when we've had a pint or three, I'm a bit 'weird'. That weird is golden. Much of the gold we've mined today came from the Late Heavy Bombardment period in the earth's history – thing about gold is, it's malleable yet conductive. A perfect conduit for information; your phone probably has gold in it. Gold is adaptable. It's strong.I know that working in fields, in the keeping and killing of stock, working on the backs of tractors and trucks has made me adaptable. There are smells I've encountered in cities that haven't bothered me but made my friends wretch; there are sights; I've felt the life drain from an animal because of the slit I made in its neck. Perhaps, while reading this, you'll think me cold. Or worse. I'm not, I'm simply aware of the reality of the everyday shit we have to do to survive, to make the things the rest of us take for granted in the markets or the clothes shops or the furniture sellers.

Farm, forest, butcher's, sewer, river: all hard work. All work I've done and would gladly do again.

The exact moment I came back around to agricultural work was when I was 19 and a close family friend's husband was out harvesting. We got the call that he'd fallen and hurt his leg. Keeping in mind that it had been a hell of an 18 months since I last worked on a farm, or did much labour except factory labour, I was happy to help. I wanted the distraction, I wanted the work. I could tell it was important. Turned out, our family friend was in ill-health anyway and probably should've been looking after himself more. We set to bailing.

As a term, bailing can apply to all the different parts of hay bailing – we were only needed to pick up the bails and stack them on the trailer. Working on his own, he should have had a conveyor (a portable conveyor belt that has square-bail-sized ridges on the belt, that can be raised or tilted, and looks a little like a flat escalator to nowhere). He didn't. He should have been working with a few people to stack. He wasn't. The stubbornness of farmers knows no bounds. He was just lucky he fell in a leftover fertiliser patch: it softened his fall.

That day we spent four hours in the afternoon sun stacking bails – his son, my little sister, my mam, and me. It was a hard day; it was a good day. We all ate at the farmhouse when it was done and Dafydd, the farmer, remarked, 'You've gotten better at stacking in the past few years. What have you been up to, then?' I was tired but had enjoyed the work so just smiled and considered my answer. Before I could speak, my mam said, 'He's a *man* now, Dafydd. He knows.' I looked at her and she held my gaze a second – recognition passed between us and we were both thankful. I think we've been more thankful of each other, of our family and its friends, of the countryside, ever since. That 'He knows' was the exact moment.

There's a community made of people who are willing to do the hard work. They shine golden in the sun when the stack is on.

These days, my family ask me, 'So what is it you *actually* do?' When I remind them of the novel I wrote and the things it's lead me to do, they're still perplexed. It isn't tangible to them. It isn't real. When I remind them of the operas I wrote for Welsh National Opera they smile and nod but soon enough the question returns to their faces. When I remind them that I still sometimes work on farms, in pubs, forests, or wherever money needs me to, they say, 'Ah! So a "jack of all trades and a master of none" then?' 'Aye,' I smile and think… *but oftentimes better than a master of one*. They think I'm very respectable, whilst I know it's a small performance. That instinctive performativity has become a respectful acceptance of their ways.

My taid told me, 'Where there's shit, there's gold.' In the novel I wrote, *Purefinder,* the main character's job is the Victorian city practice of 'pure finding', where people walked the streets with a bucket, picking up dog faeces to sell to leather tanners who'd use that faeces to purify the leather. There's a double-edged truth to his phrase. After three years researching and six living in London, I spent a year sleeping on my family's floors and writing the book – I also helped as a stable hand, grooming and caring for horses. That year was the most at peace I'd felt since I was 20. I was both farm worker and writer, my family appreciated financial help and my presence, they liked seeing me working on a farm and contented on my own; I'd found balance, an acceptance of my outlier class.

At 14, everything felt like an injustice.

At 20, I knew my place: my place is in the muck, happily so. I just scrub up well.

There is a great value in learning how to kill and skin an animal well, what calls calm birds, what motions calm a running flock, or when's the last moment you can dive out the way of a herd, stampeding. If you're working class, growing up in the countryside and reading this, remember: it's a blessing in disguise. You have it better than city kids – trust me, I've lived in a few cities now and it's nowhere near as free as the countryside. Go for that walk. Find the best way to the river. Go to that rave. Go. Get out there. Take jobs if they're offered. Go to the Young Farmers Club – it's ridiculously fun and not everyone's a farmer – and get to know your community. You might realise that not everyone farms.

Remember, I wrote, 'There was a lot of freedom to do

strange and unlikely things in the countryside'? There's a great value in space itself. Use it if you have it.

Now, at 32, nothing stops me burying my hands deep in shit if there's work to be done. After all, where there's shit, there's gold.

The Housework Issue (The Other One)

Cath Bore

In work, we sell our labour for money. Sometimes we are well rewarded for our labour, other times not so much. In work we're told that if we work hard we'll be prosperous. That's the golden rule, the big promise. Work hard and you'll earn money to put food on the table and a roof over your head, all the clichés. Work hard and everything will be fine.

But it's not, is it? Everything isn't fine, not at all. Working hard does not guarantee, nor equate to, a reasonable standard of living, a good life, or physical and mental health or wellbeing. Indeed it might mean exactly the opposite. And this is especially the case for working class women.

Imagine me at 17 years old, on summer holidays in the late 1980s, the first half of my A Levels finished and the second six long yawning weeks away. Cash strapped, I went into the local Job Centre. Modern Job Centres in 2017 look like banks with extra security guards, but back then Job Centres were equally grim in other ways, all faded tiled floors and scrubbed scratched wooden desks. Instead of jobs hidden on a website on a computer in the corner they were displayed on cards on the walls. This day, I found a card with the welcome phrase 'no experience necessary' printed in bold, black letters. The job was, as it turned out, for a temporary cleaner at Mill House, a residential home for the elderly. Mill House had a decidedly workhouse ring to it, but they paid £2.55 per hour, four hours per day, for one working week. I totted it up in my head. Four hours times five. That's 20 hours. Twenty times £2.55 equals fifty-one pounds. Fifty-one pounds! That was more money than I'd ever had. I plucked off the card and took it to the always annoyed woman on the main desk who rang up the employer to find out more details. The vacancy (that sounded posh), was available because the usual cleaner was on holiday, and could I start today? Like, now?

Might as well, I thought. It's fifty-one quid innit.

Moments after I stepped over the threshold of Mill House, the manager handed me a stand-up vacuum cleaner and a bucket of cloths, brushes and cleaning sprays. No questions asked, apart from my name and National Insurance number, the latter I didn't have on me but that was ok, 'cos I could bring it in tomorrow. It's not like now, when you need every health and safeguarding check going if you want to work with the elderly or vulnerable. Regulations have changed over the years, and quite right too, but other aspects stubbornly remain, such as the fact that cleaning for a living is the same lowly profession now as it ever was.

At age 17 I didn't think about the statuses of different jobs; I thought fifty-one quid was loadsa money, because to me, it was. And nor did I realise the woman who did the cleaning job Monday through Friday had to live on the money she earned, and permanently at that, unlike me who spent it all on books and makeup and records. And also what I still failed to learn after the week was over, and even after getting a weekend job there on a more regular basis afterwards, is that there is a mile of difference, hundreds of miles, thousands, between giving one's own house or flat a quick once over on a Sunday while the roast is on, the gravy bubbling away fragrantly on the stove, potatoes turning nice 'n' crispy, to the relentless chore of working as a cleaner.

Physical labour, because that's what cleaning is, is tiring and monotonous. It does not pay the same rate as a labourer, a role largely carried out by men, but the amount of physical work is directly comparable. The lifting, scrubbing, wiping, muscles flexing, skin stretching, pulled over joints, the sheer amount of dirt. Cleaning makes you dirty, the dirt ending up on you. Cleaning gives you rough hands and an old face. Cleaning leaves you with the energy to do sod all else after your shift and that includes cleaning your own house, never mind someone else's.

And it doesn't stop there. If you work as a cleaner, people confuse you with the rubbish you pick up. I've thought about the reasons why. Some people like to look down on others, it makes them feel superior. That's one. She's an easy mark, the working class woman in the washed out nylon uniform scuttling about with an own-brand version of Pledge and a bright yellow duster, the one canny enough to keep her head down and not cause a fuss. Most cleaners are working class women,[1] the low pay and status sees to that. Easily replaceable, there's always another working class woman not exactly eager to take another's place but ready to, because she needs the money. People don't value what

---

1. Article: Women in the labour market: 2013. (2013, August 25). Retrieved from https://www.ons.gov.uk/employmentandlabourmarket/peopleinwork/employmentandemployeetypes/articles/womeninthelabourmarket/2013-09-25

they pay so little for, and the working class woman is cheap to keep or discard at will.

In researching this essay, I spoke to Alison, who cleans offices. Experienced as she is, she told me of her shock the day a member of the office staff tossed a screwed up piece of paper onto the floor as Alison was emptying the waste paper basket. 'You've missed the bin,' said a colleague sitting across from her. 'It's okay,' shrugged the woman, well in earshot of Alison. 'The cleaner can pick it up.' Alison had worked there for months, the longevity of her employment failing to save her from being treated as a nameless faceless serf, a servant neither needing nor warranting any respect.

Such disrespect is commonplace; yet denied, indignantly. 'We even invite our cleaner to the office Christmas do!' it was announced at me in my research, as if cast iron proof of a cleaner's equality and status. Not to mention evidence that the speaker was not prejudiced, of course. It is a lucky cleaner, I bounced back, who can afford to eat at a fancy restaurant. Or even a rubbish one, come to that. I wonder if the cleaner in question actually went on the night out with all the people earning thousands of pounds per year more than her. I doubt it somehow.

Cleaners are not only working class, but often older women at that. The work they do goes largely unnoticed. They work out of hours, after an office or workplace has closed for the day or before it opens for official business in the morning. Cleaners work under the radar, and win attention only when something goes wrong. When a place is dirty or stinks, we see and smell it clearly enough. If clean and nice and tidy, people assume – what? It gets that way on its own? Or maybe they believe magic pixies sneak in overnight. As women mature, we blend into the background or are pushed there, elbowed to the side, preference given to the fresh faced and young. Choices for working class women narrow with age, and cleaners provide a healthy living or working environment for others, not themselves. Cleaning is thankless and on top of that, it is where minimum wage is king, and most workers in the sector struggle.

Cleaning is the ultimate zero hours contract. I have cleaned in retirement homes, student halls of residence, and private residences. Enlightened employers for some councils and private student accommodation providers pay living wage, but let's not kid ourselves; the living wage still falls short. It fails to provide security and peace of mind in emergencies. If you're on minimum or living wage and an essential item you need in order to live comfortably breaks, like your cooker or boiler, you're buggered big time. Kinda flies in the face of the work rules, the ones that say if we work hard we get to have nice things.

I can tell you now that people get embarrassed and uneasy when I tell them about my previous side line. Some pretend they don't hear me correctly, or swerve it by making a joke about scrubbers. Attitudes are very telling, and stretch right across the board. If we believe the work of women who clean houses and offices carries a shame, and is below the contribution made by the rest of the working population, then what does it say about us? In March 2017, three black women councillors attending an International Women's Day conference in London were asked by security staff if they were there to clean.[2] Staff insisted the query was meant in jest. Of course there are a number of issues around this, the immediate being the stereotyped assumption that any BAME woman at an official event must be on the periphery, or performing a service role rather than be a vital part of discussion and debate. A point was made being here with

2. Adeoye, T. (2017, March 15). Black councillors at women's day event asked 'are you cleaners?' Retrieved from http://www.bbc.co.uk/news/uk-england-london-39268521

this 'joke' – you think you're the same as us, but remember, it could all go wrong for you at any moment. Don't get too cocky, BAME women, you could still yet end up cleaning. It's a know your place remark, a classic case of othering, a nod that 'you don't belong.' On the flip side, I question the councillors' indignant responses too, the perfect bite back being 'and what's wrong with cleaning for a living?' and I believe one of the councillors commenting on social media, 'the struggle continues sisters,' is borne of righteous anger and, in part at least, snobbery. Valuing the work of all women, after all, is a fundamental feminist issue.

How ironic that the status of being a cleaner is so low, yet having a cleaner oneself is a status symbol. The oft repeated myth that women feel guilty at having another woman clean is exactly that, an untruth. Not in my experience they don't. Most people I know who have a cleaner bloody well tell everyone about it, and frequently. Employing a cleaner is not a bad thing, let me say that now. I had a rather strong exchange of views with a male alleged feminist socialist who chest thumped and opined 'the middle class should clean their own f*cking houses!' I put time aside to inform him that his view fell short of treating a cleaner, and the work she does, with respect. Cleaning is a job like any other. If people are too busy or don't want to clean and have the money to employ someone, I see no problem. The male socialist feminist dismissed my views. Having worked as a cleaner isn't sufficient evidence of my authority on the subject, as it turns out.

So no, employing someone to clean your house is not wrong. But what is wrong is a casual approach to that employment. When I worked in private houses, I was never offered holiday pay, Bank Holiday pay or sick pay. If my employers went on holiday themselves it was a case of 'we won't need you next week.' I have no children but if I'd ever got pregnant I'm guessing a maternity package wasn't on the table. Such disregard, and yet, cleaners in private residences are expected to be keepers of all the secrets and privacies they see and hear there.

The human psyche is a complex and most arrogant one at times. Take the trend of pressing grandiose titles onto jobs seen as unskilled, a practice held up for mockery by the *Daily Mail* and the like. 'Housekeeper' flashes up an image of a take-no-nonsense matronly type swishing about a boarding school in an Enid Blyton book; 'cleaning crew' carries a 'go get 'em' sensibility, shiny-faced superheroes on the attack against the enemy that is germs and filth; 'caretaker' and 'janitor' are male and authoritative, in long coats carrying screwdrivers and mending non-specific but very important things. 'Facilities staff', 'facilities generalist' and 'cleaning operative' fool no one – meaningless words with no character or depth. The new labelling not only takes the piss but infers that if you're a cleaner it needs to be covered up, concealed. The stark reality of what you do needs to be dressed up as something – well, nicer, because there's a shame to it otherwise. How can anyone who cleans have any sense of dignity? Do they think themselves special, these Mrs Overalls, these Hilda Ogdens? I mean, imagine!

Cleaning, getting your hands dirty, is wrong, is the message. Perhaps that message started with Margaret Thatcher's 1986 opinion 'A man who, beyond the age of 26, finds himself on a bus can count himself as a failure.'[3] Although the authenticity of this quote is in doubt, it was the essence of that decade's belief system: success and happiness measured by status and money alone, high unemployment rates in working class communities a palatable price worth paying for low inflation and more wealth

---

3. Bevilacqua, M. (2013, April 8). Maybe Margaret Thatcher Didn't Hate Buses As Much As We Thought. Retrieved from https://nextcity.org/daily/entry/maybe-margaret-thatcher-didnt-hate-buses-as-much-as-we-thought

for the already well heeled. Maybe the fear of failure was there before that, I'm unsure; I'm not old enough to remember. But what I do know is that the fear of being brought low is very real for many, and they seek to distance themselves from that low, in case it is catching. Manual work, and the thought of having to do it, frightens people.

The fact is, if you clean, then you are a cleaner. And there should be nothing about this needing to be concealed or given window dressing. Workers having enough to live on, and more workers employed so the workload is not so high, would generate a more satisfying outcome, but gentrifying job titles gifts employers a get-out-of-jail-free card on both of these things. Employers of cleaners can be hilarious in their brass neck. One told me they were 'willing' to provide cleaning materials, if needs be. An assumed sentimental attachment to wire scourers and bleach, the tools of the cleaning trade, like an artist loves her paint brushes or a writer with her favourite notebook? I'm still unpicking that one. Maybe it was intended as a backhanded compliment of sorts, a 'you're the expert' attempt at flattery. The inference being, if I used my own bleach I'd work faster, and put more effort in, or work through my lunch hour maybe? Bless them for such naiveté. Empty compliments are not a reward. More money however, is. And respect. But that's not going to happen, is it? Not while we carry on looking down on women who clean.

We, working class women, and all of us, have been sold a lie. The fabrication that if we work hard, do the right thing – whatever that means – then we'll be ok and get the good stuff. We'll get the status, and a good sense of pride, and if we're not ok we deserve our poverty; it's our own fault because we're not working hard enough. How do we measure it, how hard we work? By how many hours we work? How much sweat squeezes from our pores? How much our muscles ache? How exhausted we are at the end of a shift? Do we measure it by how much coffee we have to drink (because we'll collapse of exhaustion otherwise)? Or how prosperous we are? If we're financially stable and want for nothing, we must be working hard, right?

Wrong.

The inconvenient truth is that a badly paid and low status job with no prospects like cleaning keeps you poor. Hard work does not lift people out of poverty or issue status, not if you scrub toilets for a living anyway. We've been fed the lie and we suckle it up, guzzle it, smacking our lips in approval afterwards. Yes, we've been flogged a lie alright; one with a massive price tag. And though few of us can afford it, it's one we're more than happy to buy.

Living On An Estate Gave Me A Community I Never Knew I Needed

Gena-mour Barrett

I've lived in what I still consider my 'new house' for ten years. It's a small, three-bedroom home in South East London, oddly situated in an area that's a stone's throw away from both a dingy chicken and chip shop, and some of the poshest houses I've ever seen. It's a confusing amalgamation of the life I used to know, and the life many Britons strive for. Back in my old neighbourhood, community and kinship were an important part of everyday living. Here, in our coveted houses, you could go for almost a decade without knowing your neighbour's name.

The first exchange I had with my neighbour took place over a garden fence in the summer of 2016. It was a warm summer evening and I'd come home to hear the soft murmurs of my mother's voice, alongside one I didn't quite recognise, coming from the garden. Upon investigation, I found my mum in deep conversation with the man who lived next door, both of their heads peering over the rickety fence that stood between them.

'G, meet our neighbour!' my mum said, a request I obliged, albeit somewhat suspiciously. I'd learnt shortly after moving to the area that people didn't really *speak* to each other. In fact, in the nine years I'd lived next to our neighbour and his family, we'd never shared a word.

After a few minutes though, it seemed we had a lot in common. We'd both previously lived on council estates (mine in Grove Park, his in Peckham), and shared our experiences of summer barbecues and afterschool antics in the makeshift communities we'd come to love. 'Do you like living here?' I eventually asked, a question I'd been pondering myself since The Big Move. He paused, scratched his head, and wrinkled his nose before echoing my sentiments exactly:

'Well... it's a bit lonely here, innit?'

Before moving to our semi-silent haven, I lived on two council estates, both in South East London and within a mile of each other. The first was a lofty block of flats that overlooked a large green and an enclosed area with several rows of washing lines (or more accurately, a glorified football pitch and a *phenomenal* venue for playing hide and seek). We lived on the very top floor, which, in my six-year-old opinion, held an abundance of advantages. I lived only three doors down from my best friend, and probably spent more time in her home than my own. I could see the famous London skyline from my bedroom window, and would often waste hours transfixed by the continuous blinking of the red warning light on the roof of One Canada Square in Canary Wharf. And I even got to watch the London New Year's Eve fireworks display from the comfort of my very own balcony on the night of the new millennium, a sight few others have surpassed in brilliance, even now. The most important advantage, however, was practical. *Living on the top floor means that if a burglar were to run loose on the estate, they'd **have** to start* *with the bottom flats first*, I thought. The fact that I lived on the fourth floor and had to climb a never-ending amount of stairs to get there (or else brave the grimy, spit-ridden lift that had a worrying tendency to break down) was thus a small price to pay. We were safe, I was safe, and I spent a happy eight years there before my father passed away, and the trauma forced us out of our home and half a mile to the estate where I'd spend the rest of my childhood.

For all the talk of housing estates being grim, troublesome eyesores to the British public, or even a 'national embarrassment', I never found it to be this way. During his plans to annihilate so-called 'sink estates' under Tory policy, David Cameron wrote in a 2016 article for *The Sunday Times* that he blamed housing estates for a large proportion of Britain's social problems. He described them as epitomising the challenges of blocked opportunity, poor parenting, addiction, and mental health problems. He accused them of having 'designed in crime'. He spoke of his concern about 'how cut-off, self-governing and divorced from the mainstream' estates are. Cameron even blamed housing estates for the riots of 2011. Needless to say, the perception of estates in Britain as a whole has been *fucking poor*. But for me, the weird and wonderful world of the estate was the exact opposite of its demonising rhetoric. In both of my experiences, everyone knew everyone, and it was common courtesy to throw a quick 'you alright?' to whoever walked by. However, moving from our flat to a *maisonette* – a deceptively fancy word I initially thought meant 'tiny mansion', but actually just meant 'basically a flat spread over two floors' – came with some significant differences.

The bare bones of the typical estate were still there: the big green, the slightly run down bike sheds, the largely working class residents (including my mum, who was working three jobs to provide for the both of us after my father died). But instead of just a front garden, we now had a communal back garden, and we'd traded a grimy lift for a long canal that ran across the back of our block through to the park on the other side of the road. Even the name of where we lived, 'Marbrook Court', sounded fancier, and though we still lived in council housing, it was clear we'd moved up slightly in the estate food chain. This meant, of course, that in addition to all the other 'bonuses', our estate was noticeably whiter. Before, we were one of three black families in our row of flats alone. Now, we were the only black family in our row and, estate-wide, a considerable minority. I didn't know it yet, but this would be a recurring theme as I started secondary school and my mum and I 'moved up' and out of different areas. Every step ahead on the social mobility ladder was also a step towards a much *whiter* ideal.

That isn't to say that the estate wasn't without its problems; indeed, life was far from perfect. The police were called more than once to warn a group of young boys to stop terrorising the older residents of the area, and my diet largely consisted of 5p sweets, chicken and chips, and kebabs because lack of money meant we lived a life of affordability and convenience. Issues like drugs, alcoholism, and poverty quietly existed in the background of my experience, even if I couldn't quite identify them at the time, and one night we woke up to the sounds of twigs crackling and the ominous flashing of amber lights, only to find that the trees lining the canal outside had been set on fire by some boys from another neighbourhood. The trees stayed scorched and dejected for months afterwards, a symbol of our area going, in my neighbour's words: 'to complete shit.'

Nevertheless, for an only child living in a single parent household, the estate life suited me very well. We congregated on balconies, sat for hours in other people's houses, and at any moment you could hear the deafening shrieks of a mother calling her child to come in for dinner or the racket of kids riding their bicycles on the pavement outside. If living in a house affords you the privilege of privacy, the privilege to live away from commotion and, if you so choose, never have to fraternise with those that live around you, then living on a housing estate allows you to delight in the exact opposite. The noise and the mayhem were a comforting constant, and the fact that these people weren't just my neighbours, but my *friends*, was wonderfully reassuring. Some of my favourite childhood holidays were spent with a handful of neighbours in a caravan in Cambersands, and long summer nights were spent 'playing out' with the other kids, never too far from my mother's sight because the estate was too damn small to get lost in in the first place. These were the poorest years of my life financially, and yet the richest in happy memories.

Television, however, would tell a very different story. Shows set on council estates were rife with stereotypical images of dark, depressing tower blocks, non-stop violence, and drugs on every corner, which served to reinforce its negative perception. The Channel 4 drama series *Top Boy*, released in October 2011, was set on the fictional Summerhouse housing estate in Hackney, and told the story of a group of people involved in gangs and drug dealing. While the show endeavoured to tell an authentic story, bringing to light subjects that can affect estate tenants all over, its depiction of life, along with so many other shows of the same setting, was undoubtedly bleak. Even the opening of Channel 4's Manchester-based *Shameless*, which began airing in 2008 and was considerably less dark than *Top Boy*, portrayed an environment of incivility. In the opening of the very first episode, main character Frank Gallagher introduces us to his family and life on Chatsworth estate. At one point, he explains: 'A few things, see, are vital to a half decent community. Space, yeah? You need wide open spaces where everyone goes mental! And neighbourliness, fantastic neighbours!' It's a statement that would probably be valid if it weren't for the fact it's said at the exact moment when the tenants are happily setting a car on fire, lighting fireworks, and laughing as the police arrive.

It wasn't until the release of E4's *Chewing Gum* in 2015 that I was able to see my upbringing better reflected on screen. Turning the depiction of the dismal estate on its head, it focuses on a strong community that's materially poor, but rich in spirit, much like the environment I remember. *Chewing Gum*'s creator and lead actress Michaela Coel, who also grew up on an estate, intentionally shoots the series during summer to avoid the typical dreary portrait of the high-rise flats that's so common of the TV shows before her. Watching it feels just as warm as lying on the big green on a hot, sunny day, and makes me yearn for the estate I loved – but one show cannot change decades of the same damaging representation. Time and again, the message for Britons, especially those who lived (or still live) on housing estates, has been made loud and clear – *you should be ashamed to live here*.

It's no surprise then that the main objective (for those who could) was to leave the estate. As I entered my early teens, my mum began speaking more and more about mortgages and pining for her own garden, a space that would truly be hers. I, on the other hand, was comfortable where we were. I'd never wanted to live in a house, and was confused as to why my mum was so concerned with acquiring one. But as my mum went from three jobs, to two jobs to one – as a teacher – it was more and more clear that she was outgrowing our living environment. One year she spent an entire summer holed up in the cupboard we'd converted into a 'computer room' studying for her PGCE teaching qualification, while the rest of our neighbours sunbathed on the green or drank on the balcony. The lack of privacy on the estate had stopped being a cute quirk too, when my mum bought a new car and was met with shouts of 'Where the fuck did you get the money for that, then?!' from the balcony. It was then, my mum told me, that she knew it was time to move on.

My moment of realisation came much later, but started with school. I arguably hit my intellectual peak at 11 years old when I was accepted to Newstead Wood School in Orpington, a grammar school my year six teacher claimed I'd 'never get in to.' Before then, I'd never heard of 'Orpington' or even 'Kent' for that matter, but as soon as I started I was confronted with the huge gulf in lifestyle between me and my peers. I distinctly remember the first time visiting one of my school friend's houses, and being introduced to a very different kind of estate: the distinguished 'gated community'. While they all lived together in the private compound, the houses were completely segregated from the outside world (you needed a special PIN to even get through the gates), and were distinctly separate from one another. It was the antithesis of my own life; I walked past houses with balconies, six or seven bedrooms, and giant fountains standing outside. My friend even had a pool. It was then that I recognised that where I lived wasn't 'the norm', and that the rich and poor divide was actually even closer than I thought. In fact, we shared a classroom.

The day we arrived at our new home and found dog faeces at our front door, I suspected we may not be welcome. We'd moved to an area that was even less racially diverse than the previous one, and unlike the estate, nobody knew or cared who we were. Worse still, we'd recently heard of a racist attack that had happened two streets from where we now lived, and worried that the faeces may have been the result of racism too. Even though it was clear I was slowly growing out of the estate, just as my mum was, it didn't stop me pining for the life I'd lived there, or worrying about what moving away would mean. *Who would knock for me to check if I was home? Would I still speak to my neighbour? Were we leaving because we suddenly thought we were better than everyone here? Would we ever visit at all?* My mum insisted life would be better for us, but I wasn't convinced. On our very first night, while my mum and I lay on a mattress on the floor because the bed frame was still en route from the shop, and the sound of our new neighbour's TV permeated the wall, I began to cry. Noise was no longer a comfort to me, but a loud reminder of how much I didn't want to be there. I'd traded a life of coming home to friends sitting out on the green or speaking to a neighbour out on the balcony with coming home to a desolate street and speaking to no one. It was, as my newly introduced neighbour would tell me ten years later, well and truly lonely.

I am lucky, and will always deem myself lucky: for the educational opportunities I've been afforded, my mother's ambition (which is undoubtedly where I get my own from), and the fact we live in a wonderful house together. Still, despite the idea that your only aspiration living on an estate should be to leave, I continue to question just how much better life actually becomes once we move. The truth is, I felt safer living on our rundown estate among people I trusted than in a house, isolated and alone, among people I didn't. I've grown accustomed to living here now, and it's hard to imagine going back to where we were before, regardless of how much I've glorified it in my mind. But, no matter where I go, no matter how big the house, and no matter how affluent the area, I will never underestimate the value of a good, resilient community. It is this that sets apart the housing estates I've lived on from anywhere else I've lived since, and it's why I owe so much of the person I am today to the estates that raised me.

Hop-Picking:
Forging a Path in the Edgelands of Fiction

Lee Rourke

I.

Way back in 1937, when writers held a firm foothold in the world – a smaller, slower, less fragmented world that facilitated for them a voice which could command the utmost respect from swathes of readers far and wide (in ways writers of today can only dream of) – George Orwell (a real-life walking-talking contradiction of class and interpretation) wrote in *The Road To Wigan Pier*, his gritty, heartbreaking paean to the working class:

> '*This business of petty inconvenience and indignity, of being kept waiting about, of having to do everything at other people's convenience, is inherent in working class life. A thousand influences constantly press a working man down into a passive role. He does not act, he is acted upon. He feels himself the slave of mysterious*

authority and has a firm conviction that "they" will never allow him to do this, that, and the other. Once when I was hop-picking I asked the sweated pickers (they earn something under sixpence an hour) why they did not form a union. I was told immediately that "they" would never allow it. Who were "they"? I asked. Nobody seemed to know, but evidently "they" were omnipotent.'[1]

It's a quote that has haunted me for most of my life.

For a start, let's think about that looming noun '*indignity*' in the first sentence, which has its origin in the Latin *indignari*, to be regarded as *unworthy*. Quickly followed by the gerund '*waiting*' with its origins in the Germanic *wahhon* and the Old North French *waitier*, to *watch with hostile intent*, to be *awake* to something. As working class individuals (ignoring the varying complexities of this label for a moment) we are aware of our own unworthiness, constantly watching ourselves dwell within it, and we feel hostile towards it. This sense of unworthiness and hostility has stuck with me all my life, I have spoken to other working class writers and the same '*it doesn't feel like I should be doing this*' sentiment always rears its ugly head. The idea that we have risen above our preordained place in society, that we have broken ranks and are loosed upon the world, without reigns, or others' guidance. What is it to feel unworthy? And what does waiting really mean? To be kept waiting? What are we waiting for? To finally find our own sense of worth? To be free from the shackles of work? These questions are vital and unending – yet, I am sure, there are many, those who haven't experienced this

---

1. Orwell, G. (2001). *The Road to Wigan Pier*. London: Penguin Books in association with Martin Secker & Warburg.

burden of eternal unworthiness, who have never questioned themselves or their actions in this way, nor have they been forced to become expert watchers of themselves and others like them, outside looking in, hostile outsiders.

Yet, if we are so hostile to ourselves and those around us, why do we just let things trundle along, like this unworthiness is the most natural thing in the world? Why do we seemingly do nothing about it? Why such passivity? First, we have to answer the question of passivity. What does Orwell mean when he says '*a thousand influences constantly press a working man down into a passive role*'? Maurice Blanchot, the French literary theorist, explains passivity as:

> '*...measureless: for it exceeds being; it is being when being is worn down past the nub.*'[2]

It is beyond the totality of ourselves, it defines us because it has already worn us away, erased any hope of alternative activity, i.e., another life. This is what Orwell means when he points out the working class's '*passive role*' in society, he wants this paradox to stick, with all the intensity of a fish bone in the throat: how can our symbol of collective activity, the *working class*, be collectively passive?

Blanchot's great friend and mentor, Emmanuel Levinas, understood this dichotomy, and he found a use in it, too, something quite radical, calling it:

> '*...a passivity more passive than all passivity.*'[3]

---

2. Blanchot, M. (1995). *The writing of the disaster - Lécriture du désastre*. University of Nebraska Press. (p. 17)

3. Levinas, E. (2013). *Otherwise than being, or: Beyond essence*. Pittsburgh, Pa: Duquesne University Press. (p. 15)

What Levinas means when he says this (something he repeats throughout his work) is that passivity might not be 'passive' at all, it might be its complete opposite, an activity. An argument the philosopher Simon Critchley is keen to iterate:

> 'He [Levinas] wants to emphasize passivity but not the kind of passivity that's opposed to activity. Levinas wants a passivity that's more passive than all passivity, an ultra-passivity that might itself be a kind of quasi-activity or a passivity that's beyond the opposition of activity and passivity.'[4]

This is exactly the type of passivity Herman Melville had in mind when creating his great symbol of the working man: Bartleby, who one day simply says: '*I would prefer not to*'[5] when asked by his boss to do some task or other in his office. How can any of us forget that phrase as it's used by the static, impeccably passive Bartleby over and over again, one of the greatest imaginings of radical passivity? But, as always, it comes at a price, we never really get away with it. Susan A. Handelman, in her great work about Levinas, points us towards an important facet, a flaw maybe, in this idea of passivity, describing it thus:

> '*The term passivity is used to describe the subject as opened, hollowed out, traumatized, wounded, deposed,*

---

4. Critchley, S. (2015). *The Problem with Levinas* (A. Dianda, Ed.). Oxford: Oxford University Press. (p. 71)

5. Melville, H. (2007). *Bartleby the Scrivener*. London: Hesperus Press.

and subject to the other.[6]

Working class passivity, then, is our collective wound, our mark left behind from the event of being working class itself – the idea of having this forced upon us through no fault of our own: the existentiality of birth (*'birth was the death of him'* to quote Samuel Beckett[7]). Like Bartleby, we are already-always wounded, whether we admit it or not. We are outsiders looking in on ourselves looking out at *'a thousand influences'* that create in us a sense of action through passivity. But don't be fooled; again like Bartleby, our passivity is our double-edged sword, our form of attack (and, if necessary, something we are quite willing to fall on).

And all of this before we even begin to consider the concept of *'they'*. Because we all know one thing cannot exist without the other, right? But who are *'they'*? This shadowy, mythical presence that keeps the working class in our place? Who are our hard-working hop-pickers talking about? Let's revisit the point I made above, via the lens of Susan A. Handelman's scrutiny of Levinas: that the passive *'hollowed out, traumatised, wounded, deposed'* working class have become *'subject to the other'*.[8] What is meant by this sense of the *'other'* and why is the supposedly *'passive role'* subject to it? Is the collective pronoun *'they'* used in this context just to refer to people in general? Or does this

---

6. Handelman, S. A. (1991). *Fragments of Redemption: Jewish Thought and Literary Theory in Benjamin, Scholem, and Levinas*. Bloomington: Indiana Univ. Press. (p. 259)

7. Beckett, S. (1982). 'A Piece of Monologue', *Three Occasional pieces*. London: Faber & Faber.

8. Handelman, S. A. (1991). *Fragments of Redemption: Jewish Thought and Literary Theory in Benjamin, Scholem, and Levinas*. Bloomington: Indiana Univ. Press. (p. 259)

ordinarily vague pronoun serve to single out a certain type, or group? A target group, even? In phenomenological terms we must begin to associate the hop-picker's sense of '*they*' with Husserl's sense of '*otherness*'.[9] For Husserl, '*the other*' was a form of *intersubjectivity* where one group of people follow one thought group or mindset and another group follow another collective thought group, in which every individual has their own interpretation. Individual beliefs become the beliefs of the collective group, and vice versa, hence our unfixed definition of who '*they*' are. In Orwellian terms, '*they*' is inferred to be those in charge, or more precisely the '*thousand influences*' who serve to keep the working class in their place (this, of course, can be anyone, from the upper classes, bankers, captains of industry, the super-rich, oligarchs, politicians, capitalists, etc). An ever-present, unquantifiable enemy. The term '*they*' can be used collectively, or however the individual chooses, its very vagueness lends itself to collective/individual malleability. The perfect label.

But what's all this got to do with writing or, more importantly, being a working class writer? Well, quite a lot actually.

II.

I think it's far easier to describe myself as 'working class' than as a 'working class writer' even though, on the face of it, I don't live what can be considered a working class life anymore. But I am 'working class'. Inescapably so. What I most definitely am not is a 'working class writer' even though, just under the

9. Husserl, E. (1982). *Ideas Pertaining to a Pure Phenomenology and to a Phenomenological Philosophy—First Book: General Introduction to a Pure Phenomenology.* The Hague: M. Nijhoff.

surface, I most definitely am. I don't want to complicate the issue here, I just want to elucidate this dichotomy in a way that makes sense to me: I am a working class man who doesn't live a working class life who writes working class books that aren't working class.

There. I've said it. I do hope you understand. I'm not being deliberately awkward or facetious. Honest.

I am from Manchester, the city Jeanette Winterson described as:

> '...*in the south of the north of England. Its spirit has a contrariness in it – a south and north bound up together – at once untamed and unmetropolitan; at the same time, connected and wordly*.'[10]

It's a city of contradictions; world-changing (think of the Industrial Revolution; the birth of Socialism, the Co-operative, the Manchester Ship Canal, Marx and Engels, the first atom being split; the first computer being developed; Madchester/Acid House, etc.) yet distrustful of outsiders, proud yet understated. I've always preferred Eric Cantona's description myself:

> '*I feel close to the rebelliousness and vigour of the youth here. Perhaps time will separate us, but nobody can deny that here, behind the windows of Manchester, there is an insane love of football, of celebration and of music*.'[11]

Mancunians like to have fun, to disrupt the established order

---

10. Winterson, J. (2012). *Why Be Happy When You Could Be Normal?* London: Vintage. (p. 13)
11. Eric 'The King' Cantona.

of things in their revelry (the late '80s 'Madchester' scene is a fine example: The Hacienda, The Thunderdome, Acid House, Happy Mondays and the Stone Roses can be viewed as a collective two fingers to the rest of the country and especially London), there are certain things I cannot shake off. Mancunians like to do things their own way, outside of preconceived ideas or established default modes. Anything 'Manchester' creates is born out of its awareness/distrust of the other (especially London). Manchester is a wounded city (just type 'Peterloo Massacre' into google to tap into the psyche of the average Mancunian, think about the IRA bomb of 1996, too[12]), its wounds run deep; when they are conquered we want the world to know.

I grew up in a house with no books. My mother and father simply didn't read them, they preferred the newspapers and completing the crossword puzzles. I was never, to my knowledge, encouraged to read. It was my Auntie Anne who enlightened me to literature, whose house was full of books. This has always stuck, I carry it around with me, I mention it at dinner parties, or among 'Literary' friends, like an old man showing off his war wounds, or that scene on the boat in the film Jaws – is this sentiment a product of my class? The displaying of old wounds? The idea that books are for '*other*' people? Am I wounded by the idea that just because I'm working class I missed out on the simple pleasure of living/growing up with a household full of books and, more importantly, 'readers'? Hell yeah, I am! I'm put in mind of something the author Len Deighton once said – you can substitute 'write' for 'read' if you want (rather ironically Len Deighton is an author I've never read):

> '*I think the reason working class people don't write books is because they are encouraged to believe that only*

---

12. And, heartbreakingly, as I edit this text, the attack on the MEN Arena.

certain people are permitted to write books.'[13]

There's much truth in this quote, and much to think about. We all know the well-worn Marxist interpretation of the rise of the modern 'novel' – but it's worth repeating. The novel rose to its zenith in popularity during the 19th century, a time which also witnessed the rise of the bourgeoisie in society and the advent of the Industrial Revolution. In short, the bourgeoisie had more leisure time i.e., spending time with family, travelling around Europe, going to the theatre, visiting art galleries, and, more importantly, reading novels, so the novel grew to reflect bourgeois taste – it effectively incorporated all of these components into its make-up. The working class, on the other hand, had no leisure time at all, they were far too busy working. Novels simply weren't for us. The modern novel has never been able to shake off its bourgeois roots – it has become its default mode system of values. Society isn't as divided as it once was so these same bourgeois value systems are tolerant of working class culture, so it has developed a need for working class writers to penetrate and reflect working class issues and life (just like the bourgeoisie novel) through a mode of aesthetical, dialectic realist fiction. Rather ironically, this is a materialist need in the original Marxist sense, whether '*they*' like it or not (it's also bourgeois taste that demands the modern 'lyrical, psychological humanist' flourishes in this equation, too). It is also where I sadly part company with Marx and Engels. What was once Marx and Engel's revolutionary demand for all writers and artists to achieve class 'truthfulness' and 'pure art' through materialist, aesthetic realism is now a

13. Len Deighton Quotes. (n.d.). Retrieved from http://quotesgram.com/len-deighton-quotes/

mere expectation of bourgeois taste.

How ironic, or, should I simply say, predictable?

III.

If, like Len Deighton states, the working class aren't meant to write novels, *per se*, what do working class novelists do? Sadly, by and large, working class novelists do one of two things (or both!): a) write the same type of bourgeois novel pre-existing writers do, thereby fitting into the already established bourgeois literary default mode, or b) write the gritty, clichéd accounts of working class, inner-city misery they are expected to write for '*their*' entertainment.

These two paths are anathema to me. I have chosen my own. It's been hard, some people have understood, most haven't. And I wouldn't change it for the world.

'*I am a working class man who doesn't live a working class life who writes working class books that aren't working class*'? What do I mean by this? First it's best to ask: what are we expected to write as 'working class' writers by established bourgeoisie value systems? The clichés that follow this question are endless: we are told to hold up a huge psychological mirror to ourselves and reflect back to the world our gritty realism, our miseries, poverty, petty dramas, etc. The stuff, detritus, offscourings, whatever '*the other*' uses as symbols for us. It's repetitive, boring, useless; it keeps us in our place as supposedly working class writers. We are categorised this way, '*they*' like it like that. It's easier for them to deal with us, to understand us this way. Nothing makes me more angry, and it is why I have never attempted to replicate the 'real' in my own writing.

I'll never forget something the artist and (anti-)novelist Stewart Home said to me many years ago:

'In order for a novelist to be truly revolutionary a novelist has to write bad novels.'[14]

I remember nodding and not really saying much in response – I thought he was being flippant for a start – but the more I thought about it, the more it made complete and utter sense. If the revolutionary working class novel is now a mere bourgeois expectation then Home's words are more than timely. We have to disrupt bourgeois taste and reading pleasure by writing what 'they' consider to be '*bad*' novels. So what, in fact, is a '*bad*' novel? Stewart was talking about a common enemy: the default mode of established literature (what critic Mark Thwaite labelled *Establishment Literary Fiction*[15]). He wasn't saying that the answer to writing novels that broke convention was to write them badly, in terms of badly composed sentences and structure, he meant bad for the established bourgeois reader to read. He wants to write novels that destroy, take apart and disrupt the bourgeois notion of what a novel should be.

This idea of disrupting reading pleasure has always stuck with me. I have never wanted to entertain, I have always wanted to disrupt. It's why my debut novel was never going to be about family, art, theatre, historical dalliances, or finding authenticity in far flung corners of the globe, but about a man who does nothing, just sits on a bench, doing nothing; no plot, no personal narrative arc, no redemption, no psychological pain, no reality, nothing. Simply a novel about boredom. The very thing novels aren't supposed to be. For me, the best literature is the

14. I'm sure he said this to me in a bar in Whitechapel at a 3AM Magazine event.
15. Thwaite, M. (2007, April 20). Against Establishment Literary Fiction. Retrieved from http://www.readysteadybook.com/Blog.aspx?permalink=2007 0420104237

stuff that assaults the mind, which throws any preconceived ideas out of the window, that does away with the lousy, bourgeoisie psychology of the novel and (to use a phrase for the novelist Tom McCarthy) '*tune[s]*' into the '*rich trash of literature*',[16] to use and reuse it in ways to tip the balance, to upset the *status quo*, and never to cement it in canonical position. It is literature that is written for no one – writing for no one, in fact – but always against '*them*', '*the other*', our sense of '*they*', whatever you want to call it. It does things its own way, nothing is fixed.

It is ultimately selfish.

I approach all of my writing this way: I write for no one, yet always with my idea of who '*they*' are without seeing them. My own idea of them. I think of them as nobodies. I do not care for readers' tastes, whims, loves, hates; readers are nothing to me even though I care about disrupting these pleasures within them. I write for me, and me alone. I am a selfish bastard. I am a contradiction. If anyone does read my writing, I want to disrupt the pleasure of reading within them. I want to leave my mark. I want to create a wound.

The saddest thing for me is: I am on the edgelands of fiction here, I feel like a stranger, there aren't many of us who want to disrupt anything, and certainly not the pleasure of those who buy our books. I walk this path mostly alone, I bump into like-minded souls from time to time, but it's rare, and getting rarer. But, for me, this path is everything. I have invested so much of my life clearing a path for myself, forging ahead, navigating my own route that I now know it's too late to turn back – there are too many twists and turns, dead ends to remember, for a start.

---

16. McCarthy, T. (2017). *Typewriters, Bombs, Jellyfish: Essays*. New York: New York Review Books.

Hop-Picking

I feel like a stranger.
Yet, I keep on talking.

IV.

Let's return to Orwell's Hop-Pickers, our hard-working *'sweated pickers'*. I liken myself as a writer to them: I work tirelessly, repetitively, mind-numbingly, painstakingly towards creating something, which, if I'm lucky, is abruptly taken away from me, made into something else by others, for others to supposedly enjoy, despite there not being much in return for me. The working class writer is the Hop-Picker: the resolute worker, picking away, working alone, with that omnipotent, mysterious, ever-threatening sense of something that might never exist: our sense of *'they'* (whoever *'they'* are), the continual spectre that forces us, whether we like it or not, to keep on working, to keep on producing for *them* – this is what sets us apart, builds our character, forges our art – and whatever our art is, depends on our own idea of who *'they'* are. The working class writer feels forced to work within a world we feel we don't belong. It puts me in mind of something the great literary critic Stephen Mitchelmore wrote recently regarding the working class,[17] in which he discusses (among other things) the impact of Paul Celan. It is a quotation he uses to sum up the working class writer's place in the world. I think it is fitting to end this rant, this mere utterance here, with the words of others. This can be our beginning: the working class writer, then, is:

---

17. Mitchelmore, S. (2017, February 6). Literature belongs to those who are at home in the world. Retrieved from http://this-space.blogspot.co.uk/2017/02/literature-belongs-to-those-who-are-at.html

'...a stranger not only in the social and cultural world: there is a veil between him and nature, between him and everything. He always finds himself face to face with the incomprehensible, inaccessible, the "language of the stone". And his only recourse is talking. This cannot be "literature". Literature belongs to those who are at home in the world.'[18]

18. Mitchelmore takes this quotation from: *Celan, P. (2003). Collected prose, Conversation in the Mountains (R. Waldrop). New York: Routledge.*

Reclaiming the Vulgar

Kath McKay

I would like to reclaim the word 'vulgar'. When did the word become a pejorative term, and how does its use affect those it is used against? I argue that it silences people – and causes a huge waste of talent. From the 14th to the 17th centuries, vulgar meant 'common, ordinary', from the Latin 'vulgaris': 'of or pertaining to the common people, multitude, crowd, throng.' It began to have the sense of 'plebeian' and 'unrefined' around 1550 and 1650 respectively. The interpretation of 'coarse or ill bred' is first recorded in 1643.[1]

So, being working class is 'vulgar'. An antonym for vulgar is refined or cultured. Another one is literary, or bookish. Therefore, you can't be vulgar, i.e. working class, *and* be bookish or

---

1. Vulgar Synonyms: Word Origin & History. (n.d.). Retrieved from http://www.thesaurus.com/browse/vulgar?s=t

literary. As soon as you are bookish or literate, you are middle class: Alice-in-Wonderland logic, and a lie.

Another definition is 'lacking sophistication or good taste'. Who defines good taste? And who cares? I'm going to start with some of my own experiences.

*

A middle class woman I know once asked where I'd been on holiday.

'Tenerife.'

'Playa de las Americas? I've never been myself, of course.'

I wanted to say that Playa was much nicer than she thought, and that no, we'd been to Santa Cruz and El Médano, where my Spanish friend lived, and that Tenerife is pronounced with an accent on the last e, but I thought 'nah,' and grunted. She wasn't interested in my holiday, and had slotted me into her stereotype.

2004, Nairobi Airport, middle of the night, after a week with budding writers in Malawi. African families sat on the floor sharing food, or lay down; women wrapped clothes around and curled into themselves. White couples, middle aged or elderly, perched stiffly on chairs, in sensible khaki clothes and hats. When a young white woman with a lovely face walked past, I watched their little moues and tuts at her dyed blonde hair, high heels, white short skirt and white sleeveless vest, as if they owned the continent and could dictate your dress.

*

Having a job above your class is an affront to some middle class people. After bereavement, I arranged a substitute for my adult education class: a man wrote on the evaluation forms, 'The substitute teacher was much more professional than McKay, a teacher, not a writer.' I had published more, but my achievements were not as worthy. With a more informal style than my substitute, I sometimes cracked jokes. She was serious, with a clipped voice, and gushed. This man could not see me as 'professional' because he did not rate my opinion. I was stung by the criticism, and his coldness and inhumanity.

An antonym for professional is blue collar. An antonym for blue collar is middle class. Another antonym for professional is proletarian. If you are working class you can't be professional: you have to become middle class to be professional. Alice-in-Wonderland again. Are we supposed to disguise our origins in order to be taken seriously? Is how we say things paid more attention to than what we say?

Contrast that with a recent experience giving a reading in North Shields, where a man made me laugh with his comment: 'I really enjoyed your novel, but ee lass, you killed off the wrong character. That Di was so annoying.' That man had manners, and made me think about his point.

*

I grew up in Kirkby (an 'overspill' town) outside Liverpool. We were transplanted in clearances from central Liverpool slums. In Kirkby everything was supposed to be 'new', although there'd been settlements from 870 in the Bronze Age. This airbrushing of history happens constantly – in Leeds, I found an Afro-Caribbean neighbour crying over local flats getting bulldozed: 'I grew up there. There'll be nothing left of our history.'

It's often implied that working class people have no history, or that their history has no importance. Tim Winton's story 'Aquifer' in *The Turning*, is set in the '60s 'Battler's blocks' near Perth, Western Australia – suburbs thrown up to house thousands of people. Everything is supposed to be new, ignoring the ancient aboriginal settlements that came before. The story is a brilliant exploration of digging down to the truth underneath that lie, down to the underground waters underneath the ancient brown land.

In a recent *Guardian* article about memorable houses in English literature, I saw not one council (or modest) house, as if such 'vulgar' dwellings could have no pull on the imagination of writers.

We rarely met anyone middle class. There were 'posh' private houses up near Kirkby town centre, but the town was solidly working class. Occasionally, my mother would refer to someone without principles as 'trash', but I had no real sense of being vulgar until I left home.

My father was a docker and my mother worked at Birds Eye and Kraft, the new factories built to deliver women from domestic slavery through frozen food. I don't suppose they thought about vulgar, they were too busy trying to survive. My mother always had a well-developed penchant for ornaments. On rare days out, she would buy a souvenir: New Brighton, Southport, Rhyl, and later, London. She liked to fill up the place with 'things'. Greyson Perry has a lot to say about how working class taste is celebratory, and expresses joy. My mother certainly did. After she died, we argued over who got her ornaments – the bright cloth parrot that sang 'Born Free' ('company', she called it), the electric fish, the musical figures dressed in green that play 'When Irish Eyes Are Smiling', her multi-coloured-flashing-lights Christmas tree. A sense of her personality and humour came through her objects, and an idea that life was not to be taken too seriously. This capacity for the 'piling on of things' breaks through in many of us from working class backgrounds. Yet the middle classes can only celebrate this type of style in an 'ironic' way.

Meantime in Kirkby, people started bringing back sombreros and castanets and fans. My mother never went abroad, but she was always delighted if anyone brought her a trinket – a small piece of Australia or Spain or France. She was a storyteller, loved 1940s films, had a great sense of drama, and knew the importance of timing and a punch line. We learnt to tell stories early. But it took me a long time to think that our stories were worth writing.

*

I spent a lot of time as an adolescent sitting on a wall. Especially after the rise of street crime, politicians talk about getting kids off the streets, as if young people are a vulgar embarrassment and should be sanitised away. But many people don't have gardens, and in mediterranean countries, it's the norm to sit around in public squares. In 'Aquifer', Winton wrote, 'My parents were always struggling to get me inside something, into shirts and shoes, inside the fence, the neighbourhood, the house, out of the sun or the rain, out of the world itself it often seemed to me.' Most kids want to be outside, but quasi-public spaces, with private security guards, are becoming the norm. Having no money is vulgar. Being in a shopping mall without money is a threat.

As an adolescent with little to do, I joined the Girl Guides and asked my English teacher to sign my Writer's Badge form, after writing a story about a horse. The only experience of horses I had was watching The Grand National on TV. Girls were supposed to like horses: our comics were full of them. He signed the form, but I sensed his disappointment. Yet how could I write about my parents' arguments, or drying knickers in the oven before school, or the escaping steam from a tin of Fray Bentos Steak and Kidney pie? I was silenced.

At school we learnt Spanish, and were told we had the accent for it: 'That gob in the back of your throat – *gente, garaje*, and *girasol*.' Later, people said that working class kids were taught Spanish, not French, 'because it's easier,' an insult on many levels.

*

I left my mono-class background for Queen's University, Belfast, and had to crack codes in that polarised society. A working class Protestant friend invited me to her house. She wouldn't smoke in the street, as that was 'common'. She came from a 'respectable' family, unlike me, with our freckly, pale faces, scuffed shoes and falling down socks. Most of the time I busied myself doing student things. But politics was everywhere: people getting killed in the streets; our Scholastic Philosophy lecturer jailed for refusing to fill in the UK census; students with relatives inside. On finishing university I realised that some middle class students had done well, after making out they'd hardly studied, and were stepping straight into jobs: 'Daddy had a word.' Could I 'have a word?' They laughed.

In French classes I met middle class people who, with their politeness, soft voices and confident accents, acted as if they had more right to France than anyone else. I was learning how the middle classes cherry-pick aspects of a culture that suit, and show them in a more refined light. By then I knew from my brother, with his 'feral' childhood roaming fields and canals, that there was another France. He went on demos with French friends and discovered to his delight that 'ordinary' French people knew about food, and read books, and went to work, and argued politics. Like us.

Work and money were danger areas. Most 'editorial' jobs turned out to be mainly typing. I went for a job interview at

Spare Rib. By this time I had one child, and the job was advertised as two or three days a week. The pay was so low, I asked whether I'd still be able to claim benefits. They looked embarrassed, and said that that nobody had ever asked them that before. It was obvious they all had other sources of income. I didn't get the job. Talking about money was vulgar.

My son's friend's mother 'forgot' to pay me back £10 I had shelled out on an outing for her son. Because I really needed the money, I was too embarrassed to ask for it. Shortly after, I read an article she wrote, which began, 'Working class women are economically oppressed.'

I had a part-time job with a lefty organisation in Tower Hamlets. My colleague couldn't comprehend that I didn't have a bank account and wanted paying in cash, hiding his disbelief in a studied politeness. The difference in manners between the working class and the middle class was filtering through. When I moved to Leeds with young children and, desperate to make friends, called round on a woman who had invited me, she turned me away: 'It's not convenient,' without arranging another time. An empty invitation.

*

Giving readings about my novel *Hard Wired*, I have had discussions about the stereotyping of working class women. Di is a character drowning her grief in drink and tobacco for a while. Like most parents, she wants the best for her offspring. Some people couldn't hold these two things in their head.

Grayson Perry talks about class in a 2010 article:

'Taste is the real battleground of the classes. My middle class wife cringes if I walk round the house naked from the waist up – to her it is the height of aggressive vulgarity… I think it's fine to trample over polite, middle class taste as long as you know you are doing it and understand the context. Jackson Pollock probably got away with urinating in Peggy Guggenheim's fireplace, but we are no longer in the 1950s when a working class accent was an exotic accessory in the salons of the chattering classes.'[2]

There are unwritten rules of taste. A sofa out the front of your house is seen as vulgar, but a sofa ('garden furniture') out the back is fine. The whole outside/inside thing is a minefield: sitting on the front steps is 'common' (unless you are in a brownstone in New York), but sitting in a back garden is fine; eating chips on the street outside Leeds Market – common?; on Aldeburgh beach with a chilled bottle of wine – acceptable?; 'street' food – edgy? Certain fabrics are seen as vulgar, and have moral weight attached to them. Down with clothes made of polyester and nylon (unless worn 'ironically' or with expensive accessories), up with silk, linen and cotton, or clothes made out of recycled milk bottles. Holidays have hidden traps. For the middle classes, one-upmanship rules: Benidorm is common or vulgar, as are package holidays. What's Eurocamp but a package holiday with no doors? And what's the obsession with being an 'independent traveller'? And why is 'a little place we found off the beaten track in Brittany' somehow morally better?

A middle class friend always called herself a traveller, wanting to 'get under the skin' of a place, and see the 'real' Spain, for instance. In a week? Holiday souvenirs: why is mass produced vulgar? Yet 'something I picked up in a little market' not? Flash or bling or sparkly things can be a no-no, but 'ethnic' trinkets, showing the extent of your travels – does this show 'taste'? And Christmas trees: ridiculous style-pronouncements say they

2. Perry, G. (2010, January 30). If you have ever felt a class apart, this column is for the likes of you. Retrieved from https://www.theguardian.com/commentisfree/2010/jan/31/grayson-perry-social-mobility

should be one colour, with home-made decorations, preferably edible. Piling on unmatched decorations, different coloured lights, tinsel, a fairy on top shows your vulgar origins.

*

So what about manners, and courtesy? Manners smooth the way between people, but they can also distance. Middle class manners say you don't talk about certain things, or you talk about them in veiled terms – class and money and sex.

Tim Winton described how, at a book party in London's Soho, a drunken literary editor called him 'a bit chippy', and Winton learnt that, 'it was impolite to mention one's social origins; it made people uncomfortable. Even the most casual, light-hearted reference to class was viewed as "making a song and dance about it."'[3] He says that if he is 'anachronistically' preoccupied about class, it's not because of resentment – he was a beneficiary of Whitlam abolishing university fees, and his world changed – but for him, class is still a 'live issue', with some relatives who, when Winton's head was put on a stamp, could moisten the stamp, but not write a letter 'because they're functionally illiterate. Their curtailed educations were not a manifestation of character. They were outcomes of class.' Heart-breaking.

Definitions around vulgar have got mixed up, and value judgements attach themselves to words that should merely describe. Words burrow deep into our psyche, kill passion and spontaneity, and colour how we see the world. They divide us, and make us less than human. Instant judgements are made based on appearance and voice without people being willing to

3. Winton, T. (2017). The boy behind the curtain: notes from an Australian life. London: Picador.

dig deeper. There is a huge waste of talent.

Perry talks of his heartbreak after seeing the main character in the film *Precious* put down and verbally abused by her mother, and sexually abused by her father. He comments, 'Disadvantaged young people might not have the full set of millstones carried by *Precious*, but they might well have their own inner voice saying: "Not for the likes of us." They need to be taught to tell it: "Would you mind awfully and please shut the fuck up."'[4] I wish.

An article by Tim Lott, called 'The loneliness of the working class writer', says:

'Perhaps, like theatre, we have once again become too wedded to politeness (now in the guise of political sensitivity and inner thought policing) and too wary of passion, honesty and sometimes vulgarity. The working class voice now makes the middle class reader nervous. Partly because of guilt, and partly because, as Ken Loach observed, "any working class person who speaks intelligently is absolutely abhorrent to critics."'[5]

The use of 'higher register' Norman origin words over the vernacular sometimes gives speakers a mistaken sense of moral superiority. If I had spoken differently, would the professor interviewing me for my present job have introduced me as 'Kath, from a non-traditional background'? A veiled reference to class.

In Tim Lott's article he talks of 'the death of the English working class literary novelist,' and says the passing came around the end of the 1960s and a 'significant mouthpiece of

4. Perry, G. (2010, January 30). If you have ever felt a class apart, this column is for the likes of you. Retrieved from https://www.theguardian.com/commentisfree/2010/jan/31/grayson-perry-social-mobility

5. Lott, T. (2015, February 07). The loneliness of the working-class writer. Retrieved from https://www.theguardian.com/commentisfree/2015/feb/07/loneliness-working-class-writer-english-novelists

a sizeable part of society has been comprehensively silenced, in that field at least, for a generation, probably two.' He claims the 'politics of identity has replaced the politics of class' and that 'working class' writing has come to mean little more than 'white' writing – and that people might feel as if they are making a dubious statement for choosing it, as readers or publishers. Lynsey Hanley has said how the term 'working class' often only applies to the white working class, as if black or Asian people are airbrushed out of class discussions.[6]

*

Sex: since when did it become 'relationships'? Interesting that in the past, the words for sexual parts were not classed as 'dirty', but descriptive – fuck, cunt, pussy, and cock. Only later did they get the sense of 'uncouth'.

Grace Paley, the New York short story writer, said all stories are about love or money. Let's end with a bit of 'vulgarity'. There was a line in an early *Shameless* episode which always made me laugh. A young man has been asked to have sex by an older woman. You see his face: there is no disgust, no sense that there's something odd about an older woman wanting sex, nothing about morality, or the 'rightness' of it. A split second pause. Then, 'How much?' he asks.

So who's deciding what's vulgar? Let's change the answer.

Here's to the vulgar, the common.

---

6. Hanley, L. (2016, September 27). Why class won't go away. Retrieved from https://www.theguardian.com/society/2016/sep/27/why-class-wont-go-away

The Wrong Frequency

Kate Fox

I have a strong Bradfordian accent, but I do not know this.
I am eight. It is what the rest of my family has, it is what everyone at school has. When we had been to America to visit my
stepdad's family, people exclaimed at our 'cute' English accents.
They didn't mention that we didn't sound like the Queen. We
move to rural Cumbria. In the playground, children shout at
me, 'Posh snob, posh snob.' My voice sounded different to
theirs. I know that 'posh' is a bad thing. 'Posh' is what Mum
calls Auntie Anne and her son, our cousin Daniel, who goes to
private school and lives in Bassingbourn and sounds different
to us. We laugh at him for being posh, now I am being laughed
at for being posh. So far I am learning that sounding different
to other people could go either way. It could make you 'cute'
and cause smiling faces and chucked chins or 'posh' and cause
disapproving frowns and being tripped up on the playing field.

I was also told I used big words and talked like a book. My

new class teacher had unwisely made a big thing of me getting full marks in the English and Maths tests she set for the whole class on the first day. I knew, really, that 'posh' was something more than what you sounded like. It was also about what you said. 'Snob' meant thinking you were above other people. That would be like 'being too big for your boots' or 'being a clever clogs', which Mum and Dad said I was sometimes when I argued back about whether there was a God or whether you needed A Levels to get a good job (they said no but my teachers said yes. But Dad said the teachers were 'Loony Lefties' and wrote to the local paper to tell them so when they went on strike). Perhaps I was a posh snob really and it would be best not to let on, because nobody liked it when I was. But I couldn't help myself putting my hand up when I knew the right answer and the teacher was looking upset because everybody else had learned the lesson about not being a clever clogs or being too big for your boots. Perhaps they were the clever clogs really, but I couldn't help the thrill of a question and answer matching, or a teacher's face lighting up when I showed I'd been listening to them.

Someone speaks and someone listens and lets them know they have heard; this is heady stuff for someone growing up in a family where open, straight communication is rare. But it turns out that voices are not the simple tools for this I'd hoped they would be. It would be a while longer until I'd hear and understand George Bernard Shaw's aphorism about how 'It is impossible for an Englishman to open his mouth without making some other Englishman hate or despise him.' That's why, with no trepidation, I applied for a radio journalism course after university. I wanted to be a radio newsreader. I would tell people the news, based on facts, and they would listen. I was good at reading things out – I always got chosen to do it at school. This was clearly the career for me. It did not occur to me for a second that my accent would be an issue. Later I would compare this to *Masterchef*'s Gregg Wallace announcing that he wanted to be in the L'Oreal Shampoo adverts.

I look back on my naivety now and laugh. It was born out of unconscious privilege and unconscious stigma. The privilege of not being part of a community who had been told, 'You'll have to be twice as good to get half as far.' Whispered words had to be passed on as talismans and encouragers for those who were only a generation, or less, from being barred from certain jobs and professions. Certain ethnic minorities in certain places and times, women in certain places and times.

It also couldn't be the case that there was any stigma attached to a Northern accent, any chance that it would prevent me being anything I wanted to be. Why would I know about that in 1996? We were on the cusp of moving from John Major's classless society to Tony Blair's world of 'We're all middle class now'. I didn't adjust my accent to fit in with my mostly middle class fellow students at Loughborough University. It has probably zig-zagged somewhat between the move to Cumbria and back to Bradford, then to the Midlands, but in early tapes of my newsreading, I hear a strong Yorkshire accent. My radio journalism tutor is wary. He is an excellent journalist who has only ever been able to work in his native Bradford because of his accent. That was okay at a time when commercial radio stations employed news editors and teams of journalists but now they're all being made redundant. He's worried I will struggle. I have to come in for a special voice test before he accepts me onto the course. He tells me to always make sure I submit a demo tape when going for any radio job, as they will worry if they only hear my speaking voice in interview. I hadn't noticed that there had never been a national news bulletin reader with a Northern accent. Well, there was Wilfred Pickles from Halifax during the Second World War. He was put on air in order to 'Confuse the

Germans'. Then he was taken off it after three days because so many people complained about his flat vowels. Basically, British people would rather be invaded by Hitler than have a Northerner reading the news.

I thought for a long time that it was an inner core of arrogance that meant I didn't realise this would be a problem. Now I realise it was the strong wall of denial that there is any stigma around Northernness or working class-ness and their conflation. I colluded with some denial. At university I assiduously avoided any women's studies courses or feminist reading, despite the fact I was doing a social sciences degree. That stuff didn't apply to me. I wasn't going to work twice as hard or go half as far. Or if I was, I didn't want to know about it. There were some mentions of social status but not of class. There was a lecture on Anthony Giddens, the sociologist who inspired Tony Blair's Third Way. He told us we were going to become mobile, flexible workers. We could go anywhere.

I looked forward to this. But perversely, I had picked one career in which I couldn't go anywhere and in which this immobility was explicit. It was hard enough to get a job in Northern radio stations with my Northern accent. I managed to get a six-month apprenticeship at a commercial station in the North East of England. I fitted into the news team well. I was good at asking awkward and unawkward questions. I broke stories. But the programme manager was concerned that I didn't sound like a newsreader. Much to my disappointment, and that of my team, my apprenticeship wasn't made into a job. I went to work at Rutland Radio, the country's smallest radio station in the country's smallest county. The programme manager at the radio group's main station in Lincoln had time to give me voice training. I began to sound like a newsreader. This involved lowering my voice and flattening out my accent. Code-switching, but only on air. Six months later I applied for a job back at the

North East station and got it.

A year later, there were to be cuts to the team. I applied for a newsreader's job at a radio station in Manchester. I would be reading the news on the breakfast station. But when I got there, I wasn't allowed on air to read the bulletins I'd written. An American radio consultant called Dennis had said that since there was already a female co-presenter on the breakfast show, two female voices in the same show could 'confuse the listeners'. Just call me Wilhelmina Pickles. There wasn't much I could do to sound less like a woman.

I went for a couple of interviews with the BBC in London but got nowhere. I remember making a very enthusiastic proposal about how the BBC should have more regional reporters and accents on its national shows. That was slightly stonier ground back in 2003 (though they still don't have a national bulletin reader with a Northern accent).

I had started performing my poetry and comedy at open mic nights by then and discovering that my Northernness was not a barrier there. It was something I could play with and exaggerate. It felt like it opened doors. At the same time I got a job as part of the breakfast team on Galaxy Radio in Newcastle. The programme manager liked my voice and my accent and encouraged me to read the news conversationally to appeal to their listeners who didn't want a false or authoritative tone. It felt like any problem I'd had was now solved. I just had to pick places that encouraged me. Opt for places instead where I could talk and be heard. I went into North East schools and colleges to give careers talks. Said, 'You can be whoever you want to be and make the world a more prosperous place,' in the spirit of Blairite instrumental creativity. I became a regular poet for the BBC Radio 4 show *Saturday Live*. I was aware that as the first female poet, and the first one with a Northern accent, I was embodying the type of poetry that connected with people more, rather than the academic, elitist poetry that had turned so many people off at school. I played up to this even more. Let myself be described as a 'Northern Pam Ayres' in publicity blurb sometimes. Ran writing and performance workshops in schools in deprived areas of the North East where councils said that 'parents were unable to contribute enough to their children's speaking and listening skills' and felt good that I was able to run rap battles and 'Poetry Idol' competitions with the entire school hall screaming for poetry.

Older poets sometimes raised issues around the persistent minimising of Northern voices. The way they would be caricatured as down to earth, or horny-handed sons of the soil. Everyman, unsophisticated poets. Photographed on moors or against granite whilst looking granite. They pointed out the reviews in which Ted Hughes or Tony Harrison or Simon Armitage would be characterised as 'Defiantly Northern' or 'Unapologetically Northern' which raised the possibility of it being something to apologise for. Female poets who had forged their own spaces in the blokey Northern poetic landscape of the seventies and eighties pointed out how Northern female writers were marginalised or forgotten. Somehow didn't fit the 'Northern narrative'. They couldn't be stereotyped as the chippy Northern Poet but were instead ignored. But this was a different time. Blair and Brown were all for my sort of voice, I thought. They gave public funding to initiatives like Creative Partnerships and the Cultural Leadership Programme. There were ways in. I could be heard. I could point other people in directions where they could be too. I even got Gateshead Libraries to fund a workshop for new performers in which the comedian Sarah Millican did her first stand-up set, then got Arts Council funding for more workshops and shows. This was our time. Nothing could stop Northern voices.

Then the banks collapsed. The coalition government came

in. No more Creative Partnerships or Cultural Leadership Programme. I woke up. To the socio-economic inequalities between North and South as the gap widened. To the slashing of local government budgets which disproportionately affected Northern councils. To the way that the economic gap between London and the rest of the country is much bigger than that of any other European capital and the rest of its country. To how

Londoners get 20 times more per head spent on transport, ten times more on the arts.

I began to connect this with the persistent lack of representation of Northern voices. The lack of a Northern newsreader began to symbolise so much more. The culmination of centuries in which the North was held up as barbaric and dark, as opposed to the 'civilised' South. The North West, which Lord Howells could call 'desolate' enough to frack. The way it is needed as urban, working class dereliction to distinguish rural, middle class England. How it is body and South is mind. How it is lower and the past, always the past.

I started a practice-based PhD looking at class, gender and Northernness in stand-up comedy and poetry performance. The fact that this is fully funded at the University of Leeds suggests that someone is still willing to invest in voices like mine. But my research makes me fear for opportunities for others, even as it helps me rewrite the narrative of my own family and work history every day.

The male stand-ups that I looked at are haunted by the figure of the Northern Comedian. His archetype is Bernard Manning. The Southern-based reviewers mock the gruff voices, the large bodies of Northern comedians. Their friendliness, they say, makes them club comics. I wonder if my research is reproducing my increasing chippiness. So I analyse 260 comedy reviews, half of Northern, half of Southern comedians. The Northernness is marked much more. Nearly half the reviews mention the origins of Northern comedians, only 20% mention Southern ones. Their voices are noted too. 'Treacly' or 'Sing song' Geordie voices, for instance. The sophisticated surreal comedy of Geordie Gavin Webster is recognised by his peers who voted him 'Comedian's Comedian' in 2014, but unrecognised by reviewers who dismiss him as a 'meat and two veg' sort of performer. His fellow North-Eastern surrealist Ross Noble is harder to pigeonhole as the archetypal Northern Comedian, by appearance and demeanour, and so escapes.

This seems to be a way of reinforcing class differences via embodied regional stereotypes. Some of the avowedly working class comedians are not marked by reviewers in this way. Bridget Christie, Sara Pascoe, Russell Kane are closer to what sociologists call the 'somatic norm' of the white, middle class Southerner which makes up the expected public speaker. Working class comedian Russell Brand has been named one of the top 50 most influential thinkers by Prospect magazine as comedians increasingly take on the role of public intellectuals. I would contend that if he had a Northern identity marked by his accent then his journey would have been harder. Place has an (under-recognised) role in keeping people in their place. We see it too with the splitting of the North-South narrative into working class Northern Brexiteers and Southern progressives. This is a clear and simple bending of the figures. There were as many South-Eastern working class Leave voters.

I see what the French sociologist Pierre Bourdieu would call symbolic violence, where economic inequalities are concealed by what appear to be symbolic differences in the lack of Northern newsreaders, which might be justified by saying that they're harder to understand. I also see it in the persistent archetypes of the Northern Comedian and the Northern Poet, in the endless jokes about whippets and pits and Hovis and rain and even in the Northern Powerhouse vision of the future promulgated by former Chancellor of the Exchequer George Osborne in 2014. (This featured endless images of men in hard hats and hi-vis pointing at things on construction sites and men in suits looking important while signing council devolution agreements.)

In Bourdieu's reading of class, Northernness is something that goes into the complex pot of practices which constitutes people's status. The everyday practices such as how people move their bodies, swirl their teacups and laugh at comedians, the everyday tastes such as which music they listen to, what films they watch and whether or not it's Farrow and Ball Elephant's Breath or Dulux Bubblegum Pink on their walls. It is something which is unconscious, reinforced by families and educational institutions and continually something which is contested and struggled for. The struggle is over whose culture is most 'legitimate'. Northern culture is always seen as less 'legitimate' than that of English culture. This is why the BBC and public schools have spent decades reinforcing Received Pronunciation and Standard English. They need Northernness to continue to exist in order to reinforce their own legitimacy.

Northernness can also be appropriated to provide an instant 'de-scarifying' factor for culture which is all too aware of its own legitimacy. As the BBC continues to fulfil its sometimes paradoxical Reithian missions to inform, explain and educate, there is perceived to be something automatically anti-elitist about a Northern poet, a Northern opera singer, a Northern physicist, a Northern academic. At the same time, researchers are discovering a 'class ceiling' in elite professions and acting. This is partly enforced by the cultural capital (or lack of it) which people give away when they open their mouths and Northern vowels fall out.

My vowels are no longer, if they ever were, defiant, unapologetic or rebellious. But they are sometimes playful, paradoxical and ironic. They acknowledge both the irritation and the humour in a conference photographer thinking it's perfectly okay to tell me, 'You should be a comedian,' adding, 'with that accent.' Reminding me of how Northern vowels are automatically perceived as non-serious when there is no essential reason for this to be the case. Nothing inherent in the accent that makes its bearers, as Tony Harrison said, 'one of those Shakespeare gives the comic bits to.' Reminding me of how, even now, most audiences see a woman and therefore automatically not a comedian. Certainly not a Northern Comedian. I employ irony to keep from being seen as 'posh' or 'common', whether the irony is recognised or not. It really does, of course, depend on other people getting the same references. Knowing what is being distinguished as better than what. I recently tried to explain to some Spanish people why there are certain types of gig I'll be offered because I'm a perceived as a funny Northern poet and some that I won't. Their incredulity reminded me how arbitrary this stuff is. One of them pledged to pronounce the word 'But' with a flat 'u' in future, in solidarity.

There are moments, many moments, when I am performing and transmitting on the right wavelength to an audience who hears and receives my words without my accent and all its connotations about my level of education, intelligence, income and background getting in the way. Then there are moments such as when I did my first panel show after ten years of doing poems on Radio 4: I was introduced onto *Quote...Unquote* with the phrase, 'Its grim oop North,' complete with cod Yorkshire accent, and realised the dial is still stuck on an old station. The brilliant diversity of Northern voices can jam those out of date signals – if only we get the chance to be heard.

The Immigrant of Narborough Road

Alexandros Plasatis

Summer evening, I had just moved into a new flat,[1] un-packed, and gone out to the external staircase for a smoke. I was feeling itchy. In the courtyard downstairs three Polish guys and an older English woman were drinking beer and smoking spliffs, walking in and out their flat's doorless door. Our flat had a door, but the lock was jammed shut. When my Indian flatmate finished his cooking, I got back into the flat through the kitchen window. In bed, in darkness, scratching my calves and feet, I thought of tomorrow, my PhD viva. I switched on the lights, got my thesis, tried to read it, but kept on scratching instead. I pulled the sheets off and examined the mattress, inch by inch: there you are, a bedbug. I squeezed it between my thumb and forefinger, knocked on the Romanian girl's door,

---

1. An ESRC-funded research exploration in 2015 found that Narborough Road in Leicester is Britain's most multi-cultural high-street.

showed her the crushed insect. She showed me a sticky card next to her bed: 'This is where I collect them.' She smiled.

I dragged the mattress out of the kitchen window, down two flights of stairs, dumped it next to the bins with the rotting meat from the Syrian butcher/international grocery. Through the alleyway and out to Narborough Road, into the Afro supermarket. I bought insect sprays and asked for an Old Holborn.

He pulled a Drum from under the counter. 'Half price, boss.'

No, thanks. I got my Old Holborn from elsewhere, normal price. Back through the butcher's alleyway, I looked up at the place I had just moved in to. It had been advertised on Gumtree as a self-contained room, £220 pcm, inclusive of bills. When I went to have a look, the Pakistani landlord had shown me around: shared bathroom, shared tiny kitchen, no living-room, something wrong with the door, the kitchen window was to be used temporarily as a door. He lived next door, always ready to help, he had said. I was to share the flat with the Romanian girl who worked as a hotel maid, a Ghanaian waiter and his Italian girlfriend who cleaned houses, and the Indian who was about to start at Debenhams.

'The ad said it was a self-contained room…' I had said to the landlord. He just smirked and nodded at the beer-fridge in the corner of the bedroom. I rarely drink, but I moved in anyway. And I spent my first night there fully clothed, nodding off by my desk. But there must have been loads of the tiny bastards, my skin was burning from the itch, and I scratched myself raw until daylight.

Haiwan[2]

At 8.30am I walked down Narborough Road, turned right to

2. All names of restaurants, shops, agencies, etc., have been changed.

Braunstone Gate, and was back in the university halls of residence, where, during my PhD, I had been living and working as a residence officer. My contract had finished the day before, hence the new flat. I explained to my ex-manager, a kind Turkish lady, about my bedbug situation. 'Viva is at 2pm. I need to sleep.' She took pity on me, gave me the key to an empty room, and said the cleaners were coming at 1pm, so I had to be gone by then.

The viva lasted three hours, all good, now the bedbugs could suck my Doctorate blood. Straight after, I got slaughtered with my PhD supervisor in a pub, and later that night, back in my room, I slept on the hard wooden floor, feeling nothing; the alcohol helped. In the morning, my arms and feet had bites filled with blood and pus. I cleaned them with surgical spirit and went out to look for a job.

I started the same evening as a waiter in the Haiwan Turkish restaurant in Narborough Road. The boss was fussy with his Turkish tea and it was the first and only thing he showed me how to do. He drank tea all day. He would sit at a table and raise his finger, and I had to get him his fucking tea. Then he moved to another table, raised his finger, drank more tea, went for a piss, and came back with a raised finger.

The kitchen staff were Turks, Indians, an Albanian – nice lads, we got on well straightaway. The servers were girls, beautiful and polite, Lithuanians, Estonians, Polish. The only guy was the head waiter, an Afghan. Modesty aside, I'm a bloody good waiter, having been one most of my life. So the Afghan trained me on just the basics: 'Whenever a customer wants to pay by card, you are to apologise and say that the card machine is out of order.'

'Is it out of order?'

'Of course not. Tell the customers that there's a cash point around the corner. And *never* put a bill through the till.'

Being a Greek – that is, growing up in a country where the main education consisted of how to cheat on taxes – I caught on immediately.

The job was easy and they gave me food whenever I was hungry, which was often, and the truth is that I went out for a fag a little too often, but when the boss told me three days after I started that he'd pay me £3.50 per hour (at the time the minimum wage was £6.31) and no tips, I ate a kebab and left.

A La Cant

A week without a mattress had started to piss me off, plus the biting was getting worse, despite the fact that I had poured ant powder all over my room. I had applied to a dozen universities for a lectureship job and had my coffee and smoke in the staircase – it was nice out there, bedbugless. I had been trying to contact the landlord since I found the first bedbug, but he was nowhere to be found, until, one day, I spotted him through his window and knocked at his door. His Slovakian girlfriend answered: 'He's not here.'

'I know he's there.'

He came out: 'Oh, Alex, my good friend, it's so nice to see you…'

'Why didn't you tell me about the bedbugs?'

'You don't know, my friend, but 60% of houses in this country have bedbugs.'

'I lived in 25 houses in this country and none of them had bedbugs. Get me a new mattress.'

'The mattress was new. No way.'

'YOU BETTER GET ME A NEW MATTRESS.'

'Calm down. Listen, you get one from the shop downstairs and I'll pay for it. Bring me the receipt.'

I bought the mattress, carried it up the stairs, through the kitchen window (a development: someone had piled some bricks there to get in easier), left it in its plastic cover to protect it from the bedbugs, climbed back out and knocked at the land-lord's door. The Slovakian came out: 'He's not here.'

He was there, but I was tired.

I went to town to look for work and ended up at a catering agency, A La Cant. There were about 50 people there looking for work, mostly newcomers from India and Pakistan, some Eastern Europeans, no English. We had to take a writing test – many of them couldn't read or write. I passed the test, we all passed it.

'We have a nice job for you, Mr Plasatis.'

I had written down my title as Dr, but anyway. 'What job?'

'In a ready meals factory.' I had to report at 6pm in the re-ception of the so and so factory. 'Someone from A La Cant will be waiting there for you.'

I went back home and killed some time by squeezing a few bugs and dancing to the Romanian music that came from the next room, then cycled to the factory, 40 minutes. A Portuguese guy was in the reception.

'I was told to come and report...'

'You're two hours early. Your shift starts at 8pm.'

'I was told to be here at 6.'

'You've made a mistake. Go back home, watch some telly, and get back here by 8.'

I cycled off. But on the way home it hit me: *Go back home and watch some telly and get back here by 8*. You fucking pig. I lay on my plastic bed, fully clothed. Greece was playing the first game in the 2014 World Cup. I was feeling very itchy. The phone rang at 8.10pm, while I was seriously scratching myself: 'Hello?'

'A La Cant here. I told you to be here at 8.'

'You called two hours late.'

'What does this mean?'

'You know what it means.'

'You coming or not?'

'Not coming.'

We lost three-nil to Colombia.

Meringues

Next morning my phone rang, unknown number. Ah… perhaps someone wanted to offer me a lectureship job?

'We call from A La Cant.'

'Oh, it's you…'

'We apologise, Mr Plasatis, someone has made a mistake.'

'That's all right. But tell Ronaldo to learn manners.'

They offered me another job, in the ready desserts factory, next to the ready meals factory. 4pm till late.

'How late?'

'Till the job is done. Maybe 4am. Any questions?'

No questions.

I went to the bathroom and waited. The landlord came out of his flat and I appeared through the bathroom window this time – just to take him by surprise: 'I brought you the receipt…'

'Let me keep it… I'm off to the cashpoint. Back in five minutes.'

He didn't come back.

All workers were immigrants in the factory, every single one. Only the managers were British. They put me in the receiving end of the ovens, in a small team and a small room with two tunnel-like ovens. The first oven rolled out trays of chocolate cakes, cheesecakes, etc. You had to take their temperature now and then, load them on tall trolleys, wheel them into a walk-in freezer. The rapid change of temperature made my stomach feel like a knot. From the other oven you only got meringues. All you had to do was to grab the grease paper with the meringues out of the hot tray, turn around, and place them in a basket. The trays came slow enough to tempt you to look up at the clock and see that time wasn't passing: it was soul-crushing. In those endless trays of little white meringues I saw death.

The only kindness I saw in there was in the movements of an old Indian man. He really cared about those meringues, and watching how he handled them, how he sometimes patted them after he placed them in the basket, took a bit of the pain away. The tall Lithuanian sniffed coke on the breaks and came back ready to pick a fight or tell the old Indian that he wanted to fuck his arse. 'You got such a great arse, man. Let me fuck it, I'm so *hard…*' 'Never,' the Indian always replied. The Russian lad didn't speak to anyone, and the Polish guy drank ten Redbulls per shift. When we finished work, he used to walk back to Narborough Road faster than I cycled.

The English Lady

They always played meringue wars in the ovens. It was stupid but they needed the fun. When the supervisor wasn't there, they would look right and left, and throw meringues at each other, sometimes they would fight with hot cheesecake trays. I didn't participate, I preferred scratching my bedbug wounds: the sprays didn't work, and now I had bites even on my face. The only way to get rid of them was to move house, and I did so a month after I had moved in. Surprisingly easily, the landlord gave me a check for my deposit and the new mattress.

The new place was around the corner from the bedbugs flat, an English lady had a spare room in her house. She was on benefits, and said that the council wasn't supposed to know that she rented out the room.

I hired a van and moved my stuff upstairs to my new room, while the landlady was downstairs in the living room, watching me as she drank can after can of beer: 'Fucking hell you got so many fucking books.' I finished unpacking that night, while she was listening to loud love songs on Gem 106 …*I can see it in your eyes*… smoking her spliff. I sat down on my new bed to rest, rolled a cigarette, my eye fell on my shorts: a bedbug …*Hello, is it me you're looking for?*…

In two days or so, they had taken over my room. I said nothing to the landlady (she had a bit of a temper anyway). I bought special anti-bedbug sprays online and every day, when she went to Bede Park with her beer cans, I emptied two sprays, one for the bed, one for the rest of the room. I had to wash my bedsheets and clothes regularly, which pissed her off because I was using up too much electricity. I could use the washing machine once a week she said.

Tasting the Middle Class

The check with my deposit money bounced back. And my bike had a flat tyre again. I gave the bike to the second-hand bookshop that did bike repairs too, and went to see my previous landlord. The Slovakian open the door: 'He's not here.' I walked in and told him that he had better give me the money before I get angry. OK, he would give me half. Half? I mentioned something about a deposit protection scheme. Ah, of course he would give me the whole deposit.

'Good. Let's go to the cash machine together now.'

'Why don't you trust me?'

'Fuck you.'

'Trust me. You know, for us Arabs our word is a contract.'

'But you're Pakistani.'

'No, I'm Arab.'

Fucking hell…

The Slovakian chipped in: 'Why do you talk to my boy-friend like that?'

'Fuck you too.'

'Calm down. Would you like some orange juice?'

'If you got some without the bits.'

He asked for the money from his girlfriend as a loan and they began arguing. 'I'm not giving you *my* money, arsehole!' 'I'll pay you back, whore.'

I made it towards the door, 'Right. I'm off to the council.'

£290 was in my hand.

'Come back for a meal one day, Alex. I'll cook you nice Arabic food.'

'And I'll make something Slovakian. Come back, we're family now.'

Fucking crazy bastard couple.

The bike was ready and I cycled to the factory. I worked for a couple of hours in the first oven, then they sent me for tasting. In the new room they gave me a card and said that unless there was something *very* wrong with the dessert, I was to give it the highest score. They put in front of me a Waitrose family-sized vanilla cheesecake. Excellent, I ate half of it. Then an M&S family chocolate cake appeared. Smashing, I ate three quarters. Profiteroles? Yes, please. Double chocolate gateau, lemon tart, they kept on coming. I ate until I felt sick, giving everything the highest score, until I was sent back to the ovens. Meringues were still coming out, I wanted to vomit. For hours all I did was witness the saddest sight of my life, those endless trays of white meringues rolling out towards me ever so slowly. The Lithuanian came back from his break coked-up and threw a meringue at me that hit me in the eye. I threw one back but missed the target. He threw another one and hit me in the same eye. Fucking cunt. I found an Aunt Bessie's Glorious Jam Roly Poly and crushed it on his head. He laughed hysterically and ate it, ran to the other oven, threw a cheesecake at the Indian, who ducked just in time. I threw a meringue at the Lithuanian, he deflected it with a tray, I threw another one, he blocked it again, he was good, 'Alex,' said the Redbull Polish, 'Alex, now stop,' I threw one at him too, 'Alex…' and I saw a manager watching me from a little window…

I was sent to the office, took all responsibility, I had had enough of it all anyway.

'I'm not happy for you to go back there,' the manager said.

'I'm not happy to go back there either,' I said.

That night in bed I thought of the Romanian girl's big bum and started collecting bedbugs in a little jar, maybe she would like to meet for a drink and see my collection. I woke up when the temp agency called – they had another job for me, in a sausage factory.

Putting on my socks, I saw that my feet were swollen with bites. I found the landlady drunk downstairs and told her that I'm leaving.

'Why? You moved in two weeks ago.'

'Because you didn't let me watch the World Cup final.'

'In this house, *no one* will *ever* watch football.'

'You know, about my deposit…'

But she cut me short: 'You aren't getting any of that back.'

I wanted to tell her that I didn't want it back. She would start feeling itchy soon and would need the money to get rid of them. I was being fair.

My next place was one of the weirdest places I have ever lived. It was on the hilltop of Barclay Street, off Narborough Road, an abandoned council care home for elderly people. I was going to be a live-in guardian in a place with 60 rooms and 20 toilets in its two floors, with long corridors that stank of urine. I was given three unfurnished rooms downstairs, £200 pcm inclusive. In return for the cheap rent, I had to flush all the toilets twice a week and switch on and off the corridor lights when it got dark. The industrial kitchen was a minute walk from my rooms, and the only other occupant lived upstairs, a Belgian woman in her fifties, with long, unkempt hair. She looked fucked up. But then, I guess, so did I.

White Circles

I went to Matalan to buy clothes but then thought, no, I'm not sinking that low. So I went to Primark. I bought underwear, socks, jeans, T-shirts, shoes. I left them at a friend's place. I bought a metal bedframe with legs and a mattress, and told them I'd collect it later. I bought 20 rolls of heavy-duty garden bags and went back to the English landlady's; she was passed out in the living room. I made several journeys to the wheelie bins, sneaking past her with black bags, throwing away all my clothes – everything, my shoes, jackets, shirts, trousers, absolutely everything. I only kept my grandfather's overcoat he had bought as a young immigrant in Germany. I left behind the little furniture I had, my desk, chair, lamps, bookcases. But I kept my books, hundreds of them, inside those heavy duty bags, sealed all over with brown tape.

Kurdish man and his van arrived. The English lady got her senses back and told me to fuck off. I told her I was about to. We loaded the van, collected bed and mattress, arrived at the ex-care home.

It took me hours to complete the project. I stacked the sealed bags of books in the middle of one of the empty rooms. I encircled it with a thick line of ant powder and around that, I put double-sided tape. Then another circle of ant powder and another of double-sided tape. On each bedroom door saddle I poured more ant powder with double-sided tape on each side. I called my friend, he brought me the Primark bag. I threw away the clothes I was wearing, had a shower, put on new clothes. I set up the bed in the middle of one of the other rooms: I wrapped each leg of the bedframe with double-side tape, followed by three circles of the ant powder. I lay down: 'Now try to come and get me, you little bastards.'

Late at night, the Belgian woman came down for a chat and found me cycling from my rooms down the corridors to the kitchen. She said she had been living alone in the building for four months, and that some nights she heard plates smashing in the kitchen and some mornings she would even find the smashed plates. I smiled and told her that I'm Greek, so I'm used to this sort of thing. She didn't smile. I showed her my rooms without explaining the white powder circles. She left and never came back downstairs. After a while she moved out and I had the whole building to myself. When I came back from the factory, I liked to cycle up and down the corridors, switching on and off the lights.

Working Class Hero
I think I lost a screw during my PhD in Creative Writing. Even after I had finished it, I felt I was a fictional character, as if living in a story and everything took place in a book: I was the fucked-up immigrant with a PhD who worked in factories, exploring the new working class England. I have changed a little since then, but I was still feeling like a fictional character that night – the night that I walked back down to Narborough Road, snuck up outside the Pakistani's flat, loaded bedbugs from the little jar into a straw, and blew them under his door.

Education, Education, Education

Peter Sutton

*'The whole theory of modern education is radically un-
sound. Fortunately, in England at any rate, education
produces no effect whatsoever. If it did, it would prove a
serious danger to the upper classes, and probably lead to
acts of violence in Grosvenor Square.'*
– Lady Bracknell, *The Importance of being Ernest*,
Oscar Wilde

*'Our top priority was, is and always will be education,
education, education. To overcome decades of neglect
and make Britain a learning society, developing the tal-
ents and raising the ambitions of all our young people.'*
– Tony Blair setting out Labour's priorities for office
in 2001

I was in the school office clutching a letter. In it, my A Level results, my future – I needed a C and two Ds to get into my polytechnic of choice, Bristol, to do Biology. I was doing Biology, Chemistry and English; I was one of two Biology A Level students in my year at my school (yes, two, let that sink in a second), a comprehensive on the Wirral. I was a council estate kid and I wanted to follow my sister into higher education. I got two Ds and an E but, thankfully, Bristol took me anyway.

I'd passed my 11+ and had the chance to go to a grammar school. It's hard to peer through the mists of time and remember why I didn't, in the end, go to one. I vaguely recall that the one on offer was an all-boys school and I'd been to a mixed primary and wanted to go to a mixed secondary. But greater than that was that I'd met some grammar school kids and thought they were stuck up and that I'd always be 'the council estate kid' if I went to that school. I do sometimes wonder how my life would have turned out if I'd taken the opportunity presented. Maybe it'd be like the difference between Ace Rimmer and Arnold Rimmer when one was kept back a year in *Red Dwarf*?

When Theresa May announced her plan to create more grammar schools a wit on Twitter said something along the lines of, 'If grammar schools are so good why can't their alumni differentiate between personal experience and statistical evidence?' The anecdotal fallacy that this commentator was referring to was, of course, that grammar schools are not good for social mobility. They help the few to the detriment of the many.

According to the research from the Sutton Trust[1] less than 3% of grammar school students are eligible for free school meals, compared to 18% of non-grammar school students in

---

1. Skipp, A., Vignoles, A., Jesson, D., Sadro, F., Cribb, J., & Sibieta, L. (2013, November 8). Poor Grammar: Entry Into Grammar Schools Disadvantaged Pupils In England. Retrieved from https://www.suttontrust.com/research-paper/poor-grammar-entry-grammar-schools-disadvantaged-pupils-england/

the same area. Up to 13% of grammar school students come from private schools. Yet, despite all evidence to the contrary, the Tories push grammar schools as a means of social mobility. Numerous studies have shown that, in fact, grammar schools widen the gap in achievement between rich and poor students. I didn't of course know any of this aged 12 when I chose to go to a comprehensive. There were well-off kids at the school, but the majority were from poorer backgrounds.

To go back to that point on A Levels, so few students did A Levels in my school because of lack of aspiration. Potentially also a lack of role model. My older sister went to a different school and went to university. Ever since I'd won a competition in primary school, the prize for which was a junior encyclopaedia of science, I'd wanted to be a scientist. To become one meant university. I did have aspirations, and a role model.

A few years ago I bumped into the headmaster of my primary school, and we had a chat. Of course he wanted to know what I was doing now and was impressed and excited that I had a pretty good job. So many former students, council estate kids, had made nothing with their lives. He thought it was because they didn't know that they could. There was a lack of aspiration. In this he was unconsciously echoing David Cameron.[2]

I think he's right. I had always vaguely thought about writing, about writing for public consumption that is. I never did anything about it. I'd always put authors on a pedestal, they were special sorts of people to do what they did. When I started volunteering for Bristol Festival of Literature I met lots of authors, some from as humble a background as myself, and I

---

2. Dominiczak, P. (2013, November 13). Young poor have low aspirations, says David Cameron. Retrieved from http://www.telegraph.co.uk/news/politics/david-cameron/10448134/Young-poor-have-low-aspirations-says-David-Cameron.html

started thinking seriously about writing.

It wasn't until I spoke to creative writing tutor and author of writing craft books Barbara Turner-Vesselago, at a launch of one of her books, that I started in earnest. I was helping out at the event and whilst chatting to her about the set up I said, 'I'd like to write stories one day.' She replied, 'Why don't you? What's stopping you?' It was odd, I felt that I'd just been given permission. Later that year I had my first short story published in an anthology and won a writing competition. I'd had the aspiration, but thought that people like me weren't eligible.

Anyway, back to universities. I got in to Bristol and was eligible for a grant. In my second year Margaret Thatcher's government took away the ability for students to claim housing benefit. I appeared on the front page of the Bristol Evening Post along with thousands of my fellow students protesting at this cut. In the run up to the 2010 General Election I had an online discussion with a friend who said that Labour's plans to cap university fees were unaffordable. I pointed out that when I went to university, admittedly in a time when far fewer people became students, I had received a grant, and could claim housing benefit. His response was, 'Why should I pay for you to be educated?' I asked him why I should pay for his children to go to primary and secondary school – a logical extension to his question. 'Because it is good for society,' was his response. I rested my case.

It is hard to speculate on how I would act as a potential student in this day and age, when large student debts are the norm, but I very much think that the prospect of taking on so much debt would have put me off. As it was, the grant system being imperfect, I left secondary education with a debt. But I also left with a potential to change my socioeconomic status. Today I would probably be categorised as middle class – education has been my method of gaining social mobility.

Education has long been recognised as the prime method for social mobility, but with the state of education now it doesn't look good. The road to hell is paved with good intentions and Tony Blair's government made changes that would see a lot more students attending university. Which then led to the costs of running universities increasing. Which then led to fees. Which then led to fees being a bone of contention at the general election of 2010. We are now well on the way to a US-style of private college education. The Coalition and Conservative governments' successive privatisation through stealth of our education system is rolling back the idea that education is a right, not a privilege.

The thing is, it's not only bad for social mobility, nor just for students, it is bad for all of us. The latest scandalous sell off is of student debt – the government are now selling off huge portions of student debt to corporations.

Before 2012, average debt on graduation was under £25,000 per student. The Institute for Fiscal Studies now puts that at just over £44,000.[3] Repayments come straight out of wages and the money goes to HMRC via the Student Loans Company: used in the same way as tax, to go to pay for schools, roads, the NHS etc. The Student Loans Company handles the money, from paying the universities, to collecting the payments from graduates. That is until now. The deal has just changed – student loans are being sold off to banks as 'securitised assets'. Instead of being used like tax, the payments will now go directly into these companies' profits.

The debts of students who completed their studies in 2002-2006 are the first tranche to be sold off. Unlike previous sell-offs

---

3. Crawford, C., & Jin, W. (2014, April). *Payback time? Student debt and loan repayments: what will the 2012 reforms mean for graduates?* (Rep. No. IFS R93). Retrieved https://www.ifs.org.uk/comms/r93.pdf

of student debts, this lot is income-dependent. The first batch's value that is reasonably expected to be repaid is set at £12bn.

Remember that in 2015 there was a massive stink about the welfare bill that cut £12bn of spending?[4] So why isn't there an equal stink about this loss of revenue for the government? This is a bad deal for taxpayers. Not only does the student loan system cost more despite being designed to cost the country less (due to the high percentage of students who have some or all of their debt written off) but now the money recouped isn't even going to the exchequer. This is a short term cash injection at the expense of a long term income.

If I were 30 years younger I doubt I'd have made the decision to go to university. I would have the aspiration still, but wouldn't want to rack up so much debt. My parents, who between them earned less than half what I currently earn (even considering inflation, this is a shocking thought) wouldn't have been able to help much.

I work in a department of engineers. They are all university educated. The vast majority are from middle class backgrounds. I'm the token socialist. One of my colleagues was lamenting the fact that both his children were setting off for university at the same time. The amount he was going to be paying just for their accommodation was more than half the average yearly wage of £27,000. This is, of course, why more and more students are not leaving home even when they do go to university. And yet, to him, the old system of grants was unfair to taxpayers.

It is worth noting that Gordon Brown started and enabled

4. Bolton, N. M. (2015, July 20). Labour Party sees massive revolt but welfare bill that will cut £12bn from spending is passed in parliament. Retrieved from http://www.independent.co.uk/news/uk/politics/welfare-cuts-vote-welfare-bill-that-will-cut-welfare-spending-by-12bn-passed-in-parliament-with-a-10403340.html

this process with the first sell-off of student debts in 1998. However, the Conservatives are ideological about selling off assets. They seem to be on course to privatise education. The elimination of the last maintenance grants, getting rid of the student nurse bursary, the increase in the maximum allowable student debts are all small steps on the path to for profit education.

And it's not only universities. During his tenure as education secretary, Michael Gove oversaw the sell-off of school assets on a breathtaking scale, against expert advice. But then he did famously say that Britain was fed up with experts.[5] It appears that the resurgent Conservatives are determined to dismantle the welfare state, or at the very least make the welfare state profitable. Taxpayers' money is being funnelled into company profit at an ever-increasing rate. Blair and Brown are culpable but their motives were, I feel, slightly different. They wanted the famous third way, which, considering its association with Blair, is now defunct.

I am the sum of my experiences. You can take the boy out of the working class, but you can't take the working class out of the boy. Despite my social mobility I still have plenty of friends and family that haven't escaped their working class origins. I am neither proud of, nor ashamed of, my origins – although I have been both in the past, so escape feels somehow like the wrong word. My education has afforded me a good job, a decent wage, a nice standard of living. I watch people I know struggle financially and am glad I don't have to (as much – I'm comfortable, not rich, in my view – richness is relative of course) and I worry about the future.

---

5. Michael Gove interview with Faisal Islam [Television broadcast]. (2016, June 3). On *Sky News*. Sky plc.

My sister's children have had their education and are starting to build families of their own. I think their children will not have the same opportunities I had. I hope that they do have aspirations and they do see that uncles and aunties have done well via education. One of my nephews has been identified as 'gifted' so I have high hopes. But I know that if they do well, if they grab an escape route via education, they'll be doing so despite the system. I feel that this is unforgivable. Tony Blair, for all his faults, was right, education is a top priority.

Growing Up Outside of Class

Sian Norris

It was summer 2016, the summer when questions of class and identity became ever-more pressing as the media and politicians created caricatures and stereotypes of what it meant to be working class (male, white, living in the North) and what it meant to be middle class (male, white, living in North London). As these debates and arguments raged across the headlines and political Twitter, a friend and I shared a bottle of prosecco in a sunny beer garden in the now-gentrified area of Bristol where we all live. I was telling her of my plans to do a writing residency in a local art gallery, when she asked:

'What university is it, where your dad teaches?'

'What?' I responded, my face confused.

She repeated the question.

I should have quipped: the HMS Ardent, except you can't go there now that it's buried at the bottom of the South Atlantic. Instead, I shrugged.

'My dad doesn't teach at a university. He didn't go to university.'

'Oh!' she exclaimed, sipping her drink, a shade of embarrassment colouring her face. 'Oh! But I thought… I thought that's why you're a writer. Because your dad was an academic.'

I shook my head, startled into silence. Both of us feeling slightly awkward, we changed the subject.

This conversation stayed with me long after we left the pub. The more I thought about it, the more questions it prompted in my mind. Why was there an assumption that, in order to pursue a career in the arts, my father had to work within a similar field? What did this assumption mean, in terms of recognising how I'd come to a career as a writer, and how I'd earned it? Why did my friend think that for me to be a writer, someone – my father – must have helped me get there? What message does that send about who we think gets to be an artist, and who they need to know to reach that position?

But most of all it got me thinking: what is my relationship to class, and where do I position myself in terms of class privilege? Where, exactly, do I belong when it comes to class and being a writer?

And that led me to my childhood, and living in an 'outsider' or 'marginalised' family.

Let's start at the beginning.

My mum grew up in North Wales, in a small steel town that sometimes makes the headlines when the sector is hit by financial crisis. My granddad worked in the steelworks until Thatcherism and the gutting of Britain's industry left him without a job. He went on to become a deliveryman – this was a running joke in our family because my granddad was a terrible driver who once reversed up a motorway slip road and refused to wear glasses despite his poor eyesight. My nana was a housewife, a dinner lady, and then a warden on a council-run old people's estate. The pair of them settled on this estate after they retired.

My family's background, then, was fairly working class. The town they grew up in is identical to hundreds of towns all over the post-industrial North and North Wales – a town that transitioned from bustling community to one that lost its identity. It's both depressed and depressing.

In 1982 my parents got married, mere days before my dad shipped out to the Falklands War. In the blustery and deadly South Atlantic his ship, the Ardent, was bombed. He survived. Many did not. I came along in 1984, my brother not far behind.

So far, so 1980s childhood. My mum stayed at home to raise us toddlers, my dad was away a lot on the submarines. And then, aged four, my parents split up and my mum came out as a lesbian. We moved in with her new partner, and they have been together ever since. At the same time, illness forced my dad out the Navy and he went on to college to pursue a new career in conservation.

It can be difficult, in these heady days of equal marriage and equality law, to remember just how homophobic society was in the late 1980s and throughout the 1990s – the period in which my brother and I grew up in a gay family. One way to express it is to look at legislation. Growing up, gay adoption was illegal. The age of consent was still 21 for gay men and 16 for straight couples. Civil partnerships weren't introduced until the early '00s; equal marriage seemed an impossible demand. During this time it was still accepted that children could – even should – be removed from their gay mothers if the father contested custody. When my mum came out, sex between men had only been decriminalised 20 years before.

Perhaps most significant for me and my family back in 1988, Section 28 had recently been written into law. This ruling banned what it called the 'promotion of homosexuality' in government-funded organisations. What it meant in practice was the total silencing of conversations and discussions about LGBT issues in schools.

Section 28 effectively outlawed public conversations about families that looked like mine.

I used to joke that my family violated Section 28 by existing. There we were, a happy, healthy, loving gay family. In that happiness and health, I was a walking promotion of the brilliant benefits of homosexuality.

But it was no joke. In truth, Section 28 had a chilling and silencing effect on my family and the few families like mine that existed across the UK. The law sent out a clear message: we were to be avoided and we were not to be talked about. We were a problem. We were not a 'good' family – we were instead a second-class family and children like me would be better off raised by anyone else, so long as that 'anyone else' was straight.

Silencing is a powerful tool. It inhibits your ability to defend yourself. Section 28 prevented my family from being able to push a counter-narrative. I couldn't stand up in school and say to my homophobic classmates that there was nothing wrong with being gay, nothing wrong with having lesbian mums. Because those conversations *simply weren't allowed by law*. And so we grew up almost powerless against the narrative that families like mine were somehow wrong, or deviant, but most of all *second class*.

Of course, one of my parents' most stunning achievements was the way they made sure my brother and I never felt this discrimination when we were children. They provided a loving, stable, and supportive home that cherished us; that encouraged us to be creative and adventurous and outspoken and political.

So it was only, really, as a teenager, that I became aware of how society viewed my family and what their attitudes and prejudices said about our place within it.

It's hard to describe how it feels, living as a teenager surrounded by narratives that tell you there is something wrong
with your family. People publicly and privately expressing the
view that you'll be raised to be a freak, that you should be put
into care, that your parents are somehow disgusting. And when
you're not hearing that, you're being told you don't exist: that
happy, healthy children raised by gay couples are as rare as the
unicorn.

I remember when the nail bomber attacked London's Old
Compton Street and being so frightened that hate crime was
only ever one angry, straight man away. I remember a few years
later when Labour legalised gay adoption and crying over the
newspapers: tears of joy because the law finally recognised that
families like mine could provide caring and loving homes to
children; tears of rage because the passing of the law provoked
editorial after editorial condemning families like mine as un-
healthy and unnatural. Fast forward ten years to the Equal Marriage debates and I had the same experience: joy that this was
finally happening and anger at the blatant, public homophobia
the law provoked. My mum said she cried at the news during
2012; sick of turning on the TV to hear herself talked about as a
second-class citizen, all over again.

As an adult, I was determined to use my experience to end
the silencing inflicted upon my family during the Section 28
years. I wrote editorials in national newspapers and magazines
about the experience of growing up in a gay family, spoke on
the radio about my childhood, talked at conferences about
homophobia, and supported campaigns to prevent the depor-
tation of lesbians to countries where they face persecution.
Having grown up in a world where my family was unspeakable,
I took the decision, finally, to speak.

That's my family story.

But what does any of this have to do with class and being a

writer? What does any of this have to do with the conversation my friend and I had in a sunny beer garden, and the questions her assumptions provoked in me?

I've grown up with a fraught relationship to class.

On the one hand, my family comes from a working class background. There were times during my childhood when life felt precarious. On the other, I've enjoyed many of the privileges associated with being a white, middle class woman: I own my home, I work in the arts, I went to university.

But growing up in a lesbian family in the 1990s meant that you inherently lacked a huge amount of class privilege because you grew up outside of society's class norms. You were demonised in the media. You were ignored by the education system. You were seen as unspeakable, or invisible. You lived under state-sponsored homophobia. You grew up fake laughing at culturally acceptable homophobia. And, day by day, you had that uncanny, uncertain fear that violent personal homophobia was going to come knocking on your door.

As a result, I grew up outside the class system – never really belonging to one class or the other. I never developed that sense of belonging that comes with middle class privilege; that feeling when you can walk into university or your first proper job with that brash sense of having an unquestionable right to be there. Neither did I belong to the communities where my mum grew up and where she had been silenced after coming out. I didn't really fit anywhere: I never met anyone who came from my background. I never met anyone who recognised my experience – who knew how it felt to grow up in a gay family under Section 28. I'm nearly 33 years old and I *still* haven't met anyone who shares that experience with me. I've never had that sense of recognition, of empathy, of *belonging*.

When we talk about class, we talk a lot about belonging. Growing up in a working class community it might be that experience of belonging to a town, an industry, a culture – all of which have, of course, been constantly under attack since I was born. Growing up middle class, there's a privilege of feeling you belong in certain spaces: universities, private schools, media, political or financial jobs. And as for the upper class? Well, you get to belong wherever you go. The world's been designed for you to fit right in.

Growing up outside of class, you're marginalised in a very different and unique way. You don't have that connection to a place or an industry or a shared history and struggle. You don't walk into places believing you have a right to be there. You don't have a shared language or a common experience with a wider community. You're always, just that little bit, on the outside.

There's a distance, then. A distance between me and my working class family roots. And a distance between me and the class I am ostensibly part of, *a middle class whose government spent my childhood denying my family our basic human rights.*

When my friend asked me where my dad taught at university, she made the assumption that to be a writer I must have benefited from my parents' assumed class privilege. Ironically, she is correct. Just not in the way she thought she was.

Growing up outside of class has had a huge and definitive impact on the stories I want to tell and the writing I want to do. I am determined to have the loud, outspoken, rowdy voice that the ruling government of my childhood refused to allow my family and the families that looked like mine. That experience of being silenced, of being *unspeakable,* has had an untold influence on my ambition to write, and to use my writing to tell not just my own story, but the stories that have been ignored or gone unheard.

As a writer, I can carve out the space where, finally, I belong.

What Colour is a Chameleon?

Rym Kechacha

'For last year's words belong to last year's language
And next year's words await another voice.'
– Little Gidding, *Four Quartets*,
T.S. Eliot, 1943

I learnt how to be a chameleon from my mother. Her parents were born in houses without inside toilets, and had both left school by the age of 15. She was born in Hoxton in the early sixties, went to grammar school, got A Levels, was the first person in her family to go to university. As she studied Cervantes and the finer points of the Spanish subjunctive, she also learned that nobody took you seriously if you used a double negative. She discovered that glottal stops were to be discussed in linguistics lectures, not employed in one's own speech. She got a master's degree, became a teacher, bought a house in the suburbs, employed a cleaner. She was so good at changing the colour of her tongue, moving between all the different parts of her life without getting stuck on the chasms between. You're middle class now, she used to tell me in her cockney accent. I got my grant to go to university and now I'm middle class and you are too. I'm the story of social mobility in the twentieth century, and now you're beyond snobbery or prejudice. You can do whatever you want to do and nobody will ever know where you came from.

I believed her then, but now I know her to be wrong. People always know where I come from. My mother tongue tells them.

Naturally, my father is a chameleon too. His tongue was colonised from the second he stepped into a school building at six years old, and it has never become free. He was born into a wealthy family in Algeria just as his father was fighting against the French occupation. He spoke French at school and Algerian Arabic to his mother, who could not read, write or speak French. He arrived in Britain a dark-skinned immigrant of ambiguous origin. He learnt English at a language school in Leicester Square, working in restaurants at night. Forty years later, I found his notebooks from those lessons. Pages and pages filled with English idioms, neatly copied in a childish handwriting he no longer possessed. You're the apple of my eye, it's raining cats and dogs out there, costs an arm and a leg. I imagined of a roomful of newcomers earnestly copying these phrases from a squeaky blackboard, mouthing the strange vowel sounds, daydreaming about the day when they will lose their accents and use these very same phrases and be mistaken for English men and women.

My father learned to speak two versions of this English language: one that corresponded to the type of French he spoke – cool, clear and slightly old fashioned, each syllable enunciated, never using any slang. He used this with people he thought were posh, like our teachers at school, or the doctor. Then he learned the common English, the one he spoke to my mum, the one he would use with the bloke behind the counter in the petrol station. This English made a joke out of the people who couldn't pronounce his name, this English mocked people with four-wheel drives, this English insisted he was just a poor immigrant, trying to make a living in this big bad Anglo-Saxon world.

They got upset, my mum and dad, when their little chameleons, growing up in Essex, went around boldly displaying their baby colours. They berated my brother and I for losing our Ts and our Hs, tutted when we seasoned our speech with innits, winced theatrically with each ain't that plopped from our mouths. Please speak properly, what will people think of you, I'll wash your mouth out with soap if you're not careful.

I thought they were hypocrites. They didn't speak proper, why should I? Why should my mum lose the letter H from her words when talking to the cleaner and mysteriously find it again when she talked to a colleague? Why should she swear on the phone to my gran but put on her posh voice when she spoke to the gas company? Why should my dad insist that butter takes two Ts, when he had not spoken either of them yesterday when he asked me to fetch it from the fridge?

Their tongues had private colours and public colours, and it seemed like the mark of ultimate inauthenticity that they should be able to switch between them without a hitch in their breath.

But when I went out into the world, and my colours came in, I began to understand the multicoloured tones of my parents' tongues.

> *[Received Pronunciation is] 'the everyday speech in the families of Southern English persons whose men-folk [have] been educated at the great public boarding schools.'*
> – *English Pronouncing Dictionary (1st Edition),* Daniel Jones, 1917

The tongue is an honest muscle, it never stays still. When you exercise it by speaking a certain way, it gets stronger and more versatile, but it always holds a memory of how it used to move. The ear, however, is sly. It is composed of cartilage surrounding an empty space, waiting for words and sounds to fill it. The ear is curious, ambitious. It cannot help itself. It always wants to hear more.

When I started to mix with people from all over the country, aged about 16 when I went to ballet school, I began to speak differently. I didn't do it on purpose, and nobody ever asked me to change my accent, but slowly my language began to reorient itself. My vowels became softer, I spoke more often the way I wrote, I used less slang. My everyday speech slipped away from the nouveau Cockney I'd grown up speaking and towards a generic Estuary English. Before long, I used no slang at all, and my grandmother asked me who I was hanging around with. Just the dancers at school, I said. You sound posh, she sniffed. You're doing Received Pronunciation. They're gonna put you on the radio soon.

I've thought about that term a lot. Received Pronunciation. RP. It conjures so many images of repression, so many censored tongues. The rain in Spain, rows about regional accents on the BBC, canings for carelessly short As. The phrase describes a transaction of power. Those who have power give, magnanimously, an accepted way of speaking. Those who do not have power take, gratefully, this accent which they are assured will help them 'get on' in their lives.

But is RP a gift, or is it a loan? Should a Receiver of Pronunciation go forth into the world a changed being, their tongue transformed from base lead into an eloquent gold, forever elevated from their working class status by this new accent? Or, should a Receiver of Pronunciation treat it like a magic talisman, to be kept safe in a velvet lined box and only dusted off and deployed when appearing working class is a disadvantage?

RP has been developing for centuries. In 1066, the Normans invaded this island and, overnight, the language of power, commerce and learning shifted to medieval French. Over the past thousand years, medieval French and the Old English it replaced have merged into the English that we use today, although that merger has proved uneasy. For many concepts in English, there remains a lower register word that descends from the Anglo-Saxon, and a higher register word that claims a Latin origin. I say smell, you say odour. I say want, you say desire. I say wild, you say savage. When we want to be more formal or sound intelligent, whether we intend to or not, we switch our vocabulary to favour Latinate words brought here by the Normans.

The Industrial Revolution created mass movements of people around the country, increased urbanisation and brought the tentative beginnings of universal literacy. The creation of a bourgeoisie also created an epic panic about language, for how were the powerful to tell who was the right sort anymore, if any old idiot with a loom or a ship or a nous for lending was going about like a lord? Easy: by the words on their tongue. For these wealth generators of the eighteenth and nineteenth centuries, RP was a one-way street. They had to do everything they could to masquerade as anciently noble to be accepted, and stopping their tongues from betraying them was the first and last job of every day.

The twentieth century was supposed to bring an end to all that. The post-war reforms allowed a generation access to higher education and a golden age of prosperity, and equality of experience and opportunity became realistic ideas to aim for.

But for me, and for so many others, it hasn't worked out that way. The story of RP is one of many wrong tongues and only one right one. RP is a cloud stretching above everyone, no matter the nuances of their accent. It does not care how well off your family in Liverpool Leeds Manchester Cardiff are, it only cares about the length of your vowels. So, it is the twentieth century, with its sagas of tribe merging and the reinvention of what identity can mean, that has seen an explosion in the number of chameleon people. The first-generation degree holder, dropping back into their childhood accent with their grandparents. The second-generation immigrant schoolchild, translating at their parent's evenings for mums and dads. Anyone from anywhere north or west of the M25 who pronounces letter sounds in their phonetically most likely way.

Sociolinguists call this 'code-switching' and say that it is natural, to a certain extent, but can indicate 'linguistic insecurity'. The American linguist William Labov noted that members of the lower middle class were most likely to experience linguistic insecurity. Not surprising. For they know that everything that goes up, eventually must come down.

> *'It is the business of educated people to speak so that no one may be able to tell in what county their childhood was passed.'*
> – *Recitation. A Handbook for Teachers in Public Elementary School*, A. Burrell, 1891

The story of code-switching in our times isn't only one of talking to an imagined 'up', doing one's best approximation of RP to impress upon teachers, potential employers, the lady on the phone at HMRC your admirable qualities and seriousness. For so many of us, it is also a story of talking to an imagined 'down'.

Why might this be so? Why, for perhaps the first time in social history, does it confer social capital to speak in an accent that implies less wealth, less status, less power? Why might we want someone to know that we have a working class background in modern Britain?

The clue's right there. *Working* class.

In medieval feudal thought, a person belonged where they were born. God, or some other deity, had ordained that everyone had their place, and to stray from it would be a sin. The modern era changed all that. It became a virtue to be striving for something higher and better in this earthly life, not waiting for one's rewards in the next one.

Working, working really hard, labouring exhaustedly at whatever society deems worth labouring for became the celebrated way of being. And wealth, power, and status are what society deems worth labouring for.

To be able to code-switch into any kind of working class accent means that you're a striver. It means that you didn't inherit your advantages, that you have a real-life rags to riches story. It's why business tycoons on the television call people mate. It's why politicians, trying to appear as down-to-earth-kind-of-blokes, will discuss the price of a pint of milk in election season.

But what about the rest of us? What about those of us who have not managed to buy our way out of snobbery and are judged both on our working class accents and our lack of them?

That's where the chameleon comes in. It's the reptilian fight-or-flight instinct, mixed with acute mammalian social anxiety, switching the colour of your tongue before you can think about it, or protest, or bring linguistics into the conversation.

You want your grandparents to be proud of you, but you don't want them to hoot with laughter when you open your mouth. Listen to you, with that posh accent you've picked up at that fancy university, speaking like the Queen. Think you're better than us now, don't you? You want to be real with the man on the fruit stall in the market, you want him to know that you don't think you're better than him. Look, you want to say. I wasn't always the bloke in the suit with the hybrid car and the organic kale juice you see before you. And I've got the rhyming slang to prove it.

Perhaps this chameleon tongue is a good thing. Manipulating words to make them do what you want them to do is an essential part of learning how to be a person in the world. We all gain when the barrier between dialects and different ways of speaking becomes porous, and the distances between us can be explained, understood and bridged. The more words and phrases that we have to express the vast range of experience available to beings in this world, the richer all our worlds will become.

And yet.

Who wants to be the person who constantly has to change to be accepted? Who wants to be the person who cannot speak first in a conversation for fear of setting the tone too low, or too high, and never being able to hitch to the right register again? Who wants to be the chameleon who doesn't know what colour she truly is?

The allure of being able to speak to everyone in the same way, without fear of being assessed for your worth on the basis of your accent feels utopian. Language is one of our best tools for expressing what we've got inside us, and discovering what treasures others might be harbouring too. We are only trying to connect, to find our tribe. We desperately don't want to be Other. It's the driving force behind so much of human behaviour, and so we will do anything to fit in to any group we find ourselves in. And we have all become so good at it.

My father achieved his holy grail and eradicated his accent, but those idioms still elude him. You are my flesh and bone, you can take the donkey to water but you can't make it shit, tell it to the grapevine. There's a strange poetry in his mangled words, but I can't hear it while I'm watching the smirks. He thinks he is passing for a native speaker. He tells me proudly that he speaks better English than the English, but he has missed the point. He has been betrayed, by the very tongue he tried to train; and whether they know it or not, his audience has Othered him for it.

A few years ago, I was in a cosmetics shop with my mother. A chalkboard sign was advertising pungent shampoo using an apostrophe for a plural. She shuddered, and grabbed a shop assistant by the arm. You've got your apostrophe wrong, she said, and the shop assistant put on the same face she puts on for any complaint. We're so sorry about that, she said. I'll send someone over straight away to fix it.

I don't know if she did. I don't think she cared that much. I don't even think my mum cared if it was fixed or not, she just wanted people to know that she knew how to wield an apostrophe.

I have a telephone voice. I no longer drop my Hs like I used to, and I try to enunciate every T. I try to use considered and varied vocabulary to express myself. But then I am at a party and I'm asked if I'm Australian and I begin to get flustered. Caught. Something in my mammalian communication centre was telling me I should talk up, so I tried, but I did it wrong. I did not pass as a member of the questioner's tribe. I Othered myself. My tongue Othered me.

You are middle class now, I hear my mother saying in her cockney accent. You are middle class because I went to university. I grew up believing her, but now I have heard too many people frown when they hear me speak, too many people assume I haven't read that book they're talking about, had too many conversations that start, but where are you from? I mean, really from?

Now I know that no one is fooled about my origins, and I don't even know if I want them to be.

Every day, my tongue turns chameleon, shifting whenever it finds the landscape changing. I don't tell it to, any more than I tell my heart to beat or my lungs to expand, but I don't know if it even works. But I would like to know what colour my tongue is. I'd like to know what it is I have to say to the world, and how it is that I should truly say it. And I wouldn't mind seeing the true colours of anyone else's tongue, either, if they'd be brave enough to show me.

You're Not Working Class

Nathan Connolly

When Antony Calvert, Conservative Party candidate for Wakefield, tweeted about a self-described 'working class' man confronting him in the street, he made the wry observation that the man said this as he was walking into a Costa Coffee.[1] Clearly, the man could not be working class if he splurged on lattes and cappuccinos like some metropolitan elite. The working class drink mugs of milky, sugary tea and they drink it at home or in cheap cafes because they can't afford anything else. Such is their lot in life.

Last year I was prompted to put together *Know Your Place*, a collection of essays about the working class written by the working class, specifically for this reason. It was barely a month after

---

1. antony_calvert. (2017, April 17). Man recognises me at #Wakefield Westgate. "These f*ckin Tories, always looking 2 trample on t'working class, like me". Man walks into Costa. [Tweet]. https://twitter.com/antony_calvert/status/853880478117617665

the EU referendum and, despite being a dismayed liberal elite, I was also a working class lad in the working class heartland of Liverpool.

Liverpool voted to remain, despite being working class. I voted to remain, despite being working class, despite occasionally feeling guilty after buying a Costa I can't afford, despite working in publishing. The contradictions stacked up, and, while the working class were demonised and scapegoated as the uneducated masses that brought us to this catastrophic point, I heard remarkably little from the working class themselves.

Over 30% of parliamentary candidates are privately educated. 71% of senior judges. In the media, where I'm sure everyone gets a Costa on their way to work in the morning, that figure is 44%. Newspaper columnists will find that 43% of themselves were privately educated.

These figures aren't worrying if you believe that a working class youth who educates themselves and goes to university and gets a job in the media, or is elected to parliament, automatically stops being working class and becomes middle class. Because that view ties into a vision of the UK that we would all like to believe. It is an upwardly mobile country where the only thing holding you back from success is your own ability: if you don't want to be working class, then don't be.

That vision of this nation ignores a lot of things, but perhaps most importantly, it ignores the experience of what being working class actually is. It ignores the experience of walking into a room and knowing that you don't belong in that room. It ignores, like many things, how often the working class are ignored. It ignores all the people who drag themselves from their bed to try to make their life better and try, try, try to make their children's lives better. It ignores their frustration, their exhaustion and it ignores their requests for help. It tells them to just try harder…

I work in publishing. I tried to work in publishing for a long time, but I was told that I needed to move to London and take an unpaid internship. When I told supportive people that I couldn't do that, I always wondered if perhaps I just wasn't trying hard enough. In the end I set up my own publishing house.

Does that make me middle class now? If it does, then it ignores all of the social, cultural and economic limitations that initially held me back. Does that all vanish now? Is the slate wiped clean? Does all the work my working class mother did to educate me and get me to go to university and support me mean that now I'm middle class? Or, is it something as simple as Costa coffee and avocados for lunch that makes you middle class?

When this article is published will I be accused of being middle class? You could find a reason, I'm sure. I did go to university. I do like avocados. There is a vision of the working class that we like to cling to: a romanticised, fetishised idea that is still rooted somewhere around the publication of *The Road to Wigan Pier* in 1937, an account of working class life written by a man educated at Eton.

Delegitimising the working class is a step towards removing working class voices. If we want working class writers, actors, politicians, and judges – and if we want those institutions to understand working class life – then we need to expect the working class to be educated and intelligent, perhaps even cultured, perhaps even partial to a high-street coffee chain latte. Otherwise, we're just telling them to know their place.

Acknowledgements

This book has been a joy to work on, but it has also been considerably more work than I first anticipated when sending that original tweet to Nikesh Shukla. It would be no exaggeration to say that this book wouldn't be here, or being quite so widely read, if it weren't for all of that original enthusiasm that we received when we started. *Know Your Place* genuinely has been a team effort and I'm grateful for all of the help.

Therefore, it only remains to acknowledge those who helped us along the way. I should begin with Nikesh, whose original tweet prompted all of this, and whose early advice helped us get it going.

This book has also benefited from the amazing support of the UK's literature festivals who have championed it, in particular Kate Feld of Manchester's The Real Story who was a backer and vocal supporter from the very beginning.

In fact, much of the UK's literature sector were supporters of this book and deserve to be thanked for their generous sense of community and companionship. Most important are the independent publishers who are a constant source of support and inspiration: Bluemoose Books, Comma Press, And Other Stories, Peepal Tree Press, Influx Press, Galley Beggar, Dodo Ink and 404 Ink.

I'm also indebted to Margot at Kickstarter, Yvonne Singh for her *Guardian* piece and Sam at *The Pool*.

And… it's with great shame that I admit I was not responsible for the title of *Know Your Place*, as that honour actually belongs to Andrew McMillan.

Finally, and most importantly, is Amelia, who brought this book to life.

Crowdfunding

We funded *Know Your Place* through a crowdfunding campaign on Kickstarter. All of the people listed overleaf backed this book before it was real, and it is because of them that you are able to read this book today. Dead Ink and I owe them a great deal of gratitude for helping to make our original vision a reality.

Thank you.

Adam Farrer

Adelle Stripe

Agnes Bookbinder

Agnieszka Czepulis-Rastenis

Aidan Baker

Aisha Jiagoo

Aki Schilz

Alasdair Mathieson

Alex Blott

Alex Burton-Keeble

Alex Koss

Alfred C. Bie

Ali-Breeze King

Alice Davis

Alice Fischer

Alice Stringer

Alžběta Franková

Amanda Coe

Amanda Gavin

Amanda Nixon

Amber Greenall-Heffernan

Amy Story

Amy Wong

Andrew B. Wootton

Andrew Kenrick

Andy Haigh

Angela Malone

Angelis

Anna Beecher

Anna marlen-summers

Anneliese O'Malley

Anthony Gaughan

Ariel Lo

Arlene Finnigan

Ash Lyons

Austen Harris

Ava Ijeoma Charles

Ayyub Imtiaz

Bamidele Adewuyi

Barbara Harper

Barry Newman

Becca Inglis

Ben Finley

Benjamin Kritikos

Bethan Highgate-Betts

Bex Hughes

Blair Rose

Bobbi Boyd

Brian Smasal

Buster Blue

Caitie-Jane Cook

Caleb Stitzel

Carina Bird

Caro Ernst

Carrie Gibson

Catharine Braithwaite

Charles Browne-Cole

Charles Morris

Chia-Yi Hou

Chloe Taylor

Chris & Caitlin Grieves

Chris Parkinson

Chris van Gorder

Christine Henry

Claire L. Heuchan

Christine Stephenson

Claire Fisher

Claire L. Heuchan

Claire Squires

Colin Wilkinson

Collette Bird

Corinne Goodman

Craig Forshaw

Curtis James

D Franklin

Daiden O'Regan

Dan Coxon

Daniel Carpenter

Daniel Ross

Danielle Child

Danielle Culling

Danny Mendoza

Darren Connolly

Dave and Anne Cordery

David Bell

David Ewing

David Hebblethwaite

David Hull

David King

David Milo Fryling

David Pichardo Aguirre

David Proctor

Debbie Prior

Des Malone

Di Leedham

Douglas Gallacher

Dylan Rivers

Eireni Moutoussi

Elena Morgan

Eley Williams

Elizabeth Billinger

Elizabeth Lovatt

Elizabeth Wynn

Emily Benita

Emily Griffith

Emily Morris

Emily Oram

Emma Barlow

Emma Benson

Emma Tomlinson

Eric Haines

Erin Catriona Farley

Esta Rae

Euan Monaghan

Eugene De Rozario

Fabian Way

Farhan Samanani

Farzana Khan

Fausto Llopis Pena

Fay Rebecca

Fergus Evans

Fiona Gell

Fiz Osborne

Fizzy Oppe

Frances Sleigh

Frank & Sally Kania

G Isaac

Gabriel D Parr

Garrie Fletcher

Gary Kaill

Gemma Harris

Gemma Holgate

Gemma Sowerby

Gena-mour Barrett

Georgia Smith

Geraldine Mallinson

Giuliana Viglione

Glenn Saitch

Gordon Anderson

Graham Beer

Graham Eatough

Greg Bowman

Greg Healey

H

Hannah Jewell

Hannah Simpson

Haroun Khan

Harriet King

Harry Gallon

Harry Sideras

Heather McDaid

Heidi Gardner

Helen Binder

Helen Bradbury

Hilary Alexander

Hilary Bell

Holly Godwin

Iain Aitch

Ian McMillan

Ian Urquhart

Irene and Roy Coker

Irreverence Inc.

Isabel Costello

Isabelle Veysey

J. Davis

J&L Jackson

Jack Redfern

Jack Windle

Jacqueline Lee

Jacqueline Rice

James Green

James Marsters

James Ockenden

James Patton

James Smith

Jamie Hewitt

Jane Alexander

Jason H. Luna

JC Hoskins

Jeff Holiday

Jennifer Walden

Jessica Badger

Jessica Bowyer

Jill Murphy

JJ Bola

Jo Unwin

Joanna McMinn

Joanna Moult

Joanne Lee

Jodie Lampert

Jodie Lewis

John Eden

Jon Aitken

Jon Auty

Jonathan Ruppin

Jonathan Wakeham

Josef Matschy

Joshua & Stefania Davis

Joshua Beever

Julia Curtin

Julia Haase

Julia Kingsford

Juliet Pickering

Juliette Holmes

Justin Olmedo

Justine Taylor

Karen McKay

Karl Deckard

Karl Henry

Kate Chambers

Kate Feld

Katherine J. Wilkinson

Katherine Mackinnon

Katt Frisch

Keith Ramsey

Kelly Schweizer

Kevin Leo Duffy

Kholoud Alqutub

Kimberly Hamilton

Kirstin Lamb

Kirsty Connell-Skinner

Kirsty Marie McNeill

Kirsty Murray

Kit Caless

Kovács Róbert Dániel

Kristopher Doyle

Kush Bylykbashi

L Fellows

Laura Bryars

Laura Charlton

Laura Clay

Laura Fisher

Laura Harker

Laura Jones

Laura Wright

Linda Ewen

Lindsay R. Taylor

Lindsey Matthews

Lindsey Tyson-Green

Lisa Roberts

Lisa Rull

Lizzie Huxley-Jones

Louie Stowell

Louise Bucher

Louise Hutcheson

Lucy Moffatt

Lucy R. Hinnie

Lulu Allison

Lynds Fineran

M H Mays

Maggie Edgington

Mairi Oliver

MAMDP at UWE

Marcus Brownlow

Margot Atwell

Maria Fusco

Maria Kaffa

@markoneinfour

Mark A Chambers

Mark Nicholas Wales

Martin Geraghty

Martina Zandonella

Mary Grover

Mary Young

Matt Black

Matt Harris

Matt Locke

Matt Stone

Maxine Blane

Megan Boing

Meghan Reed Gordon

Melanie J McPhail

Michael H Whitworth

Michael Langan

Michaela Deas

Michelle Marshall

Miguel Angel Coello Cetina

Mike Murphy

Mike West

Ms. V. G.

Naomi Booth

Naomi Frisby

Natalie W (Well Blactually)

Natasha R. Chisdes

Ned Eironwy Jones

Neil Chue Hong

New Writing North

Nic Sage

Nicasio Andres Reed	Peter Jackson
Nicola Joanne Lees	Peter Sutton
Nicola Mostyn	Philip Matusavage
Nigel Atoxic	Poppy Peacock
Nigel S. Cowan	Rachael Laburn
Nikesh Shukla	Rachel Cant
Nikki Jewell	Rachel Craddock
Noel Johnson	Rachel Darling
Nora Mouallali	Rachel Heath
Nudge Staden	Rachel Miller
Nyle Connolly	Rachel Moody
Octavia Bright	Raef Boylan Esq.
Olivia Phipps	Ramsey Kechacha
Oo Sheng Hui	Raymond Newman
Oscar Carballal Prego	Rebecca Kleanthous
Owen Treacher	Rebecca McCormick
Patricia Anne Giverin	Rhiannon Kaye
Paul Climie	Rich Walker
Paul Hancock	Richard Kemble
Paul Howarth	Richard Sheehan
Paul Long	RL McCormick
Paul Michael Clarke	Rob Fordham
Paul Rutherford	Robert Swan
Peggy Hughes	Robin Hargreaves

Robin Vandome	Sarah-Jane Roberts
Robyn Drury	Scott Kroyer
Roisein McNulty	Shaheen Jiagoo
Roman Hermanek	Shane Boothby
Rory Foster	Shane W Berry
Ros Bell	Shelley Harris
Rosalind May	Simon Middleton
Rosie Canning	Simon Niklasson
Rosie Clarke	SJ Bradley
Ross Annesley	SJ Holgate
Ross Jeffery	Sladjana ivanis
Ross Madgwick	Sophie Cameron
Russell Johnston	Sophie Cormack
Ruth Urbom	Sophie Goldsworthy
S. Lee	Sophie Hannah
Sandra Djuzic	Sophie Hopesmith
Sandy Mayers-Green	Sophie McKeand
Sandy Wilkie	Spencer Fothergill
Sara Zo	Stephen Blankenship
Sarah Barlow	Stephen Kelman
Sarah Franklin	Steve Spittle
Sarah Garnham	Susan Barker
Sarah Hamilton	Susan Sinclair
Sarah Watkins	Suzanne Lee

Tamar Millen

Tara Shepersky

Tara Sibson

Tasha Turner

Terence Hogan

The Selkie Delegation

Thom Rawson

Thomas Joseph Wood

Thomas Sargeant

Tiffany Marcheterre

Tiia Ylosmaki

Tiril Pollard

Tom Coles

Tom Coll

Tom McKay

Tom Plaskon

Tom Prior

Tom Vlietstra

Tracey Connolly

Vanessa Bellaar Spruijt

Vanessa Kotiadis

Varun Mangla

Victoria Haslam

Vikki O'Neill

Vikki Reilly

W. R. Saavedra

Wei Ming Kam

Wordscapes

Yasmine Awwad

Yvonne Singh

Zeba Talkhani

Zoe Blackburn

The Kit de Waal Scholarship

A number of the authors featured in this book have kindly donated their fee to the *Kit de Waal Scholarship*. The scholarship funds marginalised writers to study Creative Writing at *Birkbeck, University of London*. If you want to support working class writers, the creators of this book would like to direct you to Kit's scholarship. More details can be found on the *Birkbeck, University of London* website.

About Dead Ink...

Dead Ink is a small, ambitious and experimental literary publisher based in Liverpool.

Supported by Arts Council England, we're focused on developing the careers of new and emerging authors.

We believe that there are brilliant authors out there who may not yet be known or commercially viable. We see it as Dead Ink's job to bring the most challenging and experimental new writing out from the underground and present it to our audience in the most beautiful way possible.

Our readers form an integral part of our team. You don't simply buy a Dead Ink book, you invest in the authors and the books you love.

www.deadinkbooks.com

Contents

To Alexandra, with whom the sun shines
twenty-four hours a day

and to the memory of my mother, an explorer
of the farthest regions of grace

Acknowledgments

I t takes the help of many people to complete such solitary pursuits as writing a book or sledding across Ellesmere.

I'd like to single out: In Norway, Kåre Berg, Per Egil Hegge, and especially Susan Barr for their hospitality and for offering their thoughts on Otto Sverdrup. In England, the great Geoffrey Hattersley-Smith and also William Mills and Shirley Sawtell of the Scott Polar Research Institute. In Sweden, Sven-Åke Jonasson for so freely sharing his Björling material. In Poland, crustacean researcher Jan-Marcin Weslawski. In Russia, the late Valery Kondratkov. In Greenland, Torben Diklev, Inalunguaq Joelsen and David Qaavigaq. In the United States, Janet Baldwin at the Explorers Club library in New York, Len Bruno at the Library of Congress, Philip N. Cronenwett and John Schwoerke at Dartmouth College, Genevieve LeMoine and the librarians at Bowdoin College, to Robert Bryce, for patiently fielding dozens of e-mails. Leonard Guttridge, Tom and Kathy Hornbein, Mary Kunzler-Larmann, David Mech, Paul Schurke, and John Tierney. I'd like to thank Bowdoin College Library for permission to quote from the journal of Fitzhugh Green, and Dartmouth College Library for permission to quote from George Rice's journal. A special thanks to W.L. Gore & Associates for the Shipton-Tilman grant that allowed me to reach Krüger country on southwestern Axel Heiberg.

The Canadian list is particularly daunting, but I'd like to say a word about three generous people. Lory James and her hardworking crew at Banff Designs provided the clothing that has allowed me to travel Ellesmere without a single case of frostbite. Bob Davies, formerly of Canadian Airlines and now with First Air, took a personal interest and has been essential in helping me fly north every year, sometimes with twelve pieces of baggage. And in conversation after conversation, Renee Wissink, former Chief Park Warden of Quttinirpaaq National Park, dazzled me with his knowledge and understanding of the island. Truly, a warden of the old school.

Others who gave of their stories and time, or with whom I enjoyed Ellesmere moments, include: Seeglook Akeeagok, Scott Akin, Jim Allan, Larry Audaluk, William Barr, Carolyn Bateman, Lyle Dick, Miles Ecclestone, John England, David Gray, Anne Gunn, Richard Harington, Vicki Hurst, Peter Jess, Terry Jesudason, Aziz Kheraj, Tom Kitchin, Peter Kobalenko, Janis Kraulis, Waldemar Lehn, Graeme Magor, Karen McCullough, Al McDonald, John McDonald, Doug McLeod, Elaine Mellor, Frank Miller, Jeffrey Qanaq, Peter Schledermann, Martin Silverstone, Josef Svoboda, Ray Thorsteinsson, Cameron Treleaven, Barry Troke, Karl Z'berg, and all of the Royal Canadian Mounted Police officers in Grise Fiord over the last fourteen years.

The charismatic Boyce Partridge of Operation Hurricane in Eureka gave good company, a flight to the fossil forest, and a surprise care package of ham sandwiches that showed up in Alexandra Fiord just as I had OD'd on peanut butter. Major Stéphane Marcoux hosted Alexandra and me in Alert, and the Honorable Art Eggleton, Canada's Minister of National Defence, gave us the rare privilege of visiting the station. James Little, the editor of *Explore* magazine, picked up the substantial tab for my Björling adventure. Martin Fortier of the North Water project and Richard Dubois, captain of the *Pierre Radisson*, allowed me to experience Ellesmere by ship.

I'd never applied for a writing grant before, but as this project stretched into a marathon trek, anything short of robbing banks became fair game. The Canada Council and the Writer's Reserve program of the Ontario Arts Council helped at critical junctures. The Leighton Studios program at The Banff Centre provided a little cabin in the woods where some of these chapters were written. Denise Bukowski convinced publishers in North America to believe in a project without an obvious "overarching narrative." My photography agents, First Light in Toronto and Stone/Getty Images in Seattle, sold enough of my wilderness imagery to buy me that most important research tool, time.

A note on spelling: Explorers rendered the names of their Inuit companions in a variety of creative ways. Today there are accepted orthographies, but they sometimes make these historic figures unrecognizable. For clarity, I've opted for traditional spellings: Peeawahto instead of Piuaatsoq, Kudlooktoo rather than Qilluttooq, and so on.

Finally, I'd like to thank my editors, Melanie Fleishman and Kathy Beyer. And most of all, my partner in daily life and in extreme journeys, Alexandra.

"No climate can rightly be considered good, though bananas and yams may flourish, if men decay."

—Vilhjalmur Stefansson

"Like land of mystery in a dream or gateway to a forbidden world of untrodded wonder."

—H. P. Lovecraft

Greely   Rice   Peary   Cook

Nares   Sverdrup   Stein   Green

Björling   Krüger   Nukapinguaq   Joy

Stallworthy   Wissink   Hattersley-Smith   Akeeagok

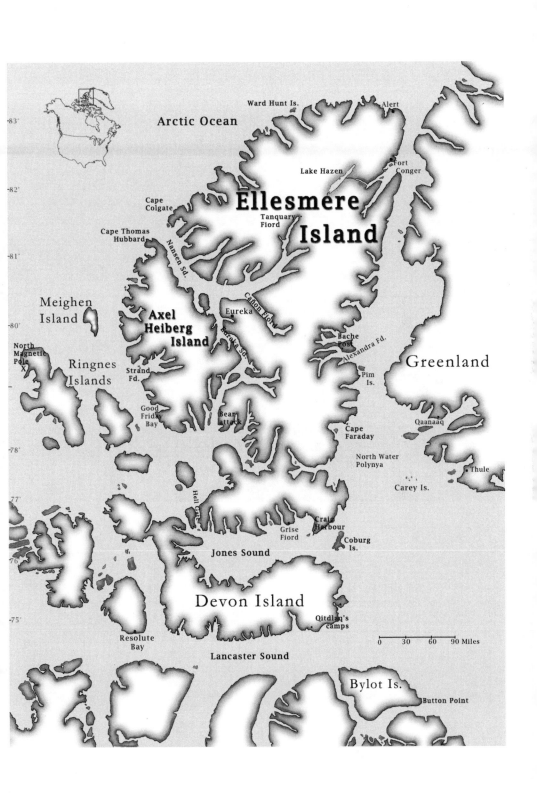

Arctic Ocean

Ward Hunt Is.

Alert

Fort
Conger

Lake Hazen

Cape
Colgate

**Ellesmere
Island**

Tanquary
Fiord

Cape Thomas
Hubbard

Nansen Sd.

Cañon Fiord

Eureka

Bache
Post

Alexandra Fd.

Greenland

Meighen
Island

**Axel
Heiberg
Island**

Eureka Sd.

North
Magnetic
Pole
X

Ringnes
Islands

Strand
Fd.

Pim
Is.

Bean
attack

Good
Friday
Bay

Cape
Faraday

Qaanaaq

North Water
Polynya

Thule

Carey Is.

Hell Gate

Craig
Harbour

Grise
Fiord

Coburg
Is.

Jones Sound

Devon Island

Qitdlag's
camps

Resolute
Bay

0   30   60   90 Miles

Lancaster Sound

Bylot Is.

Button Point

The Coast Guard icebreaker *Pierre Radisson* in arctic mist.

Prologue

The pack ice ground together with a comforting shriek. Crashing waves snapped an antenna near the bow, and sparks flew from a wire. I clung with both hands to the railing above the wheelhouse as the snow flailed. To the east winked the low specks of the Carey Islands, where two young explorers vanished in 1892. To the west, the maw of Makinson Inlet, where Inuit migrants endured a winter of starvation and murder. All along Ellesmere Island's austere coast, glaciers never trodden covered land never seen, framing stories never told.

Home at last.

Home is not where you live, it's where you belong. To me, the cold of Ellesmere Island was invigorating, its solitude lyrical. Its historic tragedies had a reality that current events did not. Here, the ice age still lived, shaggy relics called muskoxen pawed for dark lichen, and the last camps of explorers stood as if freshly abandoned, the inhabitants swallowed up moments before by some arctic Bermuda Triangle.

Where is Ellesmere Island? Think of the little metal disk that sits on top of a globe: Ellesmere is under that. Over the past fifteen years, I have put in some 3,500 human-powered miles here—more than any known traveler except the great Greenlander, Nukapinguaq. But I was not on foot now. I was on the *Pierre Radisson*, a Canadian Coast Guard icebreaker helping scientists from Canada, the United States, and Japan study the North Water polynya. Ellesmere science fascinated me as much as Ellesmere history but ships are terrible conveyances. I sympathized with those Inuit who left an explorer's ship after a single day because they found life on board oppressive and its comforts upsetting.

Space was liberal on this 105-yard behemoth, privacy adequate, food excellent. The captain was a gentlemanly French-Canadian who let off steam by giving tango lessons in the officers' lounge, and passengers and crew alike were bright and friendly. Still, I understood why so many naval arctic expeditions had ended in disaster. Ships were societies of the sedentary. Nightly dancing in a smoky bar was the only physical relief; the least active ones, it seemed, danced the best. I put in polite appearances but always felt like a wallflower at the prom and soon slunk away to pace the outside decks in the deepening polar night. Now and then, as on this stormy afternoon, I glimpsed the world I sought. Onshore lay a life of perpetual motion across a gloriously agoraphilic landscape. Here on the *Pierre Radisson*, I had never felt so close to home, yet so far away.

Every day, researchers lowered a large circular framework called a rosette into the ocean. Tubes with radio-controlled lids collected water and plankton at various depths. After dividing the samples, the mostly postgraduate chemists retreated to their sheet-metal trailers that had been temporarily soldered onto the *Radisson's* deck and hurriedly processed their data before the next rosette cast. "People back in Quebec said to me, 'You're lucky, you're going to the Arctic,'" declared a marvelously obsessed expatriate Iranian named Behzad. "I told them, 'We see nothing. We work.'"

Indeed, most spent their days in darkened labs cluttered with flasks and laptop computers and pails of what looked like tiny shrimp and wriggling grains of rice. I'd studied science at university but had given it up, feeling that, as Rimbaud put it, "I know what work is, and science does not move quickly enough." Behzad had zeal and urgency and a razor-sharp mind, but many others seemed to be methodically stockpiling data that was only tenuously connected to the Big Picture, any Big Picture.

I'd heard of extremophiles before this journey. Magnificent word, denoting microscopic creatures, usually bacteria, that not only survived under extreme conditions but needed extreme conditions to survive. Not for them, the beguiling comfort of room temperature. They sought the extremes of pressure, salinity, or temperature that other creatures avoided. Tissues laced with natural antifreeze, they could be frozen solid without their cells rupturing. They thrived in the superheated steam baths beside volcanic vents. Ocean pressures that could crush nuclear submarines were feather kisses to them.

They were the metaphor of Ellesmere. Here, the explorers, the animals, the plants, the very rocks were extremophiles. In this topsy-turvy world, the compass pointed west. For much of the year, the sun shone either twenty-four hours a day or not at all. No middle road. It was cold or hot; it was night or day; it was stunningly calm or terrifyingly violent.

Home.

The sort of place you either loved or hated. Lukewarm feelings were for tepid climes.

There are many such places. "This desert, all deserts, any desert," declared Edward Abbey. His true love was the vast American Southwest. I had felt the pull of this desert as well, but Ellesmere was special. Over the last two centuries many had heard its siren call.

No, Ellesmere was not just one of a hundred interchangeable deserts. It's easy to fall in love with a place, but it's what you have in common that sustains the relationship. Ellesmere's physical beauty, its cold, its nontechnical terrain, its isolation, its tolerant wildlife, its twenty-four hour sunshine, its unwalked expanses, its alien flavor, all felt like a purer form of my own inner geography.

Jody Deming was the chief U.S. scientist on the *Radisson*. She specialized in extremophiles and had come to investigate whether cold-loving bacteria, or their enzymes, functioned in Baffin Bay's 30°F sea water. She too was an extremophile and she came to symbolize for me the people who were drawn here.

Like her microscopic subjects, she sent out enzymes that broke down the barriers of everyone on board. At forty-seven, she was as open with us as a young woman sharing her deepest feelings with her best friends. Deming was at a convulsive time in her life. She was exploring aspects of her womanhood as exuberantly as she investigated her benthic microbes. ("Maybe microbiologists are so immersed in biology that we're not afraid to explore our own.") She had dyed her hair and pierced her ears for the first time. She confessed to enjoying the novel sensation of PMS.

Deming was so talented and successful that she'd overcome most of her early low self-esteem. But a sweet vulnerability remained. After a conversation which spanned everything from the Texas ranch where she grew up to jealousy among scientists of the highest caliber, I felt deeply privileged, until I spotted Deming, half an hour later, in an equally intense discussion with the ship's chief engineer. Many of us, it turned out, enjoyed at least one such remarkable tête-à-tête with her during the voyage.

Most of the time, Deming remained in her lab, monitoring bacteria on a rickety fluorometer and lost in grand thoughts. But when she emerged, the extremophile in her came out. If she was not having lively conversations about visits to old Hawaiian strip clubs, where the dancers performed amazing feats with their vaginas (Deming went backstage to ask for pointers) she was taking dancing lessons from the captain, or attending the nightly lectures, during which she invariably pointed out some universal application of the most seemingly limited data. She reminded me of Kierkegaard's knight of faith, who effortlessly found eternity in the commonplace and who, through the most commonplace actions, embodied eternity.

But I was not a knight of faith, and could not make ordinary environments extreme. I needed the wild landscape under my feet. Most of all, I needed to walk. While Behzad and Deming stalked about the ship with the all-consumed air of those for whom every second has meaning, I gazed through binoculars at the distant coast of Ellesmere and recalled the many times its extremes had gripped me with a similar magnificent obsession.

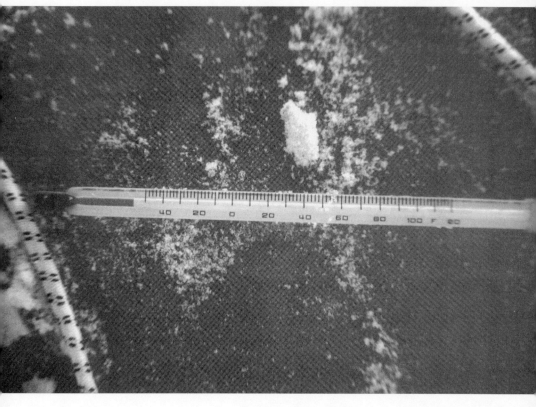

Minus 58° F: an alien world where plastic bags snap like potato chips.

Chapter One

Into the Void

One day, years earlier, I had come home with a new backpack, the largest I could find. "What's that for?" my girlfriend of the time had asked.

"Not sure," I replied. But its size made it look serious, which seemed important.

My one previous attempt at winter camping had been in high school, when four of us shivered all night in cheap sleeping bags lined with Space Blankets. As soon as dawn broke, we hurried back to the car with a new-found understanding of Napoleon's retreat from Moscow.

This time I decided that if I were going to do something crazy, I would do it intelligently. I stopped reading fiction and began to study outdoor equipment catalogs, how-to books and naturalists' musings. The writing was unintentionally entertaining: Bjorn Kjellstrom's *Be Expert With Map and Compass*, with its illustrations of smiling figures in beanie caps finding their way hither and thither with the aid of their trusty compass and Kjellstrom's pointers; John Rowland's *Cache Lake Country*, with its thumbs-in-the-suspenders prose: "Sam was plumb scared to death . . . he was in a fix and no mistake"; *Backpacking*, by R. C. Rethmel, with its appendix on winter camping provided by the author's "good friend," James (Gil) Phillips, who used polyurethane foam to the absolute exclusion of all other insulation. Snapshots of Gil in full regalia showed him looking warm enough, but he was standing in what was evidently a sunny yard in New Mexico. A dog in the background panted from heat.

Only rarely did a kindred spirit appear in this wasteland. Calvin Rutstrum first won my heart as the only winter guru not to solemnly intone, "If your feet are cold, put on your hat." Although his way of the wilderness was more traditional than what I envisioned following, his workable ideas were timeless. Rutstrum also had a love of solitude rather than a dislike of mankind. He was didactic, like most self-educated men, but his noble character tempered the pontificating. He wrote into old age, long after he should have put the pen down, but this octogenarian's last words, in his last book, were a touching thanks for the life he had lived.

I took to naturalists for whiffs of the good writing I missed in how-to manuals. The early Edwin Way Teale was distinguished by some of his fine lyric passages; Aldo Leopold by his tang; Jean Henri Fabre by his sense of wonder; Rachel Carson by her passionate use of facts; and Thoreau by the depth of his reflections, and by his eyeballs. His eyes had that mixture of sadness and purity that is sometimes found in the faces of the truly great. They were as magnificent as August Strindberg's forehead. One would never find those eyes in the sockets of a clod.

Gradually, I became aware that I wanted to do an extreme wilderness trip, which seemed to include winter camping. I worked from three principles. First, since gear "used on Everest" was readily available, while gear "used at the North Pole" was not, I assumed that high-altitude mountaineering and extreme arctic travel required similar equipment—bombproof tents, five-pound down bags, offset-baffled parkas. Second, traditional equipment was for those who had mastered field repair and general woodsmanship; ignoramuses such as myself were safer with modern stuff. Third, I chose the best of everything—lightest, warmest, toughest, biggest—and only from what I perceived to be A-list companies. When you get to know equipment, you can make item-by-item judgments, but from the armchair it's impossible to tell the necessary from the overkill. So I erred on the side of caution, reducing the cost of these Rolls Royce packs and Lamborghini bags by presenting myself to companies as an outdoor writer. Most were happy to offer me wholesale prices which, in this industry, usually meant forty percent off. Soon I was equipped for the Worst Journey in the World.

I had no idea how much food to bring on this theoretical trek, but I had recently trained as a marathon swimmer, logging six miles a day in the pool. That much exercise leaves you free to eat as much as you can, and I discovered that I simply could not hoover in more than 7,000 calories a day. My jaw ached from chewing, I got hemorrhoids from all the activity of a supercharged metabolism, and I ran out of things I wanted to eat. Even a whole strawberry shortcake every day palls after a while.

By default then, 7,000 calories seemed like a good dietary target for an extreme cold-weather expedition. Hard spring sledding, I learned later, only burns about 5,000 calories, but during the midwinter cold of my first expeditions I needed the extra 2,000 calories to stay warm. In the end, making the most extreme choices in food and equipment worked.

■

Although I originally fixated on Labrador as my wilderness ideal, a chance trip to Ellesmere Island turned my world upside-down. This was the most extreme place in North America. It drew extreme people, nurtured extreme plants, harbored extreme animals, and showcased extreme phenomena. It was everything I wanted. I forgot about Labrador.

I soon learned that the difficulty of traveling on Ellesmere is nothing compared with the difficulty of getting there. There are no roads, no boats and only one scheduled flight, twice weekly, to the lone village of Grise Fiord on the south coast.

The quest to reach Ellesmere begins two hundred and fifty miles to the south, in Resolute Bay on Cornwallis Island, "perhaps the most dreary and desolate place that can well be conceived," according to one early description. The town of Resolute lies two thousand miles due north of Winnipeg, in a part of the Arctic known as the Barren Wedge. Northern plants can endure almost anything, as long as they get one month of decent weather in which to grow. But summer in the Barren Wedge is typically windy, dank, and foggy, so Cornwallis Island has the lushness of a gravel pit. First-time visitors are astonished when they fly another five hundred miles north and step into Ellesmere's alpine meadows and warm sunshine.

Resolute is actually two villages: an "unlovely huddle" of intercon-nected government buildings near the airport, and the Inuit village. The two are connected by a four-mile gravel road of excruciating dullness that the truly desperate sometimes hike to kill time.

As the last stop of jets and the staging area for science and adventure in the High Arctic, Resolute has a certain character. Visitors have plenty of time to explore this when bad weather grounds all aircraft for days. Six days is my record, but this is by no means exceptional. One weatherman in the Barren Wedge was stranded for a month and lost his entire vacation.

A passion for Ellesmere is like an addiction to heroin: You have to sub-sidize the craving through humiliating pursuits. Hitchhiking on half-empty planes used to be a respectable means of northern travel, and early arctic obsessees—including such notables as photographer Fred Bruem-mer—rarely paid their own way. Communities put them up until they found a charter flight to hop on. Today it is sometimes possible to hitch-hike back from Ellesmere, but planes to the island are usually full, and to show up in Resolute without firm plans is to risk never getting out.

In recent years, travel has become a little easier for me because I can barter my knowledge about the island. But just how does someone, for whom two thousand dollars is a lot of money, accumulate twenty jour-neys to the most expensive wilderness destination in North America?

My first trip was a magazine assignment, covered partly by an outfit-ter and partly by tourism agencies. More wealthy magazines, to ensure objective coverage, send their writers as paying clients, but smaller pub-lications rely on outfitters to cover the cost, which is negligible if the tour is already going and there is space. Smart outfitters also give photogra-phers the occasional freebie, because good photos are vital for trade show exhibits where they find new customers and for brochures which tanta-lize repeat clientele. My love of photography, which was born and de-veloped on Ellesmere, is partly to credit for four of those twenty trips.

Another Ellesmere stratagem is to buy a piece of someone else's char-ter. Sometimes there is enough space left over for one or two people and their gear. In the spring, adventurers attempting the North Pole need pe-riodic resupplies, and their expedition managers in Resolute are always open to recouping part of their costs. The difficulty is that you never know the dates of the resupply flights ahead of time or whether they will have room. You show up in Resolute and take your chances.

In summer, tour operators may also sell a place on their flights. This is a better arrangement because their dates are fixed. However, most tours are full or almost full, and it's hard to confirm your spot until shortly before the trip leaves. Outfitters understandably prefer to fill their planes with customers paying five thousand dollars for the full service rather than with independents tagging along for a few hundred bucks.

If flights don't go exactly where you want to go, you may sometimes side charter. Most travelers aren't aware of this option. It's as if, flying from New York to Chicago, you paid an additional small amount to be dropped in Detroit, just off the flight path. Twice I've side chartered the "sked" to Grise Fiord. The regularly scheduled flight to Grise is cheap, and it's not far from there to interesting places. Once, a charter to Eureka made a ten-minute detour to drop us on western Axel Heiberg Island, a remote destination that would have cost four thousand dollars to reach on our own. Cost, including detour and our share of the charter, eight hundred dollars.

These little finesses, when they work, make Ellesmere accessible. But sometimes all options fall through. You sit in Resolute for a week, camping behind the airport or watching your dollars fly away at one of the local hotels. The charms of Resolute wear thin. You have worn thin on Resolute's citizens. The airline managers stop looking up when you walk into their office for news. The Polar Continental Shelf Project, with its many Ellesmere charters, will not accept your offers of good coin, leading you to be somewhat cynical about that science agency's well-publicized financial straits. The resupply flights of the North Pole adventurers are full with sponsors and friends. "There's another resupply in two weeks, though." A promising flight falls through: Weather delays have allowed two groups to combine their charters, so instead of two half-empty planes, there is now one full one. Steel doors clang shut. At least two more days in Resolute before the next ray of hope.

You accept the ancient wilderness principle—travelers need either lots of time or lots of money. You have come prepared to serve time, but once in a while, time is not enough. The only way out is with a credit card.

When I first went to Resolute hoping to extend the north's hitchhiking tradition by another few years, it was understandable that I should feel like a moocher. I was. My partners in crime likewise commented on how they felt like "stray cats" or "bag ladies" in Resolute. Sometimes we came prepared to spend substantial amounts of money and still felt like second-class citizens. Resolute's icy heart had seen too much. Too many foreign polar bear hunters willing to drop $20,000 in four days, leaving thousand-dollar tips in their wake. Too many North Pole expeditions with half-million dollar budgets. Too many planeloads of doctors and stockbrokers. Too many cruise ships disgorging ladies in furs (mink, not caribou) and men with glaring, corporate eyes who plunk down two thousand dollars for a narwhal tusk during their one hour on shore. Resolute is like Las Vegas: impossible to impress, no matter how much money you throw away.

Once, using airline frequent-flyer points and hooking rides, I traveled from Toronto to Ellesmere and back for two hundred dollars. But, at worst, Resolute could be so disheartening and humiliating that I would return home never wanting to go north again. Yet, like cold, fatigue, soft snow, high winds, and partners from hell, I soon forgot Resolute and remembered only Ellesmere.

■

Ellesmere's most extreme time of the year begins in September, when the sun sets after four thousand consecutive hours of daylight. By late October, Ellesmere is locked "in the black coffin of the Polar Night." Of all ordeals, explorers most dreaded the next three months. "A world without sun is like a life without love," wrote Nansen.

During these months, expeditions continued their skeleton scientific programs, but mainly everyone read, smoked, played cards, argued, and slept twelve hours a night. The length of journal entries typically plummeted from one or two pages a day to three or four lines. At Christmas and New Year's, much ado was made of the special menus, usually written in mock French, with such delicacies as Salmon à la Paleocrystic or Muskox Tongue in Arctic Sauce.

Lectures, singalongs, and weekly theater helped break up the monotony; the reason that prospective arctic volunteers were asked at their interviews, "Can you sing or play an instrument?" Officers tried to teach some of the illiterate men to read. Short walks, half a mile to a mile a day along a trampled route, prevented total physical decrepitude. Most groups put out a weekly newspaper, full of gossip, line drawings and bad inside jokes. Usually, these newspapers died quickly. "We, the editors, found it interesting," reported one.

Snow magnified the reflected starlight so that even without a moon, it was possible to see a little. "The line below will give an idea of the size of type

LEGIBLE AT MID-DAY

"wrote one explorer. Another claimed that the full moon equaled the light of a candle at forty-nine inches. Reducing the darkness to numbers was one way to cope with it.

The darkness was not nearly as trying as the social friction of this confined life. Once, even two members of the fabled Royal Canadian Mounted Police lost their poise. "I told him to pay attention to his own affairs," reported one. "Immediately he invited me to take off my hat and fight. I refrained from this method as long as possible, but in December he carried it into personal affairs and it came to blows."

Intense pastel colors wash the frigid February sky, making this the most beautiful time of year. For the Inuit in neighboring Greenland, this is the end of the winter depression called *perlerorneq*, literally, "to feel the weight of life." Custom dictates that the first time the Inuit see the sun, they take off one mitt and hold their bare hand in the air. The more devout also smile with half their face. Traditionally, all lamps in the community are put out and relit with fresh oil and new wicks. The world is reborn, and for Inuit and explorers alike, the exciting sledding season is about to begin.

■

I didn't know exactly how cold it was that night, but I knew it was cold. It was as if the thermometer were in freefall. Sleep was impossible. I couldn't stop shivering inside my sleeping bag. My breath formed delicate catkins of frost on the tent ceiling over my head. These fairy chandeliers, indicators of at least −30°F, can't be touched, however gently, without disintegrating. Sometimes I marveled at their loveliness, but now I just tried to blow them off before they became so heavy that they dropped by themselves and hit some small uncovered part of my face like a spritz of frozen carbon dioxide. Because moisture from breathing gums up insulation, I couldn't bury my face in the sleeping bag.

It was a long night. As soon as the dark purpled, I got up. Movement was the only antidote for this cold. I stomped around outside to warm up,

then checked the thermometer. Fifty-eight below. A surge of pride over-
came the fatigue. I'd had plenty of minus forty nights, and except for the
periodic frost spritzes, I had slept pretty well. But -58°F was another di-
mension. The experience was so alien, so extreme, that I enjoyed it despite my misery, and it awakened a curiosity about the cold.

By arctic standards, most of my trips have not been particularly cold.
Minus thirty sounds bad, but it isn't really, except in a stiff wind. A good
sleeping bag can handle –30°F, just like a good backpack can handle
eighty pounds but not a hundred and twenty pounds. Life only becomes
difficult after about –44°F. Thanks to the moderating influence of the
sea, mostly frozen though it is, –44°F is sometimes the winter minimum
on Ellesmere.

Extreme cold has occurred. In 1963, scientists at Tanquary Fiord
experienced –77°F, just 4 degrees shy of the North American record
set at Snag, Yukon. On March 4, 1876, explorer George Nares reported –74°F on Ellesmere's northeast coast. Whisky placed outside
froze after a few minutes, "so a few of us had the rare opportunity of
eating it in a solid state." No doubt there were many quips that night
about hard liquor.

Sledding below –30°F is difficult because of the friction on such cold
snow. At –77°F, it would be like trying to drag a Volkswagen with no wheels
down the street. During the day, perpetual movement, four layers of clothing and 7,000 calories can overcome most any cold. But sleep would be hard.

On their winter quest for emperor penguin eggs in Antarctica, Apsley
Cherry-Gerrard and his two companions survived –76°F, the record low for
camping. "Dante was right when he placed circles of ice below circles of
fire," Cherry-Gerrard commented in his Antarctic classic, *The Worst Journey in the World*. On Ellesmere, North Pole adventurers occasionally experience –72°F at Ward Hunt Island in early March, but they usually linger
in the camp's heated weatherhavens until it warms up.

I've done two trips where the evening temperature was –40°F or less
about half of the time. Strange things happen then. Beard growth on my
exposed face slowed to a crawl, while hair under my turtleneck grew at
a normal rate. Once I couldn't feel my left foot for several days, but it was
not frostbitten. I eventually discovered that my sock had slipped down
and was subtly restricting circulation. I pulled the sock up and feeling returned to the foot a few hours later. As the weeks wore on, however, my

perpetually cold toes went numb and the nerves didn't reawaken for a month after I'd returned home.

But the real quirks of cold cannot compare to its imagined powers. Cowley Abraham, whose ship was blown south of Cape Horn into the subantarctic in 1683, found "so extreme cold that we could bear drinking three quarts of Brandy in twenty-four hours each man, and be not at all the worse for it." You have to wonder what drinking records they'd have set had they continued into the Antarctic itself!

An epic tale of frostbite, amputation, and near death appeared in 1894 in *The Strand*, a fashionable London magazine. Written by one G. H. Lees, it was entitled "Lost in a Blizzard" and was introduced by the editors as "an absolutely true narrative of actual facts . . . written down from Mr. Lees' dictation, the loss of both his hands, of course, precluding him from writing."

The incident took place one wintry day near Indian Head, Manitoba, temperature a balmy –30°F. Riding his sleigh along a lonely trail, the narrator "began to feel very sleepy, through the intense cold," and got out to walk a bit. The horses bolted; he had left his gloves momentarily in the sleigh and his hands were bare. Apparently he never thought of putting them inside his coat.

He first "ran some distance, when the cold seemed to make me faint; I lay down an hour before I could recover myself." When he got up, his hands were frozen. He then wandered for hours, tired, but "dared not sleep, knowing it would mean death." It was believed that extreme cold induced a hypnotic drowsiness, and that to fall asleep was to never wake up. However, as any camper knows, to fall asleep without enough insulation is to wake up cold, or not to sleep at all.

Frostbite was also thought to make fingers as brittle as icicles, and Lees next writes, "I crawled on my elbows, for I was now afraid of breaking my hands to pieces." At length, "being famished, I had to bite the snow off trees, though it pulled the skin from my lips." Passing over the fact that snow does not stick to the mouth like cold metal, another common misbelief is that if a civilized person misses a meal or two, he becomes starvation-maddened. This narrator had gone all of twenty hours without food.

Such myths may sound quaint now, but the bogeyman of cold remains a good excuse for dismissing the Arctic as a land of Cain rather than an Eden.

■

When we think of arctic sledding, we usually think of dog teams, but a person can haul too, and that's what I do. A simple harness of seat belt webbing slips across my chest and attaches to a seven-foot fiberglass sled with plastic runners and a nylon cover. The sled holds up to two months of supplies. When towing a sled, walking is faster than skiing, so I only ski in deep snow. Like a dog, I haul with four legs: the two I was born with and a pair of ski poles.

Manhauling has been described as "about the hardest work to which free men have been put in modern times." Victorian geographical societies rightly saw arctic exploration as less dangerous but more arduous than the tropical variety. Arctic travelers didn't die from malaria or native spears but they often had to haul their own gear on foot. This is no more dangerous than walking on a sidewalk. Less so, in fact. The one injury of my Ellesmere career happened when I was bitten by a dog while strolling to the National Archives in Ottawa.

Sledding is a lovely occupation, if you like walking. Coleridge considered a twenty-mile hike in the mountains nothing special. Beethoven composed while trekking in the Alps. Nietzsche wrote that only thoughts reached by walking have value. Bertrand Russell claimed that war would end if every young man walked twenty miles a day.

But not all cultured Europeans understood activity. In *Journey to the Center of the Earth*, Jules Verne's heroes endured "three hours of terrible fatigue, walking incessantly." Jean Malaurie, author of *The Last Kings of Thule*, a wonderful study of the Polar Inuit, makes much of walking six miles per day and "penetrating inland to a depth of nineteen miles." Even Mark Twain, that vigorous traveler from the vigorous New World, believed that walking was "merely a lubricant" for good conversation.

In his essay on walking, Thoreau writes that the origin of the word "saunter" may derive from the medieval peripatetics who claimed to be going to the Holy Land, "la Sainte Terre." Sledding is, in this sense, a lot like sauntering. An imitation of Christ whose Golgotha is healthy exhaustion. For the Western soul, exertion may do what fasting does for the Eastern one.

Of nineteenth-century explorers, only John Rae had the walking gene. This first polar athlete snowshoed a total of 6,500 miles in the Central

Arctic. Those who met him described him as "full of animal spirits" or "active as a squirrel." As for the Ellesmere pioneers, American Adolphus Greely disliked exercise so much that he couldn't bring himself to order a fitness routine for others. George Nares was typical of British leaders. Rather than a swashbuckling star ship captain who was always first in line for dangerous missions, Nares remained in the stateroom, pushing his miniature battalions across the field of war with a shuffleboard cue.

Many of these early expeditions came to grief on Ellesmere, for which *The New York Times* credited the island with the highest misery-per-visitor ratio on earth. However, all the scholarly analyses of expeditions-gone-wrong, all the excuses and the crowing, fail to acknowledge the role of luck in arctic sledding. When I landed in Churchill Falls, Labrador, to begin my first winter trek, I had no idea whether I would be able to pull 250 pounds for ten miles a day. But by chance, the route I had blindly picked followed the wind-blasted lakes of the interior plateau. Superb conditions.

A few years later, a Toronto lawyer named Pat Lewtas embarked on a similar solo quest. Unluckily for him, he chose a stretch of Yukon wilderness where he quickly became bogged down in the impossible snows of the timberland. A couple of years later he went to Baffin Island, but, due to his bad-luck route, faltered again in the rough ice of shallow inlets. On his third try, over the hard snows of the Barren Lands, he accomplished a flawless six hundred mile hike from Cambridge Bay to Arviat in central Nunavut.

Many early British sledding experiences happened to occur in the same idyllic snows as Lewtas's third journey. In the windswept Central Arctic, snowshoes are unnecessary. So, when Nares explored northern Ellesmere in 1875, only one or two men brought them. After their miserable sledding mileage, Nares endured unflattering comparisons with those earlier, glory days of British sledding. Even in modern times, one armchair expert dissected several expeditions and concluded that 208 pounds per sledger was the maximum sustainable load. Nares's men averaged 240 pounds. Therein, he says, they erred.

But the Arctic is not all the same. Conditions vary over large areas and from bay to bay, hill to hill. One freak snowfall can ruin a trip. Thus, a 208-pound limit is meaningless. In good snow, 300 pounds is easy; in bad snow, 100 pounds is murder. The best windpacked snow is so hard that even ski poles make little impression, and a sled of almost any weight will glide effortlessly; hauling through powder snow is one of the Arctic's worst ordeals, or best cardiovascular workouts. The Nares expedition had to drag their one-ton sleds through powder, over the worst pressure ice in the world.

Since snow conditions make all the difference between an easy thirty-mile day and a hard three-mile day, it was disappointing to discover that the supposedly many Inuit words for snow is a myth. The myth began in 1940, when a talented amateur linguist named Benjamin Whorf misinterpreted an old anthropology text which stated that Inuktitut has four root words for snow. Whorf had never been to the Arctic, but he seemed to understand that for northern peoples, snow types are important enough to deserve their own nouns. In a somewhat casual vein and with no good reason, he wrote an article claiming that, "To an Eskimo, this all-inclusive word [snow] would be almost unthinkable; he would say that falling snow, slushy snow, and so on, are sensuously and operationally different, different things to contend with; he uses different words for them and for other kinds of snow."

Whorf's article was picked up by the mainstream media and soon lodged in the public consciousness. Since then, the "many" Inuit words for snow have taken on a life of their own as a clever cultural symbol. "Many" became fifty, fifty became a hundred, one hundred became two hundred. I recently saw three hundred on a public television spot about Inuit culture. The record hyperbole is currently four hundred, proffered some years ago by a magazine writer in need of a juicy metaphor.

Since Whorf, scholars have tried to debunk the myth, but without much success. It is, in the words of pop linguist Geoffrey Pullum, "too good to be false."

Finding out exactly how many Inuktitut words there are for snow is a thankless task that bogs down in philological hair-splitting about the definitions of "word," "snow," and "Inuktitut." Suffice it to say that English has as many or almost as many, if you count such terms as corn snow, powder, slush, and windpack. Moreover, the two or four or dozen Inuit snow words differentiate not between fine gradations of traveling snow, so wonderfully useful, but to more mundane concepts such as snow on the ground versus falling snow. Apparently, like us, they just refer to traveling snow as great, pretty good or crappy.

Digging into the myth did leave me with one small reward. A California professor informed me that the Chamorro language of Guam has thirty-seven words for coconut. I haven't dug further into it, preferring to believe that the truth behind the myth is alive in the Tropics, if not in the Arctic.

■

A sledder's day begins in low gear. The nights in the sleeping bag are too sweet to abandon easily. They have an infant's reassuring lack of responsibility. Legs are tight from the previous day's exertions and must be periodically stretched with cat-like luxuriance. If you have been disciplined the night before, leaving two hours between supper and bedtime and not overdoing the fluids, the need to pee will not wake you prematurely.

The eternal daylight eliminates the need for a rigid schedule. It doesn't matter whether the traveling day finishes at six in the evening or one in the morning; it all looks the same. As long as the miles get done, you can indulge yourself as much as your limited resources allow.

After a good sleep, I sometimes spend a defiant extra hour in the sack, stretching and savoring the uterine warmth. Finally, bracing myself like a swimmer diving into a cold lake, I unzip the sleeping bag, ignoring the ripe odors, put on puffy camp clothing, step outside, pee, get the stove going for hot chocolate and melt snow for cereal. While lingering over breakfast, I melt one and a half quarts of water for the trail. Iceberg ice tastes the best, and as it melts, it sometimes sizzles like bacon frying.

For the first few days, breaking camp takes three hours. Once the routine becomes automatic, it's down to two hours. With no dawdling, it can be done in one. On every trip, efficiency has to be relearned.

The first three hours of sledding are the hardest of the day. It's not that sledding is pain but you have to put the comfort of camp behind you. Only then does sledding feel natural. The stiffness in your legs has disappeared by then, the rhythm kicks in, the mind dances, the hours fly.

Apsley Cherry-Garrard's sledders in Antarctica claimed to spend their time thinking of "grouse moors and pretty girls," but that is hard to believe. Even when the girl you love is waiting for you at home, even when you stare at her picture every night, she seems impossibly far away, like a half-remembered dream, too distant to dominate the stern arctic horizon. More likely, Cherry-Garrard's moors and lassies were topics of conversation in the tent, not mental company on the trail.

On his 1906 trek across Ellesmere's north coast, Robert Peary grimly spent whole days counting his footsteps, presumably to measure distance. "My brain is numb with the incessant 'one, two, three,'" he complained. Why he didn't use a sled wheel odometer, like other explorers of his era, is hard to understand, unless driving himself bananas was part of his peculiarly bitter form of discipline.

Every sledder counts some of the time, though; the metronomic regularity of one's steps is soothing, and it's helpful and entertaining to graph the relation between miles per hour and steps per minute. With my stride, 112 steps per minute—a typical sledding pace in good snow—covers 2.4 miles per hour; 90 steps per minute, 1.5 miles per hour. Seventy-three steps per minute means I'm on skis in bad snow and making about a mile an hour. That pace traps you in the dreary present. It does not let the mind soar with the detachment that effortlessly devours miles. I seem to need at least 85 steps per minute to achieve escape velocity.

I usually have one or two special hours each day, when a stimulated brain invents jokes or feelingly recites old poems or catches a whiff of childhood sensations so alien and fleeting that they "tend toward the outermost limit of communicable thought." Other hours feature blank staring at the landscape or scanning for wildlife, broken only by random thoughts caroming around the skull: "Will she get used to living without me? Will my left knee give out? Are those muskoxen or just rocks? I'll take off my sunglasses at five p.m. today. I don't like chocolate-covered peanuts any more. If I make fifteen miles, I'll have the potato casserole for dinner as a reward. Slight pain in right side, maybe that couple who removed their appendices before overwintering in Antarctica were right. I . . . did . . . it . . . my . . . way . . . tra la la."

Many an hour is dominated by some idiotic song that the brain, like some scratched old record, repeats obsessively. The songs come out of the blue, but the words usually have a dreamlike connection to what's beneath the surface of the mind. Once, the old Rolling Stones' song *Ruby Tuesday* just wouldn't go away. That was in polar bear country and anxiety was high. Ruby's need to be free at whatever cost seemed ridiculously meaningful. Hour after hour, day after day, the damned song played. A year later, with storm clouds gathering on several fronts in my personal life, I couldn't seem to free myself from *Bring Him Home*, the plaintive *Les Misérables* tune.

After the first hour on the trail, it's time for a quick drink. Before the invention of waterproof bottles, chronically dehydrated sledgers drank only at the noonday stop. Nowadays, many sledders use a big Thermos that keeps fluids hot all day, but my journeys began partly as ascetic exercises in self-denial. Take enough away, and how you appreciate the little that remains! Although my camp luxuries have increased, plain Nalgene bottles are one of those spartan regimes that I affectionately hang onto. The bottles lie on the sled, insulated in my down parka, and I space the day's drinking so that only the last couple of mouthfuls are slushy.

After two hours, the 1,000-calorie breakfast has lightened. Out come high-energy snacks: chocolate, chocolate peanuts, fatty cheeses. The more water in the cheese, the harder it freezes. Until late April, even asiago has to be "cut" with violent swings of an ice ax. Sometimes I can avoid these time-consuming reenactments of the murder of Trotsky by finding a grocer at home who will vacuum pack it in pre-cut chunks.

And so it goes. Midday hikes break up the sledding rhythm too much, so I push all day and try to camp in interesting spots. In early spring it's too cold for long lunches, anyway. By mid-May, heat, not cold, is the problem. You can still get frostbite in a wind, but on calm days the sun is so strong that even an undershirt feels too warm. Sledders then begin "sleeping upside-down," traveling during the cooler night. There is a fierce, unconventional satisfaction to having breakfast at eight in the evening, sledding all night and bedding down at noon.

The changing snow conditions provoke never-ending mental arithmetic about how far you'll make that day. Of all arctic skills, learning to relinquish expectations is the most important. Since you are not in control, every camp, every stop along the trail, every type of weather, should be equally accepted. Much-anticipated sites are often disappointing; minor destinations, marvellous. Because the magic moments are so unpredictable, you live in what one traveler calls "a constant state of optimistic expectation."

In particularly optimistic states, I sometimes tried to build a snow house, but the architecture was beyond me. It is hard to say which was more difficult, building an igloo or understanding its theory. An igloo, according to scholars, is not a hemisphere but a "catenoid of revolution with an optimum height-to-diameter ratio." This shape, apparently, eliminates "ring tension and shell moments." It gets worse. The best snow for block-cutting "has a density of about 0.30 to 0.35 gm/cm^3 and a hardness of about 150 to 200 gm/cm^3."

In igloo construction, as in other arts, a thousand cutaway diagrams can never replace the master-apprentice relationship. I know the principles, but my walls never lean inward enough. So my end product is not a catenoid of revolution but a cone whose narrow end tapers upward toward infinity.

Igloo, language purists point out, means house, any kind of house, so it is the wrong word for a domed catenary of snow blocks. But that's a losing effort, like insisting on using Himalaya instead of Himalayas because Himalaya is already plural, or like the explorer who insisted on calling muskoxen exclusively by their genus name *ovibos*, because they are neither oxen nor musky.

Using an igloo is like traveling with dogs: The mystique cannot be denied. It is redolent of seal oil lamps, polar bear skin pants, and sleeping mats of caribou fur. Old, infirm Inuit walking nobly off into the blizzard without spoiling it by saying, "I may be some time." Those were the days. Sometimes, those are still the days, although most Inuit just bring canvas tents on their snowmobile-drawn komatiks.

Unlike dinosaurs, igloos leave no trace of their passing ("But where are the snows of yesteryear?") so their origin is lost. One archaeologist speculates that the artistic Dorset people may have passed the knowledge of igloo building on to the Thule. There is at least an aesthetic link between the Dorsets' exquisite carvings and the thing of beauty that is a well-built igloo. "Maybe there are so many artists among the Inuit because of the traditional need to build igloos and carve harpoon heads," suggests another scholar. "Their small groups were so spread out, they couldn't rely on one craftsman per community." There might have been some selection pressure for spatial intelligence.

Explorers quickly discovered the benefits of snow houses, and ignored or embraced them, depending on temperament. John Rae and Leopold McClintock used igloos during their journeys in the 1850s, for which they were disdained by the British establishment of the time. "Anyone can go native," sniffed Sir Clements Markham. The American explorer Charles Francis Hall occasionally built snow shelters but after spending two hours and forty minutes on one in 1871, he remarked, "This is a long time to keep tired men exposed to severe weather after dragging a heavy sledge for ten or eleven hours." Three hours is actually a typical novice time; an experienced pair of hands can build one in an hour. And once in Iqaluit, I saw a man complete an igloo in an astonishing twenty-nine minutes. In the end, however, I had to resign myself to that nylon igloo known as a dome tent, for which no spatial intelligence is required.

■

Extreme endeavors, such as manhauling four hundred miles across the Arctic, puzzle most people. Many are just curious, but occasionally some old sobersides will ask Why? when what is clearly meant is, Why do you want to do something stupid like that?

The big Why dangles over all our heads, but adventurers seem to be fairer game for the question. Yet, one might just as properly ask: Why run marathons? Why birdwatch? Why work at a job you don't like? Why believe in God? Why help the under-privileged? Why get up every morning?

Now and then I come across a line that seems to buzz around the Why of adventure. "To circle or cross a place meaningful to you is a reverential act." "The difference between vice and virtue depends on whether the pleasure precedes or follows the pain." That Ellesmere travel is a pursuit of virtue sounds a lot more impressive than, "I like it."

British poet and mountaineer Wilfrid Noyce identified thirteen adventure motives (comments mine):

1. *The ascetic streak.* Hard travel teaches self-control and gives a purifying glimpse of life as a hair shirt. Refreshing for pampered Westerners.

2. *Enjoying the contrast of civilized and primitive.* Meeting a little ship after months of living on raw seal meat, Knud Rasmussen describes with pure joy how, "Ten minutes later I was on board, with my teeth deep in an Orange. A little later, I sat staring with wide eyes at a real cup of actual steaming coffee. There were such things as Bread, and Cheese, and Butter . . . " Unless you eat the seal meat, you can't fully experience the Orange.

3. *The spice of danger.* Unlike mountains, the Arctic presents little danger from falling, avalanches, rockfall, and deadly winds. Arctic travel is more an endorphin high than an adrenaline rush.

4. *Pleasures of technique, pursuit of excellence, physical movement.* You feel like a sorcerer's apprentice every time you sleep comfortably at 40 degrees below. Also, trekking twelve hours a day is very different than exercising for an hour: The physical being awakes.

5. *Lure of wild country.* High altitudes are more extreme than high latitudes, but how many mountains are three hundred miles from the nearest village?

6. *Lure of the unknown.* A powerful motive during the first few trips, when the Arctic looms as strange and compelling as Mars.

7. *Escape.* Those who are ill-at-ease in their own culture look for home in distant places. Most travelers eventually find their personal Ellesmere.

8. *Fame, fortune.* "Most nonfamous people," writes essayist Cintra Wilson, "are frequently in a state of dull torture from the lack of boundless international adoration in their lives." Because adventure seems so dashing and difficult and arouses our Walter Mitty longings, it is one of the roads to celebrity in which no outstanding talent is required.

9. *Conquest and competition (nationalism).* A little out-of-date now, but the first Brazilians to the North Pole would still create a stir in their own country.

10. *Knowledge (science).* Often simply a ruse adventurers use to clothe, as Bill Tilman puts it, "their more or less frivolous aims with a thin mantle of science." Self-knowledge, on the other hand, is a driving force. Under extreme circumstances you quickly learn how much you're the person you want to be, and how much you're not.

11. *Fascination with machines (especially the airplane).* Around-the-World-in-Eighty-Days types continue to flock to the northern skies in putt-putts of all kinds.

12. *Curiosity about people, places.* This refers largely to less extreme adventures. One can be curious about Morocco; it's too weak a term for Ellesmere. People-curious adventurers usually go where there are more people, although a few grand arctic figures, such as Frederick Cook, Jean Malaurie, and Charles Francis Hall, fell under the spell of Inuit culture.

13. *Sense of purpose.* For some of us, what the Inuit call a journey in pursuit of its tail—one that has no purpose other than its own completion—holds more meaning than practical goals.

Noyce's forty-five year old list remains the closest anyone has come to encapsulating the Why. However, it does not address the basic mystery of why some people crave adventure while others avoid it. In particular, why go to extremes?

During one trek, I developed a crackpot theory that helped pass a lot of hours. It tries to explain the thirst for adventure and at the same time answer the basic question, What made Beethoven different?

There is such a thing as genetic energy. Scientists may suspect that it exists but they do not yet have a yardstick to measure it. Nevertheless, we are all born with different amounts. It doesn't make us everything we are—there's personality too—but it determines how exaggerated these personality traits are. When our pride is stung, do we cringe slightly or conquer nations in revenge?

Genetic energy can be squandered or fully used. As with height, a good environment takes us only so far. Beyond this, we can't make giants of ourselves through "the omnipotence of unyielding human will." At a certain level of excellence, everyone is dedicated, but the higher the energy, the further you can push without hitting the ceiling or breaking down.

Energy is not the same as talent. Talent is the ability to do things easily. The sharpness of a lumberjack's ax is talent; energy determines whether he swings that ax a thousand times a day, or a hundred.

We can consciously channel some of this energy, but it tends to flow according to our predispositions. There are five channels for genetic energy:

spiritual, physical, intellectual, sexual, and practical. While renowned French author Honoré de Balzac funneled great spiritual and intellectual energy through his talent for writing, it would be hard to find someone with less physical energy. In his few moments away from his desk, all this brilliant walrus did was sit.

Great individuals all have prodigious amounts of genetic energy. This is the basic gift that sets the Beethovens of this world apart. Some seem able to focus it all in one area; with others, it "runs madly off in all directions." Some fields of endeavor require more energy than others. Intuitively, it takes more to found a religion than to establish a business empire. A ranking of great figures by energy level would be Prophet, Leader, Poet, Writer, and Intellectual. Finally, genetic energy in an individual, and in a species, decreases over time.

I inherited my genetic energy from my mother and her high-spirited family. It seems to have been just enough to glimpse, at times, how ordinary I normally was. But I had always been physically and spiritually restless, and this restlessness was enough to shape my life. It may have been what prompted me, for instance, to buy that huge pack when I hadn't camped since high school.

The more genetic energy, the farther and more often we need to go. Much of the year, I pace endlessly, barely able to sit down. The few days or weeks after a hard Ellesmere trip are the only times I feel physically at peace. Soon the restlessness begins again. I pace and plot. Without some strange project to work toward, my days feel empty. Perhaps it's personal style, to expend energy in floods rather than in measured daily doses. Perhaps it's discontent with adult life. Not enough wonder.

If I had to walk ten miles to work, then carry backbreaking sacks of potatoes all day, voluntarily sledding across Ellesmere would be incomprehensible. But not for everyone. I once hiked the Karakum Desert of Turkmenistan with a Russian named Andrei Ilyachov. He was one of the poorest Russians I'd ever met, which is saying a lot. In a frustrating country which grinds down the strong and crushes the weak, Ilyachov spent his vacations biking hundreds of miles—without food or water. He had done this for years in Siberia, southern Russia, and Central Asia. He was not only able to adapt to the hard conditions of his everyday life, but he had so much energy left over that he devoted all his free time to making his life even harder. A holy fool.

How does this relate to adventure? Today, survival in the West requires little energy. Sometimes, the ache of unused energy drives us to tilt at windmills. Then, we discover that the happiest state lies near the edge of our capabilities, and extreme journeys take us to that edge.

Camp on Eureka Sound.

Chapter Two

Raw Fear

Most extreme travelers do not begin their careers by gradually acquiring skills in outdoor courses or by five years of easy back-packing. It doesn't fit the personality. Instead, most of us learn either by apprenticing on someone else's expedition, or by taking risks. I took risks.

On my first expedition, I set out to ski three hundred and fifty miles alone across Labrador in mid-winter, no caches, no radio, no air support. It was as extreme an expedition as I could conceive at the time, in the most extreme place that I knew about. Labrador is the coldest place in the world for its latitude.

I prepared for the journey meticulously, and for two weeks all went well. Then one afternoon in early February, near the headwaters of the George River, I was crossing a frozen lake when I came across some wet ice. It was late in the day, and I was tired and impatient to reach the other side. I assumed that the moisture was just slush that wells up through cracks and rests on firm ice. A little sloppy to wade through, but perfectly safe. However, I hadn't skied many steps when the ice beneath my feet began to give way. Attached by rigid poles to the sled behind, I couldn't back up. I tried racing ahead but couldn't ski fast enough. I fell through. Only the fiberglass poles lying on the rotten ice held me up and prevented the sled from joining me in the water, where it would have dragged me to the bottom of the lake like an anchor.

For some reason, my mind stayed calm. I scrambled back onto the rotten ice and managed to remove my skis and unhitch myself from the sled harness. Then, distributing my weight, I crawled on my belly toward the sled. I was a hundred and twenty miles from anyone, and all my gear and supplies were on that sled. If it broke through, I too was sunk.

The ice was so bad that as I shimmied forward, my hands and elbows created holes wherever they rested. I removed a minimum of gear from the sled, flung it toward shore, then crawled after it till we both reached safe ice. I was afraid to spend too much time near the sled because my maneuvers were visibly saturating the ice around it.

That night in the tent, with just a crumb to eat for supper, I took stock of my situation. At any moment, the lake could swallow up my sled. My ski boots were hopeless blocks of ice. Night temperatures often dropped below minus forty. During the day, I had Labrador's terrible northwest wind in my face.

The clear-headedness that had guided me through the accident had evaporated. I was deeply shaken. Convinced that this was still a survival situation and that time was critical, I flipped on the emergency transmitter that I carried with me. It would beam my location to search-and-rescue authorities and request pick-up. As far as I was concerned, the expedition was over.

Unknown to me, the transmitter was defective and the signal never reached them. To my horror, no one came the following morning. No one came that afternoon. I kept the transmitter on till the battery died, but no one ever came. This failure of my one security measure hit me harder than the accident. I really was on my own, and it was terrifying.

At least the sled was still on the ice. I crawled out to it, surprised to find that the ice had firmed up in the clear, cold weather. I was able to retrieve everything.

Theoretically, I could have continued as if nothing had happened, but I was in no state to go on. A deep fear, such as I had never felt before, gnawed at my belly. It made me spontaneously burst out sobbing several times a day. I'd read about the paralyzing fear that occasionally gripped front-line soldiers. This was it.

I decided to diverge from my route to an empty outfitter's camp forty-five miles away. I'd spoken to the outfitter the previous summer and he'd promised to leave a two-way radio for me as an emergency measure. Shaken though I was, forty-five miles was not far to go.

The fear held me for several days until finally I became so disgusted with it, and with myself, that I shook it off by defiantly skiing on bad ice. After that, it left me alone—although when the outfitter's camp came into view, I burst into sobs one last time, crying, "My life, my life." I'd made it. I'd survived.

Then another shock. The outfitter had forgotten to leave the radio. Naïve as it sounds, I hadn't realized that some people are reliable and need to be told something only once while others are well-meaning but forgetful, busy or just sloppy. I hadn't followed up.

Now I could only wait helplessly until my family notified search-and-rescue officials on the agreed-upon day. I had filed my route with the Royal Canadian Mounted Police and even mentioned the existence of this camp, but again, I had not pounded the point home. Although the camp was established enough to appear on the topo maps, no one noticed. It was three days and about $100,000 before the search-and-rescue aircraft, flying grids, happened over my camp.

My trek was novel enough to have attracted a little attention before I left, but my disappearance, of course, was a much better story. A few, who regarded such ventures as frivolous, wrote huffy letters to newspapers complaining about their tax dollars going to my rescue. "Don't worry, if we hadn't spent it on you, we would have spent it flying practice rescues," one official told me, but that hardly helped. It was a pitiful and embarrassing end to a first expedition. Although I returned to Labrador the following winter and did the complete trek with no problems, and although it's now seventeen years and 4,000 trouble-free arctic miles later, I still feel foolish about it.

That first expedition did, however, show me a great deal. I felt as if those forty intense days had taught me the equivalent of two thousand days of ordinary backpacking. Also, despite the later fear, my calm and clarity at the time of the accident gave me confidence that I could rely on myself to act coolly when seconds counted. Since then, I have carried neither a radio nor a satellite transmitter, preferring to make conservative decisions in the field than to rely on a contrivance that might fail me when I needed it most.

I eventually discovered that the Arctic is not a dangerous place. What is dangerous is acquiring the experience to minimize the few dangers that do exist. And as I studied arctic history, I came to notice an intriguing fact: Most famous arctic disasters had relative novices at the helm. You learn so quickly in that environment that after the first trip or two, most people are no longer capable of screwing up in grand style. The timeless adventures are created by rookies.

■

On my fourth expedition to Ellesmere I was sledding along the first-year sea ice of Eureka Sound—flat as a lake, for the most part. Ring seals birth their young under the snow of first-year ice, beside breathing holes they keep open with the claws on their flippers. Polar bears eat mainly ring seals. You're pretty safe from bears over much of Ellesmere Island, but they like Eureka Sound, especially the lower part. The explorers recognized this and names such as Great Bear Cape, Little Bear Cape, Bear Corner, Bear Strait and Bear Peninsula cover the maps.

On my first evening I camped at Depot Point, on the Axel Heiberg shore. Nowadays I would explore such an historic spot. At the time it was just another campsite. Following the precise routine of wilderness travel, I threw my sleeping bag in the rear of the tent, placed the stove in the left front corner and the shotgun beside it. Every day of every trip, each item goes in the same place, in the same sequence.

I wandered over to collect some tidal ice to guy down the tent. Suddenly a polar bear rounded a piece of ice, and we found ourselves face to face. The shotgun was in the tent, twenty long yards away. It was hard to tell which of us was more surprised, myself or the bear. We just looked at each other. The bear lifted its nose and sniffed and then—I could see it make a sudden decision—started nonchalantly sniffing the ice at its feet. "You look into a caribou's eyes and not much is going on," a friend once pointed out, "but bears have a psychology." This bear just wanted to escape with its dignity intact.

I edged back to the tent with the same pretence of unconcern and brought out the shotgun, but the bear was already wandering off over Eureka Sound, nosing for seal holes. The whole charade à deux had been an exercise in neither of us showing fear.

Despite the eyeball-to-eyeball encounter, I wasn't too worried about polar bears. My camp had been invisible in the shore ice, and we'd simply surprised each other. Eureka Sound was so flat that I could usually see five miles in every direction. I had long cultivated the habit of glancing over my shoulder every so often. Polar bears do not blend into a snowscape. They appear yellowish in sunshine and greyish in overcast weather. Even from a distance, a moving object is impossible to miss in this stillness.

■

A poem in the outhouse of a botanists' camp on nearby Devon Island advises,

Though you may be enthralled
by a passion for flora
Do not ever forget
the Order Carnivora.

Globally, polar bears kill an average of one person a year. Most incidents involve young bears that haven't yet mastered seal hunting. The encounters usually take place in camp. Every fall, one or two foolish bears wander into Resolute, where they end up as rugs or pants. In 1987, a polar bear hung around the weather station at Eureka. It rested its paws on the window sill of the lounge and stared inside, like Dickensian orphans press their noses to the windows of candy stores. This made going outside a little too adventurous for the average meteorologist, and they eventually shot it.

On Somerset Island, south of Resolute, three scientists were sleeping in a tent when their dog started barking. They looked out to see a polar bear in camp. One scientist ran to the nearby quonset for their rifle. He tried to chamber a bullet but he didn't pull the bolt back far enough and the bear knocked him down. When a second scientist tried to intervene, it seized him by the neck and was dragging him to a creek bed when the third man shot the bear. Both victims recovered.

More recently, some biologists were studying thick-billed murres on wind-battered Coburg Island, off the southeastern coast of Ellesmere. Coburg's cliffs and nearby open water make it a paradise for nesting sea birds but "not very interesting as a place of residence for human beings," as explorer Otto Sverdrup put it. Only thirty-six species of flowering plants, huddled behind windbreaks, have gained a toehold on this blasted heath.

"We were into a deep sleep when a polar bear took our tent vestibule in its mouth and started shaking it," said one of the researchers. "It had bypassed all the other tents and made straight for our yellow dome, which was the farthest tent from the sea." She escaped out the back door while her partner shot the bear.

In the last twenty years, several adventurers skiing to the North Pole or the North Magnetic Pole have had close calls with bears. None of the skiers have died, but some incidents led to the deaths of bears. It is not always clear whether the adventurers were too quick on the draw.

In 1990, a lone Swiss dogsledder named Markus Bischoff was working his way across the Arctic. In southern Eureka Sound, a bear approached his camp. Eager for pictures, Bischoff photographed the bear until it broke into his sled and began eating the seal meat for his dogs. At this, Bischoff shot the bear. When he reached Eureka, he reported the incident.

Although he had been protecting his property, his seized film suggested that he had let the bear come too close before trying to chase it away. Wildlife officials charged him, but the case never reached court. That fall, Bischoff was boating with his dogs to a camp on Great Slave Lake in the western Arctic, where he planned to spend the winter. A sudden wind capsized the overloaded sixteen-footer. Bischoff managed to swim to shore, but he died of hypothermia and was eaten by his dogs. "All that was left of him was his head, guarded by the lead dog," recalls Mitch Taylor, Nunavut's polar bear biologist.

■

Several days after my first encounter, I was sleeping blissfully on southern Eureka Sound when a strange sound woke me. Sounds, like smells, are few on Ellesmere Island and can be counted on the fingers of one hand. Most are wind sounds. The wind roars; hard grains of snow scratch along the surface; loose strings on the tent beat a little tattoo on the drum-tight fly; cooking pots and fuel cans creak as they expand or contract. That's about it. In such a simple world, a new sound is very disturbing. I don't remember what it was, but it startled me out of my exhausted sleep.

I sat upright, grabbed the shotgun and flipped the safety off. No wind. There are only so many things a new sound can be. I was familiar with the scratchings of the arctic fox and this was different. I peeked out of the zippered crack in the tent door toward my sled, which I kept several yards away in the hope that a polar bear might prefer the food in the sled to the gamey odors of unwashed manhauler within. The sled was gone.

The next two minutes seemed like hours. I glanced left and saw the sled forty yards away, upside-down, its contents scattered on the snow. A polar bear was lying down beside it eating my food. "God, this is it," I thought.

Before the expedition, I'd had recurring nightmares about this. Wish fulfilments, these dreams were not. They seemed to be playing out different scenarios. I'd shoot the bear, but the bullets had no effect. Or I'd try to escape by climbing a tall chest of drawers. Or I'd dive away at the last instant: An Inuit hunter with a feel for physics had once pointed out to me that a charging bear's speed and weight meant it couldn't change direction quickly. But can you keep pirouetting away like a matador when the bear wheels around and charges again? In their surrealistic way, the dreams probed these tactics but always ended inconclusively.

"I wonder if the bears are also discussing you," my running partner had joked, when I shared the latest installment. "'Last night I dreamt I ate him.'"

I had, at least, mentally rehearsed the situation, so I followed the plan. First, make sure the shotgun is at hand, safety off. Check.

Next, put on clothes. I slept in my underwear, and I didn't want to confront a polar bear in the middle of the Arctic wearing only socks and long johns.

Third, stuff spare ammunition into pockets. Although the gun held six one-ounce slugs, I was no hunter and didn't want to die for want of ammunition.

Finally, get out of the tent and chase the bear away.

When I stepped out of the tent, I entered the full-blown nightmare. The bear had heard the nylon rustling as I dressed. It had left the sled and was striding resolutely at me, head lowered, eyes raised. It was within fifteen yards. No doubt about this bear's intent.

Next to being killed or maimed yourself, the worst nightmare is having to kill a bear on one of these expeditions. A generation ago, no one thought twice. Bear presents danger; man removes danger. One old arctic geologist shot seven nuisance bears in his career. Maybe he was a little trigger-happy, but who can judge until they've stared into the eyes of a threatening bear?

Nowadays, shooting a polar bear in self-defence is more than tragic, it's a bureaucratic ordeal. Every polar bear killed comes out of the quota of the nearest Inuit village. Since a skin sells for two thousand dollars and a sanctioned big-game hunt may earn over ten thousand dollars for the guide, a wasted bear is bad business and the Inuit don't like it. Some communities want scientists to have to post ten-thousand dollar bonds against the possibility of a defence kill. Technically, on shooting a polar bear, you must immediately contact the local wildlife officer by radio, who then comes to investigate the incident. For a modern expedition, shooting a polar bear is as bad form as eating your dogs.

The polar bear was within a few yards of me, too close for just a warning blast. I raised the shotgun and sighted down the barrel at the vulnerable hump behind the bear's neck. The shotgun was a borrowed stockless model and I hadn't fired it before. I hoped it would work.

The blast set my ears ringing and flung the barrel in the air as the pistol-grip handle slammed into my mouth. I had missed completely, but the bear wheeled in its tracks and ran away. It disappeared behind some ice and I never saw it again.

Blood trickled into my mouth from where the recoil had split my upper lip. A dawning realization: You're supposed to fire a pistol-grip shotgun from the hip. Nevertheless, my ignorance had been a blessing in disguise. Had I fired riot-cop style, I might have actually hit the bear. As it turned out, we had escaped the usual no-win outcome of such encounters: "A polar bear attack on a human ends only when one of them is dead," writes Ian Stirling, the world's foremost polar bear researcher.

The crisis was over but I was a hundred and fifty miles from anyone and I could still be in trouble if my gear was wrecked. I went to inspect the sled. The bear had cracked the hull, but not badly. Luckily, the sweeping north winds of the day before had died, or the stuff would have been blown halfway to Baffin Island. I rounded everything up. I smelled gasoline vaporizing through a hairline crack in the fuel can and I sealed it with duct tape. The bear had eaten a half-finished peanut butter sandwich and crunched open my mug to lick the frozen cocoa dregs. It had given my hardshell sunglasses case an experimental nip but had not liked the taste. All fine. But where was the big nylon duffle with most of the food?

I followed the bear's tracks for seventy-five yards to a ravine. Here lay the duffle, open and rummaged through but intact. The bear had carried it in its jaws. Rather than rip it open, it had delicately unzipped the bag by hooking a claw through one of the loops that I keep on zippers to make them easier to pull with mitts on. It had ignored the dried sausage and gone straight for the box of Belgian chocolates I was bringing as a gift to friends in Grise Fiord. Then it had wandered back to the sled to clean up the loose ends, no doubt planning to return later.

My mind had stayed clear during the attack, but as often happens, the fear hit afterward. I realized that I had no control over when a polar bear might strike. This was the High Arctic's one freak hazard, a kind of four-legged avalanche. The near-infinite visibility made me safe during the day, but for years afterward I slept like a seal on Ellesmere, waking every hour to look out the tent for something off-white and moving.

Peeawahto, shortly before his death.

Chapter Three

Getting Away with Murder

The Ellesmere obsession began, perhaps, with murder. In the middle of August, 1986, as slanting light signaled the last days of the High Arctic summer, a few of us were tramping the meadows along Ellesmere's Buchanan Bay when Mike Watts, an Ontario surgeon, spotted an open grave among the rocks. Inside lay an ancient human skull, four teeth still clinging to the upper jaw. One of us took the skull out and turned it around in his hand as if musing on the way of all flesh.

"What's that cut above the ear?" asked Mike.

On the side of the skull was a deep horizontal gash that looked as if it had been made by a small ax. The bone below the gash projected slightly: The blow had come from above.

"This injury was fatal," said Mike, thoughtfully tracing the cut with his fingernail.

We put the skull back in the grave and continued our hike. That night in my journal, I droned on for page after page about muskoxen and sculptured ice floes and the one-liners of my companions, but never even mentioned the skull. So much went on during these twenty-four hour days that the discovery of a murder victim was, evidently, not noteworthy.

∎

That original trip to Ellesmere planted many seeds, but it was the skull that haunted me. What was the story behind this violent end? How long ago did it happen? Was the killing community-sanctioned? After all, the body had not been dumped through a hole in the ice but placed in the open for all to see.

In some ways, the skull came to symbolize a dark corner of this island, where stress could drive men to murder. Seeking to compensate for my lack of interest at the time, I tried to find the skull again ten years later, but without success. I then took to delving into the Ellesmere region's other homicides. These were, after all, the northernmost murders in the world.

Eventually, murdered ghosts rattled their chains everywhere I traveled in the High Arctic. Murder prompted the flight of Qitdlarssuaq, the great shaman, from Baffin Island to Ellesmere. There, on a small lake in Makinson Inlet, more murder. Further north, at Pim Island, Adolphus Greely's execution of thief and murderer Charles Henry. Three hundred miles further north, in Greenland waters, Charles Francis Hall collapsed within view of Ellesmere, supposedly of apoplexy, but it is now believed that his doctor poisoned him. Often a cloud of uncertainty played around the corpses. Was it murder? An accident?

In 1970, the world's northernmost murder took place on the drifting ice island T-3, two hundred twenty miles northwest of Ellesmere. Ice islands are big, flat pans of ice that break off from the 3,000-year-old ice shelves that cling to parts of northern Ellesmere. The pieces drift around the Arctic Ocean for a couple of decades and are ideal platforms for ocean science. The first one, discovered in 1946 off Barrow, Alaska by a U.S. spy plane, was classified top-secret because of its value as a base. Ice islands are like large soda crackers floating in a loose polar soup. During their lifespan, they can cover marathon distances from Ellesmere to Alaska and back to Greenland. Eventually, they reach open water or break up.

T-3 was discovered in 1947. It was the third such "target" sighted, hence its name. Since 1952, researchers under the U.S. Air Force had occupied it almost continuously. At first, it was thirty-one miles across and two hundred feet thick, but by the time of the murder, it had shrunk to seven miles long, four miles wide and one hundred feet thick.

Researchers on T-3 lived in comfortable trailers and spoke by radio with the outside world. But planes could not land on the puddly summer ice and T-3 was well beyond the range of helicopters, so the nineteen men were on their own for months. In that era, such outposts were not today's politically correct environments. Even in the mid-1980s, towns like Resolute drew a lot of freewheeling, hard-drinking misfits. Porn videos blared nonstop in the background like arctic elevator muzak. Bush pilots routinely dented aircraft in seat-of-the-pants landings. T-3 was like a university dorm full of engineering students.

"Porky" Leavitt was one of these ungrounded wires. He had already attacked three people on T-3 in his quest for alcohol. On July 16, 1970, Mario Escamilla heard that Porky had just broken into his trailer and stolen some homemade raisin wine. Escamilla had been attacked by Porky before so he brought along one of the camp rifles for protection.

He found Porky next door with the station manager, Bennie Lightsy, drinking a withering concoction of raisin wine, grape juice, and pure ethanol. Escamilla told Porky to stay away from his wine and was back in his trailer when he heard footsteps. Thinking it was Porky, he picked up the gun, flipped the safety off and pointed it at the door. Bennie Lightsy entered, thoroughly drunk himself. The two argued about the raisin wine. Escamilla ordered Lightsy to get out and continued to brandish the rifle as the argument heated up. The gun went off, and a seriously wounded Lightsy died shortly afterward.

Legally, T-3 was perhaps the most awkward spot in the world for a homicide. An ice island is neither land nor ship. It does not belong to anyone. T-3 had originated in Canada and lay in the so-called Canadian sector, which extends from the coastal edges to the North Pole. But it was a U.S. station, manned by Americans. Although maintained by the Air Force, its civilian personnel were not subject to military law. Ice islands simply did not exist in international law. Lightsy's death had occurred in one of those rare jurisdictional gaps where serious crimes might go untried. "Murder in Legal Limbo," declared the headline in *Time* magazine.

Ultimately, Escamilla was tried as if it had taken place on the high seas. In 1971, he was found not guilty of second-degree murder but guilty of involuntary manslaughter. He was sentenced to three years (with possible parole after three months), but his appeal turned up enough procedural flaws to win a new trial. The retrial never occurred and all mention of the ice island homicide disappeared from legal literature as abruptly as the ice island melted away in the spring of 1984.

At his death, Lightsy had a blood alcohol level of at least .26. Curious to know just how inebriated he was during that conversation with Escamilla, I threw an Ice Island Murder Party. Designated drinkers were given charts to keep track of their drinks and the time between them. The local police agreed to provide the breathalyzer tests. We were warned, of course, that drunken behavior depends less on blood alcohol content than on personality and individual tolerance. Both breathalyzer technicians had seen chronic drinkers who appeared sober despite registering in the high .3s. Death from alcohol toxicity normally occurs at .4, though one of the constables had tested someone with even higher levels who was still ambulatory.

All of us were wine-sippers and naïve in the ways of hard drinking. Nevertheless, the volunteers gamely set to work in the interests of quasi-science. Mark Wold, a slender, fit sales rep, won the Lightsy Award, consuming sixteen shots of vodka in two hours, one every seven minutes. Since the body eliminates one drink an hour, Mark had fourteen drinks in his system when tested. His score of .177, still six or seven drinks away from Lightsy's state, says nothing about the murder on T-3 except just what level of drinking used to occur at isolated arctic outposts.

The only side effects of the Ice Island Murder Party were hangovers and a consuming desire for total abstinence that lasted several weeks.

■

All hard Ellesmere journeys are stressful; that's part of their appeal. Anxiety is high in polar bear regions. When the going is bad, you worry about covering the distance before your food runs out. When the going is good, it can only get worse. If it's cold, the sled glides poorly; if it's warm, the snow may disappear before a land crossing.

In May 1988, my partner and I flew to Copes Bay, forty miles north of Alexandra Fiord, to cross Ellesmere from east to west by a new route. Edward Shackleton, son of the legendary Ernest, had tried it in 1935, but deep snow aborted his attempt. We budgeted three weeks for the two hundred mile trek to Eureka.

The mountain pass follows a river valley beside a huge glacier, then angles west to Cañon Fiord. On our maps the route looked good, but we were soon trapped in a gorge with a glacier wall on one side and a cliff on the other. Overhanging seracs creaked and dripped overhead. Small frozen waterfalls forced us to strap crampons to our sealskin boots, climb eight or twelve feet, then haul the gear up. We were making just five miles for ten hours' work. At this rate, we were not going to make Eureka. We hoped the route would improve when we reached higher ground.

1988 was a hot year on Ellesmere. Day and night, the sun blazed from a cloudless sky. The air was warm. Winds were calm. This made travel pleasant. By mid-May, we sunbathed naked in camp, dipped our water bottles in melt puddles and watched the year's first insects warm themselves on the tent. But the snow was disappearing at an alarming rate. The pile that we banked around the tent at night would be gone by morning.

The twenty-four hour sun usually burns off the snow by early June. Then only the ice caps, the glaciers and the frozen sea remain wintry-looking, while most of the island becomes toast-brown. But this year, summer arrived a month early. Within five days of beginning our journey, every flake of snow was gone. We dragged the sleds over bare land, leaving gelcoat streaks behind us on the rocks like canoes bashing down rapids. The river to Cañon Fiord was in full flood. We needed rafts, not sleds. Eventually, we had to portage our gear overland in three loads and fell further behind our schedule.

Reluctantly, we doubled our travel time. For two days, we marched nonstop for eighteen hours. On the third day, we pressed on for twenty-four hours. The second night, I nodded off with my supper spoon in my mouth. When we finally reached Cañon Fiord, we were so tired that when I broke through some sea ice weakened by the river flow, the jolt of adrenaline nauseated rather than energized me.

Once out on the sea, our troubles were unexpectedly over. The ice was in great shape. We hauled twenty-five to thirty miles a day and managed to reach Eureka in five days.

Some Ellesmere journeys are harder than this, some easier, but every one throws unnerving twists in the traveler's path. Some of us thrive on this insecurity, or at least accept it. Others crack.

■

In 1914, explorer Fitzhugh Green shot and killed his Inuit guide Peea-wahto. Green was a member of the Crocker Land Expedition, which set out to find the snowclad summits of a mysterious island allegedly sighted by Robert Peary off northwestern Ellesmere in 1906.

The expedition leader, Donald MacMillan, had been north only once before, as one of Peary's assistants. An ambitious man, MacMillan expected the discovery of Crocker Land to vault him into the front rank of contemporary explorers. Although Crocker Land proved illusory, Mac-Millan did manage to win a place in the thinning pantheon of polar heroes. What explorers accomplish is often not as important as their knack for self-promotion, and MacMillan always affiliated himself well, in this case, with the American Museum of Natural History. MacMillan later became something of an educator, introducing many students of Bowdoin College to the Arctic through summer excursions by ship.

The published account of the murder had always seemed strange to me. On northern Axel Heiberg, Fitzhugh Green's dogs are buried in a snowstorm and die. Peeawahto won't slow down for Green, who is on foot. Green, convinced that he is being abandoned, shoots Peeawahto in the back, appropriates his team and rejoins the others. MacMillan's one-sentence summary of the event is almost comic: "Green, inexperienced in the handling of Eskimos . . . had felt it necessary to shoot his companion."

To better understand the murder, I walked four hundred miles to the scene of the crime near Cape Thomas Hubbard, then visited Bowdoin College in Maine and the American Museum of Natural History in New York to look over the expedition journals. Bowdoin College, one of those lovely New England campuses full of maple trees and greystone chapels, still basks in the afterglow of its two arctic alumni, Peary and MacMillan. The college's mascot is a polar bear; researchers at its Peary-MacMillan Arctic Museum continue to make ethnographic trips to the pair's old stomping grounds in Greenland. Bowdoin has Green's journal. Between the tattered brown covers, erasures, pemmican stains, and fear lurk between the grandly pencilled lines. MacMillan's journal is in New York. "Not our favorite topic," volunteered the librarian, when I asked for Crocker Land material. "Wasn't someone killed on that expedition under museum auspices?"

Green's journal bears the earmarks of authenticity: pages smudged from where wet mittens gripped them; writing somewhat faint, pencil does not register well in the cold. The words too are authentic. Green would write some forty books in his life, all bad. But the journal is, at its key moments, unaffected. It shows a man overwhelmed with panic.

■

The Crocker Land Expedition floundered from the start. When their ship ran aground off the coast of Newfoundland, MacMillan frantically chartered a second. Eventually they reached Etah, on the Greenland side of Kane Basin, where they spent the winter. The following February, with an army of 19 men, 15 sleds and 165 dogs to lay depots, MacMillan set out for northern Axel Heiberg and the Arctic Ocean.

MacMillan had hoped an early start would minimize open water during their travels over the ocean. But mid-February is a hard time to begin a long trek. The weak sun has just returned from a four-month absence and limps along the horizon, giving light but no heat. It feels like the sun must feel on the surface of Pluto; the slightest wind burns exposed cheeks like liquid nitrogen. In the profound cold, familiar substances acquire unrecognizable properties. Butter shatters. Plastic bags snap like potato chips. Dental fillings drop out. On the coldest days, pee crackles as it arcs through the air and freezes before it hits the ground. Little wonder that when some men fell sick, MacMillan returned to Greenland for a month to regroup.

Mid-March is still cold but feels less like a space walk. MacMillan and a smaller crew retraced their steps across Kane Basin to Hayes Fiord, unknowingly passing the skull of the ancient murder victim we discovered seventy-odd years later. Eager to avoid the sled-destroying gravel of Sverdrup Pass, they followed the fiord to its terminus at the Beitstad Glacier.

The modern Canadian Inuit of Grise Fiord shun glacier travel, but the Polar Inuit who accompanied MacMillan lived in the shadow of the Greenland ice cap and were used to it. Even today, that is the only way for dogsledders to skirt the open water that laps against certain cliffs. Two Greenlanders carved steps in the glacier wall; dramatizing difficulties, MacMillan describes the wall as nearly insurmountable, but his photo shows a relatively minor obstacle that would take just a few patient hours to overcome.

MacMillan unexpectedly lost four of his party here. Minik, who spoke perfect English, may have sensed trouble ahead and quit; a second man, fearing Minik's interest in his wife, followed. The group's geologist frostbit his toes and had to return to Etah with a third Greenlander. That left only MacMillan, Green and four natives, carrying heavy loads with dogs weakened by bad pemmican. MacMillan sent Green and two of the natives back for supplies while he and Etukashu continued ahead. They were to reunite on northern Axel Heiberg.

Fitzhugh Green, a 25-year-old naval ensign, came from good old stock; his great-great-grandfather had been a large Virginia landowner in the 1600s. As a young man, he was talkative and ingratiating, with a tendency to fawn over his betters, and he expected those whom he considered his inferiors to snap a salute when he spoke. This made his dealings with the Inuit condescending at best. Nevertheless, he and his party fetched the extra food and oil and charged back across the glacier to catch up with MacMillan.

MacMillan and Green fancied themselves the dauntless explorers leading the happy-go-lucky, childlike Eskimo. "Their life was a sublimely simple fight for food and clothing," puffed Green later. "Mine was a cruel struggle of such labyrinthine intricacy that only the genius could be rich and none be truly contented save the shrewdest philosophers."

Little did they know that the Greenlanders who accompanied them were really the distinguished ones. It was as if Peary, Nansen, Sverdrup, Amundsen, and Shackleton were all part of the same expedition. Etukashu had joined Frederick Cook on his great 1908 journey that climaxed with wintering in a stone den on Devon Island and a magnificent four hundred mile trek back to Greenland. Peeawahto had also served with Cook, as well as with Peary and Knud Rasmussen, who described him as "a comrade who was ready to make personal sacrifices in order to help and support his companions." Minik was the famous "New York Eskimo," brought south by Peary as a curiosity, raised by a white family, who attempted to reassimilate in Greenland but eventually died in New Hampshire. Akqioq was awarded Denmark's highest medal for his role in Knud Rasmussen's epic Fifth Thule Expedition and later mysteriously disappeared with the German explorer, Hans Krüger. And Nukapinguaq, a young man on his first expedition, evolved into the greatest traveler the High Arctic has ever known.

■

The Canadian arctic islands are the size of Europe, but for nine months a year their territory is doubled, because the sea between all the islands is frozen. For sled travel, the sea is better than land, and the west coast of Ellesmere is particularly good. Surrounding mountains catch most of the snow and make Eureka Sound, the six-mile-wide artery dividing Ellesmere from Axel Heiberg, a true polar desert. Sweeping north winds transform the little powder that does fall into a hard surface resembling squeaky styrofoam. Every explorer recorded a burst of speed on this arctic autobahn. And its muskoxen and polar bears made it a land of plenty for these expeditions, which all depended on hunting.

Spring weather is usually good on Ellesmere, but 1914 featured one gale after another. Fighting the north wind was exhausting; once Green fell asleep chewing his supper, that barometer of a hard day. They couldn't spot wildlife in the blowing snow. Dogs died, and men went hungry. Worried entries about the worn-out dogs recur daily in Green's journal. But eventually the three of them caught up with MacMillan. "How we found them . . . seems now a miracle," wrote Green, adding grandiosely, "I think it was the fiendish intensity of our determination which did it."

■

Except for the Beitstad Glacier, I've covered the Crocker Land Expedition's entire route from Greenland to the northern tip of Axel Heiberg. Little has changed since then. Ellesmere is theoretically easier to reach, but charter flights costing up to $20,000 create a financial barrier as daunting as the ice of old. Tour groups focus on a couple of areas; the rest of the island remains gloriously unwalked.

Hikers in the Lower 48 are never more than twenty miles from a road, but Nunavut has no roads, just isolated Inuit hamlets separated by three hundred miles of Ice-Age wilderness. Ellesmere lies 2,500 miles from the nearest highway and 2,000 miles from the nearest tree. On a map, Ellesmere and Axel Heiberg resemble Britain and Ireland linked by a frozen Irish Sea, what is known as Eureka Sound.

Many of my sledding trips begin at the Eureka weather station, because charter aircraft refuel here and it's easy to reach. A meat locker door one foot thick leads into the main building. Within this oasis, a dozen employees can make phone calls, watch videos, and eat fresh bread every morning. But no one forgets that the High Arctic is just outside. The canine pug marks in the snow belong to wolves. Muskoxen have to be shooed off the airstrip before planes can land. Despite its e-mail access, Eureka is wilderness.

Still, the true sledging experience doesn't begin till six miles out, when the Telesat dish at Skull Point vanishes from sight and you pass through a time portal into Eureka Sound, where everything is just like it was in MacMillan's time. On the near coast, the rolling, muskox-dotted hills of the Fosheim Peninsula. Across the Sound, the mystery and austerity of Axel Heiberg, one of the world's loveliest islands. There resides what John Muir called the "unexplainable mysticism" of glaciers.

Like the polar bear, the spring sledder is a marine mammal. He travels on the sea, camps on it, and sometimes drinks old ice from which the salt has leached. The ice is five feet thick, a secure platform. "White men always think of ice as frozen water, but Eskimos think of water as melted ice," Nukapinguaq would explain to some British explorers years later. "To us, ice is the natural state."

I sometimes feel that this is what I was born to do, haul a sled over Eureka Sound for eight to twelve hours a day, temperature –20°F, snow hard, winds calm, trudging, as Thoreau wrote, "like a camel, which is said to be the only beast which ruminates when walking." In good conditions, the sledder can continue for twelve hours in this vein. Hours eleven and twelve are the most revealing: They are like the final rounds in great championship fights, when all the bullshit and grey areas of the personality slough away, and only strength and weakness remain.

In April 1997, my partner and I set out from Eureka and reached Skraeling Point on Axel Heiberg after seven hours. Here, we camped among the many "tent rings, store houses and traps" that prompted the Norwegian Otto Sverdrup to give the place its name. At the south end of the Schei Peninsula, where MacMillan had camped in a blinding snowstorm, we discovered an ancient Thule settlement, built around the